PROTECTORS OF THE OUTDOORS

True stories from the frontline of conservation enforcement

Jim Chizek

Flambeau River Publishing
White Leopard Press

First edition, first printing

Library of Congress Catalog Number: 99-69426
ISBN: 0-9673510-0-6

Cover art: Irene Fleming
Editor/Designer: Diane Schwartz

Printed in Canada by Hignell Printing, Ltd.

Flambeau River Publishing
W10298 Wells Road
Lodi, WI 53555
(608) 592-3752

White Leopard Press

About the artist: Irene Fleming operates Rene Studios in Fifield, Wisconsin. Her series of eagle prints were among the finalists in a recent Wisconsin Wildlife Federation art competition.

Publisher's Cataloging-in-Publication
(Provided by Quality Books, Inc.)

Chizek, Jim.

Protectors of the outdoors: true stories from the frontline of conversation enforcement / author, James T. Chizek ; illustrator, Irene Fleming. --1st ed.

1.Game wardens--Wisconsin--Anecdotes.
2. Wildlife management--Wisconsin--Anecdotes.
3. Poachers--Wisconsin--Anecdotes. I.Fleming, Irene. II. Title.

SK463.C48 2000 363.28

This book is dedicated to my wife Shirley and my children Frank, Donald and Michelle.

Acknowledgements

Hundreds of people assisted with the completion of this book. The following list attempts to recognize all those people who are mentioned in this book, assisted in gathering material for this book,* or who appear in this book and assisted in gathering material.** Thank you very much.

Dick Abney,** Frank Adamske,** Jack Allen,** Cletus Alsteen,** Owen Anderson,** Dave Aubert, Rollie Baker, Billy Bauman, John Bauschek, Don Beghin,** Ken Beghin,** Dave Bennett, Butch Bergner, David Bogue, Robert Bohlman, Judy Borke,* Bob Born,** Osuld Bredsen, Glenden Brosig, Pat Burhans,** Bernie Burrack, Harold Burton, Helgsen Channing, Don Chizek, Frank Chizek, Shirley Chizek,** Alan Christensen, Blacky Cline, Art,Collins, Ken Corbett,** Ed Corey, Ted Cregeski, Larry Dahle, Jim Daley, Thomas Daley, Emmy Dallman, Royce Dallman, Steve Darms, Bob Davis, Thurman Deerwester, Barney Devine, Fred Dicke, Milt Dieckman,* Cunera Reif-Diedrick,** James Doyle, John Draheim, Mike Dressen, Dick Dufour, Pat Dwyer, J.P. Edwards, Dale Erlandson,** Don Euers,** Ray Faeling, Mark Farnum, Paddo Fish, Jim Flanigan,** Chuck Foley, Jon Folven, Frederick Fowle, Cliff Freeman,** Norbert Froelich, Donavan Gabbei, John Gagnon, Kim Gaffney, Al Galston, Tom Gatz, James Gehling, Marvin Gerlikovski, Randy Giese, Wayne Giese, Louie Gieson, Art Gillette,** Donald Gleason, Jim Golomb, Paul Gossens, Bob Grant, Anthony Grell, Gerry Gusick, Harry Gyarsbock, George Hadland, Austin Hall, Jim Hamblin, Bob Hamele, Max Harter,** Fred Hatch, Stuart Hayner, Lloyd Heinz, Myron Heistad, George Helga, Johnny Helsing, Harold Hettrick,** Rick Herzfelt,** Winter Hess,** Norm Hicks, Wilham “Bill” Hiebing,** Ed Hill,** Ralph Hiller, Phil Hine, Michelle Chizek Holmen, Bill Hoyt,** H. M. Hosford, Lavern Hugget, Byron Hughs, R. A. Hunt, Denny Jameson,** Tony Jellich,** Wayne Jiedy, Bud Johnson,** O.K. Johnson, Ollie Jones, Walter Kaczmarski, Marvin Kaukl,** Ken Kazmar, Mark Kelsey,** Robert Kennedy, George Kern, Mike Kit,** Ralph Kleist, James Knope, Warren Knowles, Bud Knutson, Marriner Kohlman, Andy Krakow, Jill Krakow,** Travis Krakow, Larry Kriese,** Tom Krsnich,** Jerry Kryka, Ronny Kubisiak,** Richard Kucksdorf, Paul Kuhn, Elmer Lange, Frank Ladenberger, Lonny LaFave, Neil LaFave, Nichole LaFave, Peggy LaFave, Howard Latton, Chuck Lawrence, Bill Leasch, Roger Lenzer, Ernie Lien, John Long, Darlene Lukins,** Mike Lutz,* Mac Mackenzie, Gordon

MacQuarrie, Ernie Mallard, Phil Malsack, Ed Manthei, Bob Markle, Fritz Markman, E.B. Martineau, Mark Martin, Sue Martin,** Buckley Marquardt,** Milt Marquardt, Harley McKeague, Joel McOlash, Ernie Meress, Carl Miersch,** Jack Miller, Jack Y. Miller, Larry Miller, Kenny Mills, Dale Morey,** Dennis Morgan, Arnold Murphy, Ernest Nash, Laurie Nevel, Mike Newton,** Robert Nixon, Milton Nowland, Daniel O'Conner, George O'Connor, Armin Ohnesorge, Chuck Olson, Bernie Olson, Marvin Olson, Pat Oshesky, Garner Oswald, Scott Otto, Bill Ozburn, Bernie Palas, Frank Palenik, Robert Parins, Hartley Paul, Elmer Pennington, Peter Pesheck, Harley Peterson, Rod Pevytoe, Leon Pieschek, Earl Piper,** Don Plante, James Pressentin, Staber Reese,** Albert Reif, Albert Reif Jr.,** Robert Reif,** C. Rhinehard, Francis Riley, Tony Rinzel, Al. Robinson, Dick Roehrick, Bill Rollmann, Larry Roth, Joe Rubesch,** Sam Ruegger, Babe Ruth, Joe Ryder,** Floyd Sanders, T.J. Sanderson, Nick Schaefer, Bob Schmidt, Robert Schoenhofen,** Richard Schrickel, Emil Schroeder, Al Schultz, John Schultz, Jack Schwartz, Steven Sell, Harold Shine, Robert Siegried, Louie Simons Vince Skilling, Bob Smith, Irving Smith, James Smith, Neil Smith, Robert Smith, Don Soderberg, Louie Spray, Leo Stecker, Dean Steele, Harland Steinhorst,* Dick Streng,** Norman Stowers, Clyde Sundberg, Dave Swanson, Stan Swenson, Rudy Teschan, Jack Tessman, Johnny Thomas, Edward Thompsen, Gerald Thorpe, Omar Thorpe, Lennie Tomczyk, Cal Tomlinson, John Toonen, Jim Tourtillot, Daniel Trainer,** Wayne Truttman, Len Urquhart,** Ollie Valley, Herb Vander Bloemen, E. J. Vanderwall, Don Van Straten, Les Voight, Dean Volenec,** D.W. Waggoner, Robert Warren, Peter Weatherhead, Orville Weborg, Clarance Wilger, Todd Wipperman, Allen Wittkopf, Norm Wood, Richard Wright, Dave Zasada, Walter Zelinske, Walter Zerbes and Donald Zuidmulder.

About the Author

Jim Chizek is a retired game warden and lifelong resident of Wisconsin. He was born in 1930 and raised on a dairy farm near Fifield. Prior to becoming a warden, he worked as a dairy farmer, logger and had various jobs in railroading.

The year 1955 proved pivotal for Chizek. After serving a stint in the United States Marine Corps during the Korean War, he married Shirley Plyer and began his conservation career. He was hired as special conservation warden in Ladysmith for the Wisconsin Conservation Department. Under the tutelage of Warden Ed Manthei, he began a two-year journey toward becoming a permanent warden. Manthei set an example of hard work and compassion. Chizek always endeavored to put himself in the shoes of the person he was dealing with. He never forgot a word coined by his mentor – "humbility."

The following winter, Chizek returned to Fifield to work for Game Manager Art Doll out of Park Falls. He surveyed deer wintering yards and put on many miles on snowshoes. He also drew deer-timber browse maps, saw his first starved deer and learned how to take bone marrow samples from dead deer. This unforgettable experience helped him understand and support controversial deer management practices of the era.

As spring broke, Chizek went to Shawano to work for warden Ortis K. "O. K." Johnson at Shawano. Working the spring sturgeon run on the Wolf River was an exciting adventure for the 25-year-old. Working the Wolf was considered the acid test for wardens of that era. Special wardens who survived the hard, grueling work of dragging the river almost every night for snag lines in inclement weather, were usually hired on a permanent basis.

In the spring of 1956, Chizek was assigned a training position in Jefferson where he worked as a trainee warden for Bill Leasch and Royce "Smoky" Dallman, stationed at Milton. An interesting deer season followed: for the first time in nearly a century, deer hunting was allowed in LaFayette County. Chizek reported to Warden Omar Thorpe at Darlington. Since they're were few hunters to hunt the healthy herd, Chizek and Thorpe went deer hunting on opening day and took just two nice bucks – two of just 16 killed in the county in the nine-day buck season.

Chizek was stationed permanently at Portage in 1957, working under the tough supervision of Louis "Pat" Oshesky. It was here that Shirley and Jim's two sons were born– Frank in 1957 and Donald in 1959. In 1966, after working nine years at Portage, he accepted a promotion as the district supervisory warden at Park Falls. He replaced Robert "Bob" Markle who was killed that spring in a high speed chase of fish spearers near Bass Lake in Price County. Shortly after moving to Park Falls they were blessed with a daughter Michelle.

In 1968, Chizek was seriously injured in an auto accident while working deer-shiners on the Price-Lincoln county line. After two years of rehabilitation, he accepted a job in the bureau of law enforcement at Madison. He spent the next 16 years doing law enforcement budget and planning and undercover enforcement. Chizek retired in 1986 after 30 years of law enforcement duty.

He and his wife Shirley now live in rural Lodi. He serves on the board of directors of the Wisconsin Conservation Wardens Association, the Wisconsin Conservation and Education Foundation and is president of the Friends of MacKenzie Environmental Education Center.

He previously published the book *Game Warden Centurion* and does some freelance outdoor writing.

Author Jim Chizek receives a symbolic litter box from Governor Warren Knowles and Mrs. Wisconsin at a ceremony outside the state capital commemorating Wisconsin's first litter law in 1965.

TABLE OF CONTENTS

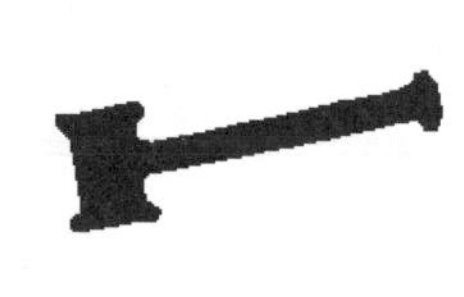

THE GAME WARDEN AND THE JUSTICE OF THE PEACE

FORWARD

The beauty of a white-tailed deer edging through a forest clearing on a moonlit night, the wonder of a shallow rock strewn shoreline covered by spawning walleye. These images trigger awe and respect for most people, but for some individuals they trigger deep urges to shoot a rifle or throw a spear without regard to conservation laws.

In his sequel to *Game Warden Centurion,* Jim Chizek tells us fascinating tales of what happens next, the battle of cunning between those who place little value on fish and wildlife, and conservation wardens who live and sometimes give their lives to protect the public's natural resources.

Protectors of the Outdoors describes the full range of experiences and emotions facing the men and women who devote their lives to protecting the fish and wildlife in this state.

You will read firsthand reports of the danger, injuries and death caused to these heroes by individuals with greatly misplaced values. On the other side of the spectrum, you will read numerous episodes of humor and friendly battle of the wits between wardens, and between wardens and poachers. These stories put into perspective the role of these individuals in their communities.

Lastly, you will be rewarded by Jim's fun-loving description of our historic fish and game justice system: the justice of the peace. For those of us accustomed to today's large, impersonal and sometimes slow court system, you will love these down-home stories about swift, and usually very effective justice.

Chizek's writings combine the best of all worlds: the first hand experiences of an excellent conservation warden, ready access to the memories of the fine men and women who have been Wisconsin Conservation Wardens, and a highly accurate, home-spun writing style.

As I read these stories, I could hear the words as if they were actually being uttered by the warden, poacher, or the justice of the peace. Jim Chizek has done it again. Sit back, throw another log on the fire, and picture yourself on the shoreline of that northern lake.

George E. Meyer
Secretary
Wisconsin Department of Natural Resources
August 29, 1999

INTRODUCTION

Protectors of the Outdoors was written in response to the many letters and calls received to do a sequel to *Game Warden Centurion*, my first book. *Game Warden Centurion* was based on the first 100 years of warden service in Wisconsin. Stories ranged from the time Rollie Baker was appointed the first "Fish Warden" in 1879, to 1992 when that book was published. *Protectors of the Outdoors* is another collection of true stories that reflect the myriad changes in game enforcement--laws, equipment and methods--that occurred from about 1920 to the 1980s.

None of the stories are routine.They are about the unusual, dramatic circumstances that wardens sometimes find themselves caught up in. Adventures of this type could, and have occurred, in all other states to county, state and federal wardens. Most of these experiences were rewarding and some downright hilarious. Some were unpleasant and at times miserable or dangerous. It is from these arenas that I choose to write.

As in *Game Warden Centurion,* I have based all stories on actual happenings and have kept the tales as authentic as possible. Please forgive me for imposing my own interpretation to parts of the stories where I could only imagine what was said or felt under trying conditions. Names have been changed to protect individuals, their relatives and friends from any discredit with the exception of Thomas "Blacky" Cline and Justice of the Peace Norman Stowers. None of the game wardens names involved in these adventures have been changed.

While working conditions and equipment have improved for present day wardens, they continue to have the dedication and adaptability of the legions before them. Today's warden must work fewer hours and spread their time among more activities.. They have learned to be more effective through utilization of better training.

I am proud to have been a Wisconsin game warden, to have provided a measure of protection to our natural resources and to have taken a small part in building the proud tradition wardens enjoy. Semper Fidelis.

Jim Chizek

BUTCHERY AT SENISIBA WILDLIFE AREA

PART I

On the morning of September 24, 1971, his thirty-second birthday, Neil LaFave kissed his pretty wife Peggy good-bye and left for work.

LaFave had worked as a game technician for many years in the Green Bay area. Most of those years he carried special warden credentials and worked closely with wardens in the area. He was well-known and perceived as very professional by the hunting public and his peers. Wardens in the area relied upon him to provide law enforcement coverage in the area and at the Senisiba Wildlife Area. Through the years, he made many game law arrests on the area and became respected for his persistence and fairness in enforcement actions. Wardens are aware that there are always a few hard-headed people who blame others for their misdeeds. Often, it's the arresting officer.

LaFave happily drove to the wildlife area. He was thinking of the surprise birthday party awaiting him upon his arrival at home that evening. He was sure he had fooled Peggy by not showing any suspicion of such a happening as he left for work. With a smile on his face at his little deception, he light-heartedly began posting "no hunting" signs at Sunset Beach Road.

Arriving home in the afternoon, Peggy hurriedly set the table with the birthday cake with its 32 candles neatly arranged. Four-year-old Lonny and two-year-old Nichole joined her as they feverishly arranged the gifts for the surprise party. The kids were filled with anticipation. Soon, other guests began to arrive.

When LaFave didn't appear shortly after 5 p.m. as expected, Peggy turned on the television to distract the kids who were anxiously waiting for the gala event to occur. Gazing often out the window to catch a glance of Neil's truck she began to worry. Finally, as the clock approached 7 p.m. she called Harold Shine, Neil's supervisor.

"Harold, Neil hasn't arrived home. I wonder if something could be wrong."

"I don't know. He was to quit at five o'clock. I haven't heard from him and it's only a matter of minutes from the wildlife area to your home. I'll run out there and see what's keeping him."

Unable to contain her fears, Peggy also called the Brown County Sheriff's office. They said they'd respond at once.

Urged by several of her party guests, Peggy agreed to look for Neil herself. She drove along the country roads which Neil occasionally patrolled on his way home. Finally her headlights picked up a truck parked at the end of a dead end road. Neil's truck! With a sigh of relief on her lips, she parked by the pickup and called, "Neil–Neil." No answer. She left her vehicle and opened the cab of the truck. "Neil–Neil," she repeated.

With no flashlight she stumbled around the truck kicking grass aside hoping nothing had happened to Neil, but still looking in case he may be laying nearby injured. Suddenly the blackness was pierced by headlights coming down the road. The car stopped behind her vehicle. To Peggy's relief out, stepped Harold Shine.

"Find anything here?" he asked.

"No, did you find anything?"

"Not really. I followed his tracks back into the wildlife area where he was posting, but lost them in the underbrush.

Peggy sighed, "I just know something dreadful has happened to him."

Trying to bolster Peggy's feelings Harold replied, "He's around here somewhere. I'm sure he'll show up any moment."

As they were talking, several Brown County Sheriff's Department squad cars drove up. Investigator Wayne Truttman stepped out, surveyed the situation and radioed headquarters for assistance.

"We need help out here," he reported. "Neil's truck is here, but no sign of him. I think some violator got to him. Contact the Department of Natural Resources and have them get some wardens out here and call surrounding counties. We'll need every available person. Have them bring hip boots, flashlights, portable radios and anything else they can think of. This is wild country. Come prepared."

Truttman organized a search around LaFave's vehicle and soon found his toolbox and a partly smoked cigar that Peggy identified as the brand he smoked.

Squads began arriving from neighboring jurisdictions along with wardens and LaFave's co-workers. Truttman directed them on a systematic search of the area. Lantern lights mingled with beams of flashlights as the search continued into the wet and spongy swamplands. Truttman assigned searchers as they continued to arrive. At 1 a.m., Truttman discontinued the search as progress was very slow in the dark, boggy area. He asked the team to return at 6 a.m., but some never stopped searching.

As the sun slowly broke through the darkness on the morning of the 25th, concerned friends and fellow workers were still searching. As visibility increased and crews were easier to control, Truttman organized a skirmish-line. The line of men moved painstakingly over the rough terrain looking for the slightest clue that may reveal where LaFave might be.

Upon his arrival, Brown County Sheriff Norbert Froelich conferred with Investigator Truttman.

"I have a large search going. We'll cover every inch of the public hunting ground. It'll take quite a long time as the area is huge," said Truttman.

Froelich murmured, "He may never be found. If some poacher shot him and buried him he'll be almost impossible to find."

"That's been bothering me, but I've told the searchers to look for any disturbed ground and if they find anything suspicious to let me know so we can investigate more thoroughly," Truttman replied.

As the day wore on, more people volunteered to assist in the search. The search intensified when tracking dogs and aircraft were brought in. A plane from Brown County Sheriff's Department, one from the Department of Natural Resources, and one from Austin Strauble Airport in Green Bay flew over the area. The planes flew low and directed the search via radio contact with ground searchers. The massive effort turned up no clue as to LaFave's whereabouts.

Meanwhile, Warden Dale Morey, stationed at Appleton, overheard the radio conversation of LaFave's disappearance–a conversation that would launch him into a long, stressful but fulfilling investigation. Like many wardens, Morey was personally acquainted with LaFave and volunteered to assist the Brown County Sheriff's Department in the search and investigation. He would leave the following day.

Back at the wildlife area, Marvin Olson, an experienced bow hunter, archer and expert at reading sign, arrived at the public hunting ground to practice shooting his bow. Upon hearing of the missing warden he joined the search. Examining the ground carefully, as one would do when looking for a wounded deer, he came upon what he thought was a deer scrape. Upon closer examination he discovered where a log had been dragged. He started to dig to satisfy his suspicion that something was buried there. His fingers easily dug through the loose soil until he suddenly struck something solid. He extracted the object from the dirt and stared in wonder at a belt buckle. He feverishly dug deeper and unearthed a human elbow. His voice betraying his terror, he yelled toward wardens Earl Piper and Norman Hicks, "I've...I've, found the warden!"

With a rush, the group crowded around the slight rise in the ground, dragged the log away and began digging with their hands. Soon they revealed LaFave's body buried with wet dirt and mud, intermixed with marsh grass and ferns. Truttman was called to the area and scraped the mud and dirt from the torso. Horrified, he stared at a massive, open, seeping wound where LaFave's head and neck had been gruesomely chopped-off-clear to his shoulders. Searching around the grave, they were unable to locate the head.

Investigator Truttman immediately posted guards and secured the area with crime scene tape to preserve evidence. He collected all the names and addresses of the people present when the grave and body was found for future reference. Sheriff Froelich contacted the Wisconsin State Crime Laboratory and asked technicians to come to the scene to help secure evidence.

An eerie feeling pervaded the swamp that dark, dreary, foggy night in the Senisiba Wildlife Area.

En route to the scene on the morning of September 26, Department of Natural Resources Pilot Kenneth Corbett, who was assisting in the search, updated Dale Morey by radio. Upon arriving at the scene, Morey was surprised at the number of vehicles and people at the site. He took note of the crowded parking lot, the Red Cross workers and neighborhood women setting up feeding stations, and the Brown County Rescue Unit parked on Geano Beach Road.

Arriving at the grave site, Morey observed as the searchers who found the body were escorted out of the area. Familiar with Morey's work on felony cases, Truttman stationed Morey at the grave site and asked him to carefully search the area for evidence. After commiserating over LaFave's body, who was buried lying on his back, Morey tediously began searching the area, aware of every step, being very careful not to destroy any evidence. Slowly, he worked out a drag trail where he found blood and hair stuck to leaves and grass, apparently splattered there by a rifle blast. He stood aghast at the story so vividly portrayed to his trained eye. Lining up the direction of the shot from a spent rifle casing, he discovered to his horror a white substance stuck to the foliage that could only be brain tissue. To Morey's experienced eye, the shot came from the north and threw the body pieces south. Analyzing the area further, he discovered another drag trail where grass, weeds and brush were considerably trampled. *Someone may have laid in wait to ambush another here.* Backtracking, Morey returned to the body to make sure no one interfered with it. The night grew darker, cooler and more eerie in spite of newly installed portable flood lights. A heavy, wet fog settled in to encompass the grisly grave and its contents.

A gigantic search was underway for LaFave's head as technicians from the state crime lab arrived. Morey directed them to the evidence he had found, which were marked by flags for later inspection and collection. Under the supervision of Harry Gyarsbock, technicians took samples from the body and painstakingly searched the immediate area for evidence before allowing the coroner to remove the corpse. As it was removed from the shallow pit, technicians collected blood, hair, and anything out of the ordinary as evidence. The body was then taken to St. Mary's Medical Center in Green Bay for an autopsy.

Peggy, who had remained at the wildlife area during the night, was devastated when told that LaFave's body had been found. Peggy's tears flowed freely as her neighbors took her home to gaze upon the celebration table prepared for her loved one. Even harder was the inevitable job of telling her children that Daddy would never return.

For the next day and a half, the crime lab team, Morey, and Brown County Sheriff's Department Deputies, meticulously searched the small area near where LaFave's body had been found.

About 50-feet south of the grave site, stuffed under grass and forest duff near a game trail, they found a blood-soaked area, LaFave's sunglasses and case, his pen and notebook and several .22-caliber rifle shell casings. Nearby, they found a tooth, blood, bone and brain tissue spewed in a macabre manner around the concussion area. The forest floor had been gouged, apparently by bullets fired from a high powered rifle. The team agreed that this was likely the place where an unsuspecting LaFave had been ambushed, slaughtered and mutilated. That evening, Doctor John Draheim, a pathologist from St. Mary's Medical Center, reported there was only one wound in LaFave's torso, a bullet hole through his left arm.

A herculean effort took place as an area about 300-feet-square was physically cleared of all underbrush and laid out in grids. The area included the grave and the ambush site. Warden Dale Morey and Brown County Sergeant Marvin Gerlikovski collected and marked evidence. Deputy Chief Warden Harold Hettrick manned the military surplus metal detector, following grid lines marked out by DNR Training Officer William Rollmann. Fire control personnel Elmer Pennington, Don Soderberg from Wausaukee and Gerry Gusick of Pound chopped brush and dug up articles. They found an assortment of wire, nails, bolts, ox shoes and parts of old utilities along with .22- and 30.06-caliber shell casings and bullets. The casings and bullets were analyzed at the crime lab and identified as being shot from Remington rifles.

On the morning of the 28th, during a visual search north of the area where they felt the murder had occurred, Brown County Deputy Sheriff Robert Grant spotted some loose soil about 60-feet north of where the body had been buried. A scattering of forest humus among the grass and leaves directed his attention to what appeared to be a round plug of sod. He grasped the grass and twigs growing from it and carefully lifted the plug from its round hole. He gingerly dug through the soft and easily scoopable dirt with his hands. Drawing a deep breath, he continued to scoop, knowing full well what he was about to find. He was startled at the grisly sight of LaFave's face starring up at him. Large slashes extending across his face made the macabre vision even more frightening. After photographing the site, the long tiring search ended. LaFave's head was carefully lifted from the shallow hole and placed in a box.

Peggy was waiting at the parking lot when the searchers carried the box to their vehicle. No one had enough courage to tell her what was in it. The shocked look on her face attested to her thoughts—*she knew!*

The investigative team concluded that LaFave had either been commanded or attracted to the game trail to investigate something. He had been shot in the temple several times with a .22-caliber firearm. The large pool of blood suggested that he had laid there a considerable time. The assailant evidently returned some time later with a 30.06-caliber rifle and a shovel taken from LaFave's truck. LaFave's glasses, pen and notebook were hidden under grass and weeds and his body dragged about 50-feet northwest. LaFave's arms had extended due to rigormortis, also suggesting that he had laid there a long time. His extended arms left a wide trail when dragged by the killer.

It appeared the assailant had stopped and attempted to blow LaFave's head off by shooting him repeatedly in the neck area with the 30.06-caliber rifle. Six 30.06-caliber rifle casings and projectiles were later found on and in the ground. The rifle did its grotesque job with the exception of a small amount of tissue connecting the head to the shoulder. This was apparently chopped off with the blade of the shovel.

Dragging the body approximately 60-feet, he dug a hole, buried the body and attempted to camouflage it by scattering the excess dirt and dragging a log over the grave. Carrying the head another 56-feet north, he cut a round hole through the sod, scattered the excess dirt, put the head in the hole and replaced the sod cap.

Doctor Draheim examined LaFave's severed head. He reported that two small holes through the brain from a .22-caliber rifle were the most likely cause of death. However, other wounds were severe enough to also cause death: the back of the skull had been crushed exposing the brain; the face was mutilated with a heavy, sharp instrument, possibly a shovel; and a broken jaw revealed loose teeth.

Armed with few clues other than the autopsy evidence, Sheriff Froelich called a meeting and appointed Captain Richard Schrickel, Sergeant Marvin Gerlikovski, Investigator Leon Pieschek, Sergeant Robert Grant and Investigator David Zasada to lead the investigation. They agreed the murderer was a person LaFave had either caught in violation that fateful day or someone who carried a deep-seated grudge from an earlier arrest. The killer waited for, or stalked LaFave with the twisted intent to make him pay for his actions. They knew LaFave had arrested a large number of game violators on the preserve and they vowed to check his arrest records and question every one of them.

The attack was delivered in an unabated frenzy of fury and indicated the assailant had built up an intense hate for LaFave. This was a clue to the identity of the killer. Vengeance had to be the reason for the murder.

As the days passed, a number of people who knew LaFave were questioned. Several local poachers consented to lie-detector tests administered by lieutenants Donald Van Straten and Pat Dwyer. All passed. The area was searched several more times with nothing of significance found.

Two weeks after the Sept. 24 murder, an impromptu meeting was held in the Madison office between Chief Warden Walter Zelinske and Deputy Chief Warden Harold Hettrick. They assigned Warden Dale Morey to assist the Brown County Sheriff's Department on a full time basis until the murder was solved. Morey was the logical choice since he had been involved in the original search and seizure and had experience with felony investigations as under sheriff of Washburn County before becoming a warden. Plus, his station at Appleton was close to the scene and he was familiar with county deputies. Later he confided. "I was chosen because I'm the best looking warden in the state." Upon approval of Secretary Lester Voight, Morey accepted the challenge on October 10, 1971.

The Brown County Conservation Alliance offered a reward of $1,000 for information leading to the arrest of the murderer. A week later it was increased to $2,300. The reward offer brought information flooding in from many sources, mostly false leads. The investigation area was enlarged to include people LaFave had arrested in the Green Bay area. A significant number of people were cleared either by questioning or through lie-detector tests.

Finally, one person refused to take the test based on his attorney's advice. That person was Gene Glencoe. Under questioning, Glencoe admitted he hunted the Senisiba Wildlife Area with a 30.06-caliber rifle, but that he didn't own the gun. The relative who owned the rifle gave it to investigators for a ballistic check. The crime lab report indicated that the rifle was not the murder weapon. None-the-less, Glencoe remained the prime suspect because he wouldn't consent to a lie-detector test. Investigators questioned his friends who said that Glencoe owned two Remington rifles, a .22- and a 30.06-caliber. One man said he'd been out shooting with Glencoe recently in a gravel pit. Using metal detectors, investigators recovered a number of .22-caliber rifle shell casings.

Wayne Truttman directed another metal detector search when it was determined that Glencoe commonly used an area north of the murder scene. Truttman had received information that the two guns being sought may be buried there. Harold Hettrick headed up a group of wardens trained in the proficient use of surplus military mine detectors to search the area. They were Dale "Swede" Erlandson,

Madison, Edward "Ed" Hill, Antigo, Dennis "Denny" Jameson, Baraboo, Richard "Dick" Streng, Chilton, Robert "Bob" Smith, Marinette, Charles "Chuck" Olson, Marinette, and Donald "Don" Euers, Green Bay.

The weather had turned bitter cold and wet as it often does in November and the search was miserable. Brown County deputies sweat and froze in the bitter weather as they swung machetes to clear underbrush. The wardens swept the area with metal detectors. The wardens felt especially put-out because they weren't told what they were looking for. At one time, Hettrick shook his widely-known 'big finger' at Morey. "If I find out you've got us on a wild goose chase I'll have your A—!"

"It's not often a peon gets to order the man with the long tails around," quipped Morey.

Nothing of consequence was found and Morey's underwear was left intact.

As the long day wore on, Glencoe and his cohorts watched from a safe distance to see what may be found. The investigation of Glencoe revealed disturbing behavior; his acquaintances feared him; when babysitting his niece he dismembered her doll while she screamed in terror; and at a party with his buddies, he jerked the head off of a live, purring kitten.

The attack on LaFave had been delivered in a cowardly manner possibly from behind and had turned into a frenzy of fiery fury indicating the assailant had an intense hate for him–a clear signal the killer was venting a pent up vengeance. Was this young man capable of such a crime? Glencoe's quirky behavior seemed to fit the bill.

Little things, while not conclusive, kept the investigators going: LaFave had arrested Glencoe the previous fall for killing a pheasant during the closed season; Glencoe's grandmother lived just south of the wildlife area parking lot within easy walking distance of the murder scene; another grave site, almost identical in size, shape and depth as the one used to bury LaFave, was found behind Glencoe's grandmother's house.

A soil scientist from the University of Wisconsin at Green Bay analyzed lichen growth on the disturbed soil from the second grave. Analysis indicated that the hole had been dug approximately six months earlier. Had the assailant prepared and laid a grave for LaFave prior to fall? LaFave's truck could easily be seen from his grandmother's house.

Glencoe had been target shooting at beer cans thrown into Green Bay with a Remington .22-caliber rifle. Investigators used a back hoe to scoop out the shallow beach area and sifted the bottom material through a giant screen to allow everything to go through except a .22-caliber bullet. They found several .22 bullets fired from a Remington rifle, but a positive match couldn't be made with existing projectiles because of corrosion. All felt the bullets were from Glencoe's gun adding another piece to the puzzle.

A cooperative search was conducted between Brown and Oneida County Sheriff's Departments when they discovered that one year previous to the murder, Glencoe had sighted-in his 30.06-caliber deer rifle at old bachelor Johnson's place on Lake Tomahawk. Johnson showed them the area where the targeting had taken place. A crew of officers shoveled two-feet of snow off the area on a bitterly cold December day and Morey utilized the military metal detector to search the area. A large blow torch was used to melt the ground where they found a 30.06 rifle casing along with nuts, bolts, nails and assorted junk. In a large popple tree near the target area, they found a bullet embedded in the trunk. A block was cut from it and sent to the crime lab along with the 30.06-caliber shell. The bullet matched the type recovered at the crime scene, but wasn't usable in court due to damage. Still, the bullet pointed toward Glencoe.

Meanwhile, one of Glencoe's alibis was destroyed. He claimed to have purchased a particular item at a local store on the day of the murder, but the item was actually purchased much earlier allowing him plenty of time to commit the murder. During the investigation, a female clairvoyant in her 80s, living over 100 miles away, contacted Gerlikovski several times. She cited her fears for him and Morey. She had a history of working with law enforcement agencies and told them things that only Gerlikovski and the murderer could know. The men found this disturbing, yet comforting; at least she felt they were on the right track.

Though circumstantial evidence was piling up, significant evidence to charge Glencoe didn't exist. Convinced that he was their man, Sheriff Froelich discussed the case with District Attorney Donald Zuidmulder.

"We may have one more card to play," said Zuidmulder. "I'm going to ask Attorney General Robert Warren to authorize the use of a wire tap."

The newly enacted law allowing the use of electronic surveillance had never been used in a murder case in Wisconsin.

"Assistant Attorney General Peter Pesheck is a law school classmate of mine. I'll call him to ease the way."

Receiving the call from Zuidmulder, Pesheck set up a meeting at the old Lorraine Hotel in Madison. Attending was Gerlikovski, Morey, Zuidmulder and Pesheck. They mulled over reams of investigative material during the weekend meeting which resulted in a 65-page affidavit. The document gave Judge Donald W. Gleason the legal foundation to issue the tap of Glencoe's girlfriend's apartment where he lived. To meet the 72-hour limit the tap was valid, a plan was formulated to keep Glencoe at home and motivate him to use the phone. Morey volunteered to keep a watch on him and make sure he knew he was being watched. It had the desired effect.

"Every place I go that rat sticks his head out of his hole," said Glencoe. Becoming nervous he finally called his grandmother.

"Hi grandma. I'm worried. If anyone asks about that gun I left with you, tell them nothing. That rat Morey is tailing me. They're up to something. Just don't let anyone have the thirty-o-six."

The search warrant was executed by members of the department of justice, Zuidmulder, Froelich, Gerlikovski, Brown County deputies and Morey. The grandmother stated unequivocally that she had no gun of any kind, but persistent questioning brought forth the whereabouts of the gun. She said that her daughter had visited her this morning and took the gun with her. Insisting that the grandmother accompany them, they swiftly drove to the aunt's place of business. She cooperated immediately, fearing further implication of herself and her mother in obstructing justice. The rifle was wrapped in plastic. Unwrapping the plastic, the found the rifle covered with dirt, indicating it had been buried for some time. The rifle was a 30.06-caliber Remington.

Crime lab testing proved beyond a shadow of a doubt it was indeed the rifle used in the murder of LaFave. The .22-caliber rifle was never found. Tapes retrieved on December 13 were turned over to Ernest Nash, a voice identification specialist with the Michigan State Police. Comparison between them and known voice prints of Glencoe proved he was the caller.

A John Doe hearing conducted before Judge Donald W. Gleason on December 15 brought forth a murder warrant for Gene Glencoe. Sheriff Froelich, Game Warden Dale Morey and Special Agent John Schultz from the state crime laboratory went to Glencoe's grandmother's home to make the arrest. Glencoe was there and was taken into custody.

"Why is Gene being arrested? I told you earlier he spent September 24 helping me can tomatoes. You even taped our interview. Now you're arresting him? I don't believe this," said Glencoe's grandmother.

His head hanging low Glencoe said, "Aw grandma, they know where I was that day."

The trial was held on April 4, 1972 with District Attorney Donald Zuidmulder prosecuting. Attorney James Pressentin represented Glencoe.

After four hours of deliberating and reviewing evidence, including the 30.06-caliber rifle that Glencoe had hidden, the jury ruled a verdict of guilty of murder in the first degree on April 13. The next day, Judge Robert Parins sentenced Gene Glencoe to life imprisonment and ordered him to the state prison at Green Bay where he would begin serving his sentence. While never admitting to the murder, he made a statement to Morey and Gerlikovski, "If I ever get out of jail what happened to LaFave will be like child's play compared to what will happen to you."

Sheriff Froelich and District Attorney Zuidmulder praised the investigators, giving special accolades to Sergeant Marvin Gerlikovski and Warden Dale Morey.

PART II

On August 28, 1981, headlines of the *Wisconsin State Journal* screamed: **Killer cuts through fence, escapes from Fox Lake**. The story described how Gene Glencoe, now 31, had cut through two chain-link fences to escape from Fox Lake Correctional Institute on August 27.

> *Fox Lake Superintendent John Gagnon said Glencoe had been transferred to his medium-security prison from Waupun a maximum-security prison, 10 months ago because of good behavior. He said Glencoe had been working as a janitor in one of the prison housing units and felt the escape had occurred between 7:30 and 8 p.m. He was reported missing at the 9 p.m. check last night. He said he felt Glencoe had acted alone because no vehicles had been stolen inside the prison.*

Glencoe escaped on a wet and windy August night. Scudding clouds made the dark night even darker and reduced visibility to almost nothing at the Fox Lake Prison Farm–an ideal night for Gene Glencoe and his girlfriend Alice Joust, of Sheboygan, to carry out the 10 month planned escape. The two fine-tuned the plan during an afternoon prison visit that day.

Joust carried out the first phase of the plan shortly after her visit. She threw cutting tools over the prison fence at a prearranged spot where buildings physically blocked the guards' vision. Around 7 p.m., Glencoe slipped unobtrusively from the buildings to the spot along the chain link fence where he knew the tools would be. Working feverishly with bolt cutters, he systematically cut through the two chain link fences to freedom.

Joust waited nearby in her auto until 7:45 p.m. when she drove to the site of the escape. She killed her lights as she reached the prison and coasted slowly to the prearranged spot, using the emergency brake so the brake lights wouldn't activate. She removed the dome lights so that Glencoe could open the doors without light exposing their movements. Suddenly the door was jerked open and Glencoe hurtled himself inside. "Drive! Get out of here!" he ordered.

Thus began the second and final stage of the notorious Gene Glencoe odyssey. A smart, cagey and very dangerous murderer of a dedicated game enforcer was on the loose. His pugnacious nature, finely-honed survival skills and woodsman's abilities would befuddle and endanger law enforcement officers for many months.

As alert bulletins circulated around the state and Midwest, the two travelled north and west. They managed to elude the law for two days by sleeping in their car and eating food brought along by Joust.

On August 30, Glencoe insisted on driving even though his driving ability had deteriorated during his 10 years in prison. Approaching Hayward from the south on highway 2, off-duty policeman Fritz Markman and his wife noticed his erratic driving. He radioed Mike Newton, a young Hayward officer on his first patrol. Newton and his partner, Donald Plante, responded to the call of a drunken driver entering the city. Hearing the dispatcher return a check of the car aroused no suspicion or alarm about who they were dealing with because it checked out to Alice Joust of Sheboygan. As they waited at the intersection of highways 27 and 63 for the suspect car to arrive, Officer Dave Aubart joined them and parked across the intersection. He had heard the conversation on the radio.

Watching the driver of the suspect vehicle setting at the stoplight, Newton noticed the man reach stealthily under the front seat.

"I think he's hiding booze Don," said Newton.

"Could be, lets take him," replied Plante.

Seeing the squad setting at the intersection, Glencoe panicked.

"Man we're in trouble now. Give me the snub nose." Reaching under the seat he whispered, "Here it is, I'll kill this guy if he stops us. I'm not going back to jail."

Quickly he shoved the .44-caliber snub-nosed handgun into the large stomach pocket of his blue sweatshirt. With red lights flashing behind him, Glencoe instantly pulled over and got out of the car. Leaving the door open, he hustled to meet the approaching policeman. Hands in the pocket of the zippered sweatshirt and grasping the Magnum hand gun, he met Newton halfway between the two parked cars.

"May I see your drivers license please?" asked Newton.

Meanwhile, Aubart drove past the two cars on their right and position himself in front of Glencoe to thwart an escape. Seeing the second squad, Glencoe quickly changed plans.

Nonchalantly he replied, "Oh sure, come with me, I left it in my car."

Turning on his heel as though to walk to his car, he suddenly reached for his rear pocket as if to produce his wallet. He turned his head and said, "Just a minute, I just remembered I..." He spun around and struck Newton a stunning blow to the face with his balled fist. Coming back, Newton slammed his hands into Glencoe's shoulders and shoved him forcefully backward. Glencoe caromed off the door post landing squarely behind the wheel. Meanwhile, Plante left the squad and ran toward the assailant who he saw struggling with the shifting knob. Hurtling himself forward, Plante struck Glencoe a slashing blow across the shoulder with his flashlight. Glencoe hurriedly jerked the shifting lever into reverse by mistake and jammed the accelerator to the floorboard. His vehicle lurched backward and ran over and broke Plante's foot.

Newton thought, *my God, my first shift and my squad is going to get hit. I won't be a policeman in Hayward very long.*

Glencoe quickly shifted into drive and careened toward Aubart, who was watching this wild activity. He turned on his red light and pulled out in front of the speeding vehicle to block his escape.

Seeing the squad blocking the street, Glencoe swung the wheel wildly to the left. He stomped the accelerator to the floor in a mad dash to slip by. A loud crash was the result as his path was effectively closed by Aubart's squad. Scraping the length of the squad, the rear bumpers of the two vehicles hooked together. The two vehicles squealed down the block with Glencoe's car dragging the squad until it finally broke lose halfway down the block. Smiling at his ability to escape, Glencoe raced down Hayward's streets. Newton's squad, red lights running and siren screaming, followed immediately behind him. Making several evasive turns on city streets Glencoe made it to highway 77 on the east end of town.

Shaking off the effects of the confrontation, Newton and Plante began chasing the unknown driver. Radioing Sawyer County for assistance they were relieved to hear a state squad was in the vicinity. They would set up a roadblock on the east end of town. State Patrol Officer Harold Burton and Radio Dispatcher Peter Weatherhead swiftly responded and placed their squad crosswise at the intersection of Airport Road and highway 77. Approaching the roadblock, Glencoe gritted his teeth to prepare himself to run it. At the last minute, he realized he couldn't avoid hitting the squad and he dynamited the brakes. Sliding to an abrupt stop, he opened the door and bolted down through the ditch into the bordering woods.

Arriving at the scene, Newton and Plante quickly discussed the situation with Burton and Weatherhead and asked them to take Alice Joust, who had been left in the auto, to jail in Hayward. They would attempt to shag the runner out of the woods, but after slogging through the woods a half hour, they decided they couldn't find him. As they walked toward the car, Plante asked, "How would you describe the guy Mike?"

"A big fist!"

"A big fist? That's a description?"

"A better description is a big fist swinging!"

At the jail, Alice Joust wasn't cooperative. She wouldn't give her name and told officers she had picked up Glencoe as a hitchhiker between Windigo Wayside and Stone Lake. The vehicle checked out to her and she gave her address in Sheboygan. In searching her purse they found an owners manual for a newly purchased gun. The manual described a .44-caliber Ruger Magnum pistol. The escapee, although not identified, was considered armed and dangerous. It wasn't until the next morning, through checking reports at the Fox Lake Institution, that the officers discovered that Gene Glencoe was the driver.

The fugitive was now in the woods. At 2 a.m., while patrolling an area four miles from where Joust's vehicle had been seized, Burton identified a car reported stolen earlier that evening. Glencoe bolted down county K and finally spiked the brakes, abandoned the car and hightailed it into the brush to again escape capture.

Sheriff Ernie Lien called in wardens to assist in the woodland search for the murderer. All wardens in the northwest area were put on standby and many participated in cabin searches where Glencoe had been sighted.

While checking deserted tourist cabins near the Lac Court Oreilles Indian Reservation, wardens Bill Hoyt from Spooner and Jim Flanigan from Siren received an urgent message from Sheriff Ernie Lien asking them to check a report that Glencoe had been sighted near their location. Their response brought them to a logging area. They parked their auto and walked around the cut over forest area.

"Jim come over here," said Hoyt. "Look at this. Someone has been walking around here alright. Could very well be Glencoe."

"Yeah, let's follow it out," said Flanigan. They followed the track off to one side so as not to disturb the spoor. Slowly they worked their way across the slash to a large brush pile. "The track seems to end at the brush pile. I can't follow it any further." Joking he commented, "Looks like he's hiding under it."

"Yeah, he's probably got a bead on you. I'm wearing my underwear, thanks to Ernie. What're you wearing?"

"This is no joke. I think the state should buy all of us vests."

Poking around in the brush pile with a stick Hoyt murmured,

"Looks like there's no one here. Lets move on."

Returning to their vehicle they radioed Lien.

"Checked the area you described. Found one fresh track, Glencoe could have been here. Nothing here now."

Alice Joust's story of picking up Glencoe as a hitchhiker did not long stand and she was convicted of aiding and abetting an escape and sentenced to two years at Taycheedah Correctional Institute.

Somehow working his way to Radisson, Glencoe stole a pickup truck. It was found abandoned two days later in Cornell where he stole an Oldsmobile. In mid-September this car was found abandoned in Menominee, Michigan. For a time, nothing was heard of Glencoe's whereabouts.

Dale Morey was now living in Black Earth and working out of the

Bureau of Law Enforcement in Madison as the Boating Safety Administrator for the Wisconsin Department of Natural Resources. Concerned about his safety, the Brown County Sheriff's Office notified Morey of Glencoe's escape. Glencoe had often threatened Morey and Gerlikovski while in prison.

Reports sighted Glencoe in Suamico and Green Bay, where authorities expected him. One report spotted him in Madison which kept Morey looking over his shoulder. Morey later explained that his shoulder became sore from sleeping on a loaded .38. None of the sightings were substantiated.

Shawano County Sheriff James Knope began receiving reports in early October indicating Glencoe was hiding out in his county. Indeed he was. While in Waupun he became acquainted with Jim and John Colgate, two brothers whose father owned land on the Stockbridge-Munsee Indian Reservation. Told of its wilderness nature, Glencoe intuitively worked his way toward what appeared to be a perfect sanctuary. Glencoe contacted Bob Colgate in early October and managed to rent the backwoods area of his land and was given permission to build a shack on it. The month of October was a busy time as Glencoe laboriously built a 12-foot-square cardboard shack supported by small cedar poles cut from nearby swamps. This was his refuge against the coming winter.

Constantly on the alert, the Shawano County Sheriff's Department checked out each report of Glencoe's presence in their county. In early December, Knope was satisfied he knew where the fugitive was holed up.

On December 9, Knope called together 50 law enforcement personnel from many counties and agencies to lay out a plan of apprehension. The group met at the Shawano Police Department office and included the following men: Shawano County deputies Chief Deputy Lloyd Heinz, Sergeant Ray Faeling, Bob Schmidt, Randy Giese, Tom Gatz, Larry Roth, John Toonen, Robert Bohlman, Dave Swanson, Art Collins, Richard Kucksdorf, Gerald Thorpe, Paul Kuhn, Laurie Nevel and Milt Marquardt; Shawano City Police officers Captain Elroy "Butch" Bergner, Lieutenant Donald Schoenhofen, Scott Otto, Bernie Burrack, Myron Heistad and Al Schultz, Oconto County Sheriff James Gehling; Menominee County Sheriff Jim Tourtillot and four officers; Brown County Deputy Glendon Brosig; Department of Natural Resources wardens Rick Herzfelt, Shawano, Winter Hess, Marinette, Wayne Jiedy, Oshkosh, Larry Kriese, Appleton, Andrew Krakow, Marinette, Todd Wipperman, Clintonville and pilots Kenneth Corbett and Jon Folven from the northeast area; Menominee Tribal Police Chief Kenneth "Paddo" Fish and 15 officers; and finally, the State Department of Criminal Investigation team of Garner Oswald and Rod Pevytoe from Madison.

Knope told that group that he had received information that

Glencoe was hiding in a shack on the Stockbridge-Munsee Indian Reservation. Indian officials knew nothing of him or the rumor.

With safety of the officers a prime concern, all persons participating would identify themselves by attaching a strip of blue forestry tape to their outside garment to ensure they could not be mistaken for Glencoe. Ambulances from Shawano and Tigerton were ordered on stand-by. To assure radio communications could not be understood by anyone monitoring them, special codes and signals were developed.

The plan was laid out in two phases: surround the suspected area of Glencoe's shack from the north and then approach the hide-out from the south. Eight teams were appointed, each with specific assignments. Winter Hess was chosen to lead teams one through four. Sheriff James Knope was in charge of teams five through eight.

Because of his experience in the woods and as a "forward observer" during the Vietnam War, Winter Hess' teams would encircle the shack from the north. The deeply-wooded character of the landscape made it the most likely escape route. When in place, Sheriff Knope's teams—five through eight—would move in from the south and confront Glencoe in his hideout.

On the outside chance that Glencoe got by this circle, a second cut-off line was set by Menominee County Sheriff Jim Tourtillot and his four deputies on the Menominee County line, and by Menominee Police Chief Kenneth Fish and his 15 officers at the Menominee Indian Reservation boundary. Roadblocks were set up on Anderson Road to the east and west of Bob Colgate's home who was suspected of harboring Glencoe. Hess faced many perplexing problems. First, he had never been in the area before and no one knew exactly where the shack was located in the vast woodland. Second, how was he going to keep 18 people on his team quiet and together? Third, he didn't know the woods prowess of his charges. And finally, what if his team accidentally stumbled onto Glencoe either in his shack or wandering around in the woods?

The night before the proposed raid, Hess summoned the aid of a State Forest Technician Robert Siegried of Shawano who provided him with aerial photographs of the area. Hess studied them with a stereoscope and located landmarks and vegetative changes that he hoped would guide him to the shack.

Early on the morning of the operation, a canine unit headed by Glenden Brosig from Brown County searched a number of summer residences on the Stockbridge-Munsee Indian Reservation to determine if reports of Glencoe using these sites were valid. Nothing was found.

Hess's group checked a metal shed on the edge of a field to be sure it wasn't occupied and entered the wooded area north and east of the supposed location of the shack at 6 a.m. They had one hour to get into position near the shack.

Hess lined up his men in teams. He placed the Department of Crime Investigative agents immediately to his rear, the wardens in the middle and the Oconto County Sheriff's officers in the rear. Winter led them silently through the whiteness of an unbroken new snow. About halfway to their proposed objective, a team member told Hess that the Oconto County officers were no longer with them. Moving very slow, and hoping the lost crew would catch up, Hess was shocked to see someone ahead of them. Squatting and squinting feverishly through binoculars, he wondered if it could possibly be Glencoe. He spotted the blue streamer worn by Sheriff Gehling and several of his officers. The Oconto Sheriff's team had caught up. Worried about the lost time, Hess quickly reorganized his group and led them swiftly forward. Watching his map and compass very closely, he brought them to a point he thought to be about 100 yards from the suspected location of the shack.

Needing something to release his and the team's built-up tension and not really sure of where they were, he confidently walked out in front of the assemblage and scratched a cross in the snow with his boot down to dirt and nonchalantly said, "X marks the spot." To his rear, a DCI agent looked at him in wonder and turned to whisper to his partner, "How the hell did he find that X in this woods?"

Hess glanced at his watch at 6:45 a.m. and quickly dispersed his team about 50 yards apart in a semicircular line. He radioed in code that this team was in position.

"5-0-3 Shawano go ahead with that 28."

"K-S-B-5-0-4 Shawano Sheriff at 7 a.m." said the dispatcher which instructed teams five through eight to begin their initial advance.

With a search warrant in hand, teams seven and eight, consisting of Sheriff Knope, Chief Deputy Lloyd Heinz, Tom Gatz, and DCI agents Garner Oswald and Rod Pevytoe, stopped at the residence of Bob Colgate who Glencoe was reported to be associated with. Colgate owned the land where the shack was supposedly located. Colgate admitted that he knew a shack had been built on his land and agreed to lead the officers to it. He was cooperative and consented to a search of his buildings.

Asked if he knew a person fitting Glencoe's description, he answered, "Yes, he lives in the shack, but his name isn't Glencoe. I'll show you the way back into the woods where he is."

Driving back on a woods road, Colgate pointed out where the officers could park their vehicles out of sight of the shack. His group went forward about 150 yards into the woods. With the shack in view, Oswald threw out an order on the bull horn. "Glencoe, this is the police, come out with your hands up."

Silence pervaded the woodland as they waited in suspense. Nothing happened. Then, Knope directed teams five and six, consisting of Shawano Police officers, to fan out and form a skirmish line. They advanced toward the area of the shack, stepping lightly. Donald "Don" Schoenhofen, Scott Otto, Myron Heistad and Elroy "Butch" Bergner were on his left and Bernie Burrack and Al Schultz were on his right.

Schoenhofen stumbled over one of the many small, cut and limbed cedar trees littering the ground amidst the tightly interwoven swamp of cedar and spruce. *Wonder why someone is cutting these trees? They're too small to use as firewood or posts. Certainly Glencoe isn't cutting them as building material for his shack. They're too small. They're freshly cut. Man tracks all over the place. Got to relieve myself.* He leaned his 12-gauge shotgun against a huge cedar, stepped a few feet away, and unzipped his bulky snowmobile suit to answer nature's call. Just then, he heard a crunching sound. Whirling to look in the direction of the sound, he sighted a pair of sorrel boots approaching beneath the deer browse line in the darkly-shaded maze of cedar. Stopping, the man stepped up on a fallen log pausing long enough to give Schoenhofen time to think. *Must be one of our guys. Maybe I should yell. No, I may be too close to the cabin. Glencoe may hear me.* Suddenly, the boots began to move toward him. The man materializing from the shadows about 30 feet away was none of his fellow officers. Recognition paralyzed his thinking and movement. *My God it's Glencoe. He's got a rifle! What do I do now?* Desperate to find a way to escape he gazed around looking for a refuge of one kind or another. Several feet from him was an uprooted tree. *Maybe I should grab my gun and dive into that hole. Gun's too far away. Don't think I can make it.*

Carrying a white milk jug in one hand and his rifle cradled in the other, Glencoe trudged closer, "Dave, how's the hunting?"

My God he thinks he knows me. Play along. Sure glad I don't have a uniform or badge showing. He would shoot me for sure.

"Not too good, getting cold, going to get out of here."

Swinging his jug, Glencoe trudged toward an open water creek.

Burrack had also seen the boots pass beneath the cedars. Not knowing who the person was, he pointed his firearm toward the man and heard the sounds of talking. He saw the boots move off. Burrack and Schoenhofen met briefly and talked over Schoenhofen's close encounter. After moving only a few feet, they saw a small shack hidden in the swampy tangle. They laid down and looked at it from under the overhanging branches.

At the same time, Oswald, Brosig, Gatz, and Pevytoe walked quietly along a well-travelled trail until they reached a wood pile, some 500 yards from their cars. They slowly peered to one side of the wood pile saw the shack. With the sun shining over their shoulders and glistening off the whiteness of the barely disturbed snow, visibility was good. They could make out a man standing in the door.

Brosig asked, "Is that one of your men Garner?"

"It might be, no, no it's not. I recognize him now, it's Glencoe."

Raising his bullhorn a second time Oswald bellowed, "Glencoe. Police. Freeze. You're under arrest!"

Glencoe swiftly stooped and grabbed a rifle that was leaning against the door sill. He darted around the shack toward the northwest.

Again Oswald's voice boomed through the bullhorn, "Police, freeze!"

Pevytoe shouted, "He's got a gun."

Gatz had worked himself up near the shack when he heard the bullhorn and saw Glencoe run, "Halt Glencoe or we'll shoot!" he hollered.

Turning, Glencoe raised his rifle and aimed at Gatz and the group of officers. Gatz fired a burst of shots from his .223-caliber automatic rifle.

Brosig saw Glencoe point the rifle in his direction and heard the burst of automatic fire. Hurriedly, he jerked his handgun into position and fired four times.

Heinz then leveled his 30.08 automatic rifle and squeezed-off one shot. Oswald had followed in pursuit of Glencoe but instinctively took cover behind a stump after seeing his rifle leveled at the group and hearing the shooting. Oswald peeked from behind his stump and saw Glencoe being hit. Glencoe fell and rolled onto his right side, all the while pointing the rifle at the group of officers. Glencoe spotted Oswald and swung the muzzle threateningly toward him. Oswald yelled, "Drop it," and ducked behind his stump. *He thought, this damn rotten stump will never stop a bullet from a high powered rifle.* Glencoe was now aiming at him. Oswald reacted. He jerked his 12-gauge shotgun to his shoulder and fired a load of double-zero buckshot at him.

Glencoe was down for good. He had fallen on his rifle and laid stomach down on the ground, his arms and legs sprawled in the snow. The booming echo of gunfire was replaced by a deafening silence. One-by-one, officers left their cover to advance on the unmoving man. A pool of blood stained the winter white ground.

Pevytoe was the first to arrive at the still form. He placed his shotgun muzzle against the back of Glencoe's head. "Don't move," he breathed. Directing the shotgun with one hand he reached down carefully and worked the rifle loose from under him and handed it to Oswald. Still cautious, the two searched for the .44- Magnum handgun he was reputed to be carrying. They recovered a 6-inch knife and began first aid.

Silent and ashen, Glencoe was alive but very seriously wounded. He was gently carried out on a blanket and loaded on the waiting ambulance manned by Roger Lenzer and Steve Darms at 8:42 a.m. He died en route to the Shawano hospital at about 9 a.m.

Winter Hess and his team heard the bullhorn and shooting and waited with bated breath. *Is he coming our way? What will we do if he does?* The radio came alive with the buzz of excited voices.

"Winter come on down. All's clear. We have him."

Breaking cover, Hess felt the tension drain from his body as he hand-signaled the team members forward. *Glad he didn't come our way. Looks like we were about 200 yards from his shack. Not bad. Wouldn't care to be any closer anyway. Get caught in a cross fire.* Nearing the man sprawled in the snow, he realized Glencoe had indeed ran in their direction. *Sure glad we weren't the people who had to shoot him.*

As Hess approached the cabin, a plane swooped low and Pilot Corbett wafted words of finality across the woodland over the plane's P.A. system.

"Bye-Bye Birdie!"

Examining Glencoe's shack revealed he had been eating breakfast when the raid began as evidenced by a partially eaten sandwich. He also had an ample supply of food and wood to keep him fed and warm. The small, patched together shelter contained a metal folding cot, a small woodstove, shelves, a chair and small table. A new pair of boots still carried a K-Mart sale tag. Obviously someone was supplying him with subsistence provisions. Officers recovered a Remington 870 12-gauge shotgun and the .44- Magnum handgun. Both were loaded. The shack also contained a large supply of ammunition.

On a tree limb outside the shack hung an air-dried and frozen deer carcass and a squirrel, skinned and impaled on a tree spike, evidence of his subsistence way of life.

Later, Bob Colgate admitted hunting with him during the fall deer season. Colgate said that Glencoe remarked about the time he hid from the law in Sawyer County.

"Glencoe said, 'There are a couple of lucky game wardens over there. I almost killed them. They had me cornered under a big brush pile and didn't know it. They stomped around looking for me and even joked about me being under the pile. If they had, I would have killed them both. I aimed my .44 mag at one of them, but thought better of killing him 'cause the other one may have gotten me. If I thought I could have killed both of them I sure would have. They didn't stay together long enough for me to be sure I could get both of them before the other one got me. It seemed each was always on the other side of the brush pile and it was a big one.'"

Author's notes:

• This story shows the cooperation that must and does exist between law enforcement agencies and how wardens fit into this cooperative effort. Wardens have expertise under certain conditions beyond the average law enforcement officer. They have knowledge of the outdoors, can read outdoor sign and have a familiarity with areas in the state that other officers do not have. In turn, other officers have much to offer wardens. It's especially comforting to know when facing a dangerous situation, that help can be at the other end of a radio transmission.

• Bob Colgate was never charged with a crime although it was evident he had assisted Glencoe in evading the law. The 30.06-caliber rifle that Glencoe was carrying when killed was later determined to be stolen from a True Value Hardware Store sometime before the incident. After Glencoe's death, Warden Don Schoenhofen was shown a raffle ticket purchased in Gresham during the preceding deer season under Glencoe's name. A hand-drawn map was found in Glencoe's shack tracing a course from his cabin to the Bowler Bank with a separate route of return to his abode. The words, "Home Free" were written at the end of the trail at the cabin location. Evidently he intended to rob the bank. Having no vehicle one would assume he was planning to traverse the 10 miles to the bank and back on foot.

• The old bachelor living near Lake Tomahawk burned to death in his house a short time after the search there.

• Investigator Wayne Truttman was later shot and killed at the Brown County Sheriff's office while bringing in a prisoner. Warden Andrew Krakow was later shot and killed while assisting the Marquette County Sheriff's Department. This story is told in "Andy."

•Proper legislation giving law enforcement the necessary authority to carry out their responsibilities and a change in policy by the Department of Criminal Investigation proved to be vital elements through the ten years of these events. Two new laws were enacted to the credit of the Wisconsin Legislature and used successfully to bring the case to a successful conclusion. The first telephone tap was authorized and used to gather evidence against Glencoe. A new law gave wardens expanded arrest authority under certain conditions and allowed them to be covered financially by the state while assisting other law enforcement agencies. Wardens have always assisted other law enforcement agencies in cases of this nature, but had they been injured or sued as a result of this assistance, they wouldn't have been protected by the state. State disability protection would not have covered them. Lastly, the State Department of Criminal Justice got involved under a new policy of assisting local authorities on fugitive captures.

•More officers could have been killed by this ruthless killer if not for the will of God and old-fashioned luck. While gathering material for this story, a statement make by Mark Kelsey a Hayward police officer struck me as appropriate, "In almost every instance when Glencoe could have killed a law enforcement officer, the officers had superior presence." The only way superior presence can be obtained is by superior cooperation between law enforcement agencies.

PARKS LOGGING CAMP STANDOFF

In the late 1940s, people in northern Wisconsin were still struggling to recover from the Great Depression and were apt to condone and encourage illegal hunting. The few people doing well economically, remembered how they supplemented their larder with covertly taken fish and game, and at times, they still couldn't resist an opportunity should one present itself. Stealing from the state, an unknown entity ruled by Madison bureaucrats, was often accepted with a sly wink and a grin. It seemed perfectly acceptable. To most, it was requisite to survival. These attitudes may have come from an immigrant ancestor that was deported or escaped punishment for stealing the king's deer.

The kill and burn frontier mentality was firmly entrenched in depressed northern Wisconsin. This long-held attitude of local citizens was further aggravated by placing a warden with the convictions of Kenneth "Kenny" Beghin at Park Falls. He was short of stature, but tall in imagination and effort put forth in conserving the resource. He soon earned the reputation of a hard-driving warden who gave no quarter in enforcing game laws. This reputation was not easily earned. Beghin encountered physical resistance many times in his short time there.

September 16, 1949 was a bright sunny day as wardens Beghin, Richard "Dick" Roehrick, Arthur "Art" Gillette and Leonard "Len" Urquhart awoke in the Tower Cabin near Conners Lake. The state-owned cabin was a natural place to stay when concentrating on an intense effort like the illegal grouse and deer hunting being reported in the vicinity.

Beghin was still recovering from a terrific beating. He had been set up and ambushed in a deer shining episode one month ago near Pike Lake in Price County. To protect himself from further assaults, he obtained a tear gas gun. He had used the gun once in a fierce struggle and now carried it at all times.

The four rode in Beghin's car as they patrolled the Conners Lake area in southeast Sawyer County where they had received numerous complaints of illegal hunting. Hearing shots west of them, they crossed the Flambeau River and headed northwest toward Loretta. When in the area where they thought the shooting had come from, they turned south on an abandoned railroad logging grade toward what was known as the Parks Logging Camp. They stopped where the old grade led to the camp and conferred about how to proceed.

Gillette suggested that he and Urquhart continue on foot to an old cabin they knew of, while Beghin and Roehrick continued along the old grade. Beghin drove the old grade and spotted a car parked at the clearing of the logging camp. They briefly discussed their next move. While making their plans, Beghin took a small .25-caliber pistol from his car and shoved it into his breast pocket.

Hearing a sound like a tractor motor, they got out of their car and continued on foot to the edge of the clearing where they saw someone on a tractor plowing a long field. Parked on the edge of the field was an old, dilapidated Plymouth coupe cut down into a farm truck. It had broken windows and a small box built on the rear that contained assorted tools and cream cans. Beside the front wheel lay a bulging gunny sack that was obviously covering something. Removing the sack, they found four sharp-tailed grouse. On the front seat of the car was an uncased single-barrel-shotgun with ammo sitting in a box on the seat. Beghin grabbed the gun through the open window, opened the breech and found the gun loaded. He closed it and said to his partner, "Well looks like we've got some business here."

"Yeah, what should we do next?"

"Let's just wait a little while. Maybe the farmer will return. I'd like to make the contact here if possible."

Ka-pow! Ka-pow! Two shots rang out at the other end of the field. They turned and spotted a flock of sharp-tailed grouse rising in escape from the frightening sound. The covey, only partially broken up, sailed gracefully up over the trees and glided downward out of sight.

Roehrick said, "The woods are full of hunters. If you want to wait here, I'll walk down there and check whoever is shooting."

"O.K., but don't take all day." Acting on a premonition, perhaps as a result of his recent confrontations, Beghin did something he had never done before–he unloaded the gun in the car. Usually, a warden waited to confront the violator with the fruits of his errant ways by unloading the gun in his presence. Walking around the truck, he reached through the broken window and opened the gun to let the shell fall on the floorboard. He closed the gun.

Alone, he crouched in the brush along side the field and waited for the farmer to plow his way toward him. As the tractor approached, he walked out to the furrowed ground where the Farmall tractor stopped.

In a loud voice he announced, "I'm a state conservation warden and I'd like to talk to you."

The burly driver jumped from the seat to the tractor tire. Hanging onto the steering wheel and with a wild look in his eyes, he aimed a wild kick at Beghin. He missed.

"You Gestapo S.O.B. Get the hell out of here."

Forced to retreat, Beghin shouted, "What's wrong with you mister?"

The man jumped back onto the tractor seat and sat staring at the warden.

Standing out of kicking range, Beghin repeated, "I'm a conservation warden and I want to talk to you."

With an oath on his lips the man jumped nimbly off the tractor.

"Get off my land you Gestapo S.O.B.!" he repeated. "I'll kill you you little S.O.B." He held his doubled-up fists several inches from his nose and stalked Beghin. Backing away, Beghin tried to reason with him.

"Man what's wrong with you?"

Backing up toward the car, he continued to try to talk him out of his actions.

"Right now you aren't in much trouble, but if you keep this up you will be."

Undaunted, the enraged, burly man pressed forward. Beghin backed up defensively as the man continued to order him off his land, swearing and savagely threatening to beat him up.

"Leave my land damn it or I'll throw you off."

Wild thoughts ran through Beghin's mind. *What am I going to do? Have to get control somehow. I'll make him think I've got help. He must know Johnny Helsing.*

"Now just a minute mister, I'll call Johnny Helsing out of the woods." Pointing to the edge of the woods he said, "He's right over there. I'll bring him over so you can talk to him."

"You keep that Gestapo bastard off my land too."

Lowering his head, he charged like a bull into the warden. Beghin defensively grabbed the man in an attempt to wrestle him to the ground. Beghin felt the incredible strength of a man seeming to be driven by inner devils. He was thrown back toward the truck thinking as he back peddled. *Man I don't know who this guy is, but I know I can't handle him. Got to find a better way.* Near the truck the man charged again and knocked him against the storage box. A cream can caromed off, landing between him and his aggressor. Off-balance and blocked by the cream can, Beghin couldn't stop the man from running to the truck for the shot gun. In a flash, he cocked the hammer, shoved the barrel into Beghin's stomach and pulled the trigger. When the gun failed to discharge, he backed up, broke it quickly and looked at the empty chamber in amazement. A bewildered look on his face, he closed the gun, grasped it by the end of the barrel and swung the gun at Beghin like Babe Ruth going for the homer. Beghin felt the breeze as the gunstock missed his head by inches. Frightened, Beghin realized he was physically unable to apprehend this brutish madman. Struggling with the tear gas gun entangled in his shirt pocket, he was relieved to feel it slide out. He fired the gas gun with his right hand

and in the same forward motion swung a haymaker with his left to the man's jaw. Neither seemed to effect him and he became more enraged. Bellowing like a wounded bull, he ran around the right side of the car, all the while feeling in his pocket for a shell. Beghin got one step short of grabbing him when he ran into the cloud of gas and his eyes teared. The berserk brute stopped and ran around the left side of the car. He stopped midstride, tears streaming from his eyes, turned aggressively in his tracks and again swung the gun at Beghin. Beghin evaded the blow and continued to pursue him. He struggled with the small handgun tangled in his breast pocket. Finally freeing it, he fired two shots over the man's head.

Frightened by the gunshots the man speeded up. Beghin put the gun in his pocket and continued the chase. Realizing the warden had gained on him and was about to grab him, the brute turned to fight. Bellowing, he threw savage blows at Beghin who reached in his pocket for a blackjack and struck him several resounding blows to the head. The final blow brought the brute heavily to the ground, the gun flying into the nearby weeds.

Panting, Beghin stood over the prostrate man, watching his trembling body and fluttering eyelids showing only white. He breathed a sigh of relief. *Whew! It's over, he's out cold.*

Then, as if by magic, the man bounced from the prone to the upright position. Fists raised and in a crouched position, he again advanced toward Beghin. "God damn you get off my land. You have no business here."

"If you touch me I'll shoot you."

"Go ahead shoot me. You haven't got a hair in your—-if you don't. That little popgun wouldn't hurt me anyway."

Not knowing what further could be done without killing the man, Beghin walked back to the vehicle, picked up the shells and the grouse and waited for Roehrick to return. Telling Roehrick what had happened, they searched for the shotgun that had fallen apart in the scuffle. They found only the stock and the barrel.

"The guy isn't running away. Stay here and watch him. I'm going to the car to radio for help," said Beghin.

At the car, sweat pouring off him from the stress and exertion, he radioed dispatcher Jim Hamblin at Hayward and asked who lived on the old Parks Camp. Hamblin called the Ranger Station at Winter and repeated Ranger Sam Ruegger's reply.

"My God that's Fritz Gridder. He just bought the place. Tell Ken not to tangle with him. He'll kill him. I know his reputation."

Upon hearing the name, Beghin paled. He had indeed heard of Fritz Gridder. If the stories he had heard were true, he had a real reason to be careful. He was known to be an inhuman brute with uncommon strength and a wicked temper. He had a long record of violating game laws, assaulting law enforcement officers and larceny. Rumors had it that he cut pulp stripped to the waist in 30-below-zero weather. He worked so hard and furious in the bitter cold that flecks of sweat would fly from his bulging muscles. It was also said that he knocked out a huge bull with a six-inch-blow and had killed a man with a single blow in a tavern brawl.

He knew the history of the Gridder family. His mind drifted back to the time when he and Warden Phil Hine had stopped a car for illegal hunting. When the car stopped, two men ran into the woods, while the other two remained in the car. As he began to run after the two escapees, Hine yelled, "Hold it Ken. Come back here. We'll arrest these two and I'll tell you about the other two later."

The wardens arrested the driver of the car, patriarch Gus Gridder, and his son-in-law, and ordered them into court for possession of an illegal deer.

"Those two you don't want to chase into the woods alone," he warned, "I'm pretty sure that was John and Fritz Gridder. They would kill you. Gus here is their father."

Beghin's mind wandered to another time in 1947 when he had made contact with the Gridder family. It happened on a cold, spring night just after ice-out. Beghin was working on fish spearing on Elk Lake near Phillips. He and Hine had silently paddled their canoe along the shore line. Stowing their paddles to maintain silence and control drift, they slowly moved themselves along by pulling on overhanging brush while watching for any suspicious activity. Rounding a slight bulge on the lake shore, they discovered three men busily spearing walleyes with an under water light–a sealed-beam headlight on a pole that was attached to a battery cable to a wet car battery. The light illuminated a large underwater area, but wasn't visible a great distance over the water. Hine whispered, "Watch it Ken, that's the Gridder outfit. They're known to be alert and cagey as coyotes. When contacted, they run or fight." Pulling themselves silently along, they moved stealthily toward the violators. Getting within 25 yards, Hine reached for his flashlight in the bottom of the canoe. He touched it and the light moved slightly, making a low scraping sound. Instantly, the underwater light went out and the men began whispering. "I heard something. There's someone around. Just set quiet for a minute."

Silently, Ken dipped his paddle into the water to test the depth. *Only about two to three feet deep. A good place to grab them.* Testing the wind Ken thought. *The wind's just right, if I let us drift we should float right up to them.* Touching Hine's sleeve, he motioned his intentions. Releasing the bush holding them in place, they waited breathlessly as their canoe drifted silently toward the area where they had last seen the light.

Suddenly the light came on and illuminated the area. The warden's craft was only about 6-feet away.

"What the hell," sputtered one of the spearers. Beghin jumped into what he thought was shallow water, only to go completely under the icy surface. Floundering to the surface and gasping for breath, Beghin grasped the violators boat and with a mighty heave tipped it over. The epithets flew. At the same time, the canoe with Hine in it also tipped over.

There were now five men in the water floundering around swearing as Beghin yelled, "You're all under arrest! We're state wardens!"

Worried that they had lost evidence, Hine searched the water as Beghin escorted the three men to shore. He found the gunny sack of speared walleyes floating on the water and the wooden spear handle and the pole attached to the sealed-beam light bobbing enticingly near the boat. The two wardens retrieved all the evidence with the three, dazed, freezing men looking on. Upon righting the spearer's boat, they found the wet battery stuck under one of the boat seats. Evidence in hand, they proceeded to haul the three to the Price County jail where they discovered who they were dealing with. It was Gus Gridder, his son John and a third man. While booking them, they were asked if they had ever been arrested before or incarcerated. Gus replied weakly, "Yeah once."

"What for?"

"Well, they said I murdered a man. But I served my time."

Later Hine told Beghin the story of the charge.

"It seems old Gus got into a disagreement with a young man in a livery stable some years back. As I understand it, he tied the man to a supporting pole in the livery and beat him to death with some heel chains. He's the same guy that John Long tangled with when he arrested him for that illegal deer. Tried to kill John with a knife. Anyone who knows John would know that to be a mistake. Nice people we deal with, say what?"

Beghin snapped back to the present as the dispatcher intoned, "Ken I repeat, Sam says don't tangle with Gridder. He's very dangerous. Sam is coming right out and bringing help. Wait for help."

"I've already tangled with him, but don't have him in custody. I definitely need help. Len and Art are in the area, call them too. They know where we are. Go ahead."

The two wardens waited at the car until Len Urquhart and Art Gillette arrived. In discussing what had happened it appeared that all knew Fritz Gridder except Beghin and Roehrick.

"This guy is no one to fool with and when we go back there we'll take him if we have to kill him," Urquhart said.

Arriving at the truck, they found Roehrick watching Gridder. He had returned to his plowing. Urquhart took charge. "I told you never to carry that damn peashooter Ken."

"It didn't make any difference, I only shot over his head to scare him."

"What a bunch of B.S., you couldn't hit him with that toy. You'd be better off throwing rocks at him. I'll show you how to take him."

Following Urquhart, the group walked to the end of the furrow and waited for the approaching tractor. As the tractor approached the end of the field, the forest protection truck arrived carrying Ranger Sam Ruegger and two other forest protection men. Stopping at the end of the furrow, Gridder stared at an apparition.

A giant of a man, Urquhart wore an eternal lopsided grin caused by a bout with Bell's palsy.

"Get off that damn tractor Gridder or we'll splatter your damn brains all over it," Urquhart spat through the corner of his twisted face in a voice like Satan.

"The hell with all of you, I'm going home," murmured Gridder as he stared at Urquhart.

Gridder jumped nimbly off the tractor while holding a two-foot monkey wrench in his hand.

"Try me," he glowered. "I'll take the whole works on. Get that weasel of a Helsing out of the woods and I'll take him on too. You'll have to kill me to take me in."

As they were trying to talk him into surrendering, Urquhart unceremoniously took an arm load of pick handles off the truck and distributed them to everyone.

"All right Fritz, have it your way. After what you've done, we don't care how we take you. Either come peacefully or else. We don't care which way. You want us to kill you? When we get done with you your own mother won't know you," he spat venomously. Leading the bat wielding mob forward and waving the pick handle like Casey on his last strike he bellowed, "We'll beat you to death if we have too. Drop the wrench now!"

With the overwhelming show of force, Gridder dropped the wrench and surrendered. After searching Gridder unsuccessfully for shotgun shells, he was placed in the back seat of Beghin's car. Gridder put both of his hands up and cradled his bloodied head, blood streaming profusely down his torso onto the car seat. When asked questions, he answered in unintelligible grunts.

Urquhart glanced at him and said, "Ken I think he's rum-dumb from you hitting him on the head."

"Could be, I sure rapped him hard. I didn't think a man could take so much punishment."

He was quickly transported to Hayward and incarcerated in the Sawyer County jail.

Several days later, Beghin couldn't get his recently purchased car seat completely clean of Gridder's blood so he decided to cover it with a car seat cover. While installing the seat cover, he reached between the seat and found a double-zero buckshot shell. It was the shell Gridder had struggled to find during the ruckus–the shell he had dropped during transportation—the shell that could have taken

Beghin's life if found earlier.

Waiving preliminary examination, Gridder was bound over to circuit court and released upon payment of a $2000 bond. At the next term of circuit court, Fritz Gridder was found guilty of possession of sharp-tailed grouse during the closed season, resisting a conservation warden in the performance of his duties, pointing and aiming a gun at another, and assault.

All the local outlaws attended the jury trial in Hayward and filled the courthouse to capacity in an open show of support for Gridder.

When the jury ruled guilty on all charges, Gillette quickly pushed his way to the back of the courtroom.

Judge Clarence Rhinehard sentenced him to serve no more than three years and not less than one year of hard labor on each count to be served concurrently in Waupun State Penitentiary. He warned him that if he didn't change his ways he would be spending most of his life there.

"Sheriff take him to Waupun."

Gillette stood at the exit door and greeted all of Gridder's supporters and advisers as they left.

"What do you think of the verdict John? Good decision, hey Joe?"

His puns were met with cold silence as the disappointed crowd filed out of the courthouse. This case deterred resistance to wardens for many years to follow.

A WARDEN'S FIRST DEER TAG

In 1942, Jimmy Chizek had finally reached the age of 12 and would no longer stay home doing farm chores while his father Jim hunted deer with his uncles. He would soon join the family hunting tradition and become part of myriad hunting tales, told and retold while growing up. He had purchased his first deer license and tag and now would take part in the longstanding Wisconsin deer hunt. His heart skipped a beat at the very thought of seeing and bagging a trophy buck.

Violating game laws was also a large part the family tradition. Putting food on the table had been an all consuming endeavor for a family of immigrants entering Wisconsin in 1914. They lived in an isolated backwoods homestead that they cleared to farm. The Great Depression had further sapped their ability to feed the second generation. Impoverished, they cut all corners to exist, including utilizing the products of the land. They weren't alone. The Great Depression forced desperate people to do desperate things. People living in northern Wisconsin during the 30s and early 40s generally believed nothing was wrong with taking a game animal or fish during the closed season or by illegal methods, so long as it was not wasted or sold.

The young Chizek relished each and every beguiling tale told at family gatherings of big bucks killed, of those that got away, and of constantly challenging the game warden. Many nights were spent listening to thrilling stories, sometimes to well after midnight.

On Jimmy's first official deer hunt, his uncle, dad, and a few others headed to Dead Man's Slough. Many a hunting tale had been spun in his living room and kitchen about hunting this area. They left their car beside the North Fork of the Flambeau River in Sawyer County near Babcock Island and Dead Man's Slough. Jimmy's imagination ran wild. The name Dead Man's Slough conveyed a notorious feeling, a feeling akin to a dead man who by devious means ended up floating in the slough, either drowned or murdered many years ago.

Was he a lumberjack or a shacker left over from the logging days? Or a human derelict residing in one of the many abandoned logging camps of the era, drifting from one camp to another and never becoming known to the local populace? Never told the circumstances to his satisfaction he wondered. *How did this place get this mysterious name?* The telling and retelling of the strange story varied so much that no one was sure how the unfortunate man had ended up in the slough. *Could it be I'm finally at Dead Mans Slough?*

As in all hunting and trapping, the most fertile area lay across the river on Babcock Island. To get there, they crossed the Flambeau in a leaky, flat-bottomed derelict boat. Long ago abandoned by some unknown person, everyone used the boat to get to Babcock Island. Arriving early, they had gained the opportunity to use the boat and thus to hunt the favored spot.

Sitting on the narrow rear seat in the total blackness soon to be dissipated by the rising sun, Jimmy held his breath as uncle Curt Tiller stood in the center of the scow and poled through the swift current. Rattling menacingly, the pole slipped and slid off the rocky bottom, crunching against hidden rocks. The flimsy craft tipped dangerously, scooping water over the gunwales. Unconcerned by the danger, Tiller swung the pole unceremoniously back and forth, his shifting body weight causing the boat to wallow and slide sideways in the current.

Jimmy always had a great admiration for his uncle Curt. It seemed he always got the biggest buck, trapped the biggest and orneriest bear and told the best stories. There were hair raising stories of lynx and timber wolves caught, and sometimes sold illegally. A chapter of past experiences, episodes and scrapes with game wardens, and how to outsmart them, seemed a requisite at each gab session. Enough spice accompanied each tale to impress a young impressionable boy.

Safely across the river, the four hunters walked at a steady pace for about a half-mile through several inches of fresh fallen snow.

Culminating a great day of hunting, they dragged the two deer they had bagged to the rivers edge. Arriving as the evening blackness fell, the return trip across the roiling Flambeau was to be more harrowing to the young 12-year-old than the morning trip. Again he rode in the rickety boat with uncle Curt, the weight of an eight-point-buck increasing the peril. Concern showed on his face as he watched the torrents of water now pouring over the sides.

Noticing the strain on the young mans face, Tiller temporarily stopped poling and let the boat drift aimlessly, "Don't worry. I can't swim. I'm not going to tip us over. Besides the water here isn't very deep, probably not over my head."

"But I'm shorter than you. Is it over my head?"

"Maybe," he murmured undisturbed. "But you can swim."

"But the water is awful cold and swift."

"Don't be afraid. We're not going to tip over. Besides I don't want to lose your dad's buck."

Heaving a sigh of relief, Jimmy jumped from the boat as the current slammed the gunwale against the rocky shore. Heaving mightily he dragged the buck from the boat. Watching Tiller cross the river for another hunter and his deer, he again thought of Dead Man's Slough. *Maybe the man drowned using a boat like this one.*

The following days brought less success at Dead Man's Slough, with one small buck being killed. Thanksgiving day brought several inches of new snow, making the trek through the woods more difficult. As the sun broke through in the afternoon, it became a beautiful bright winter day. Standing on a deer runway, Jimmy spotted his uncle striding swiftly toward him.

"Come with me. We've got some work to do."

"Work? Did you get a deer?"

"Never mind. Just come on along."

Bewildered he followed his uncle. Something's up. I can tell uncle is excited. He keeps looking behind every bush as though he's afraid of something.

Tiller turned off the trail, muted by the new snow, picked up his earlier track and followed it into some brambles. Rounding a thicket they startled several crows, who flew away cawing raucously in protest.

Glancing at the area the crows had inhabited, Jimmy was startled to see a small dead buck partly covered with new snow. "How'd he get here? Looks like he's laid here awhile."

"Tiller replied, "Just help me clean him up."

"But his belly is all green. Isn't he spoiled?"

"Never mind. Grab his leg and hold him on his back so I can gut him."

"But, but..."

"Never mind just help me."

His mind running overtime Jimmy wondered. *Why would anyone gut a spoiled deer?* One of his eyes has been pecked out by the crows. He remained quiet as the gutting was completed. Washing his hands in the fresh snow, Tiller pointed, "Now help me drag him over into those bushes." They then carefully extended the fore and hind legs in a full-stride position. With a satisfied grunt he kicked snow over the buck, stepped back and surveyed his handiwork. "Now we can go hunting again."

Wondering about Tiller's actions, Jimmy later asked his father why he would do such a thing.

"I don't know. You can rest assured he has some use for it. Maybe he will drag it out after the season and feed it to his chickens or something."

The fifth day after the close of the deer season, Tiller stopped at Jimmy's house. "Get your deer tag and come with me."

"What for?"

"Never mind. Just bring your tag. we're going for a ride."

Always anxious to please his uncle and join in anything he was involved in, he quickly found his unused deer tag. Tiller, noncommittal about their mission, headed the old Chevrolet west on highway 70.

Arriving at Dead Man's Slough, Tiller quickly chopped ice from around the boat with a single-bitted axe. Sliding the old scow into the swift current of the Flambeau, he breathed, "We're going to get that buck."

"But why, he's spoiled."

"Yeah I know, but I have a use for him."

"What?"

"I may tell you later. Right now let's get the deer before it gets dark."

"What if a game warden comes along?"

"We'll tell him we're out for a walk. This is the last day we can legally transport a deer after the season. Don't worry, there are no wardens out here."

At the deer they brushed off the snow as Tiller said, "Give me your tag."

Handing his uncle the tag, Jimmy swallowed hard. *My first deer tag is going on an illegal deer. Guess it's all right though or uncle wouldn't do it.*

Slitting the gambrel of the buck, Tiller snapped the tag on.

"Now we're legal. This is the last day we can transport a deer. If anyone asks, it's your deer from the deer season that we couldn't get out of the woods."

Heading east toward home Tiller was jubilant. "That's not a bad looking buck."

"He's spoiled."

"Yeah, he'll do just fine for what I want him for."

Driving into Short's Tavern at the intersection of county B and highway 70, Tiller drove around the tavern parking lot so the deer tied on the front fender could easily be seen from the tavern window. "Come on in. I'll buy you a bottle of pop."

Heads of commiserating beer drinkers turned as Tiller blurted, "Does anyone want to buy a deer?"

Stunned, Jimmy didn't know what to say or do, his thoughts a jumble. *My god he's going to sell the deer. It's got my tag on it. I could get into a lot of trouble.*

He was brought back to reality as one of the hunters at the bar answered. "I may be interested. My buddies each have one. Is that your deer on the Chevy?"

"Yep, $20 and he's yours." Gesturing toward the window his finger extended, "Nice little buck. Be good eating."

"Well he looks O.K. from here. Let's go out and take a closer look at him."

"Sure come on. He's a six pointer."

Terrified at the turn of events, Jimmy hung back. The four left the tavern to look at the deer. His stomach cramped. He knew something terrible would happen when the hunters saw that the deer was spoiled. *I bet they beat uncle Curt up. Not only that but what if one of the other hunters tells a game warden about this? Or worse yet, what if one of those hunters is a warden? I've heard wardens sometimes set in taverns to catch people selling deer.* Pulling himself together, stepping from the tavern he heard Tiller warn, "Lets get this over with before tongues start to wag. You never know when a warden may show up. If you want the deer give me the $20 and get out of here."

It suddenly became clear to Jimmy why Tiller had insisted on tying the frozen deer on the car with his belly down. He doesn't want them to see the green on the stomach or the eye pecked out by crows. I wish this was over with.

As the young hunter who had shown an interest walked closer to the deer, Tiller said, "You want the deer or not? If you do, lets get this over with. If you don't want it, O.K. we're leaving."

Hesitantly, the young man said "Yeh, I guess I'll take it. Looks nice. I'll take it."

Smelling success Tiller whipped out his hunting knife and slashed the metal tag. "Quick put your tag on."

Hurriedly, the young man unwound the tag from his hunting cap and snapped it on the deer. Tiller held his hand out. "Twenty dollars please."

As the man dug through his wallet to locate the twenty dollar bill Tiller yelled, "Jimmy cut that deer loose and load it on their car."

As one of the hunters moved to assist in the loading, Tiller interjected. "He don't need any help. He's strong as an ox."

The hunter shrugged and stood back as the young lad nervously fumbled with the ropes. He picked the stiff carcass up and placed it behind the other two deer tied on the fenders where it was difficult to see the belly or the eye. *Now I know why uncle was so careful in laying the deer out in this position. He knew it would be easier and faster to load on someone's car.* Suddenly marveling at his uncles ingenuity, he quickly tied the deer on and turned.

"Better get on the road before someone blows the whistle on us," said Tiller.

The three hunters quickly entered their car and wheeled out of the drive. With a satisfied smile on his face, Tiller turned to his nephew.

"Lets get out of here in case they stop and look at that deer and come back."

Tiller stepped into his car and raced the motor to urge the young man on, "Come on, shake a leg."

"Where are we going?"

"Away from here," chortled Tiller as he drove in the opposite direction the hunters had taken.

As fate would have it, circumstances bring about strange happenings. Twelve years later, 25-year-old Jimmy Chizek wrote and passed the wardens examination and was appointed as a permanent Wisconsin conservation warden. He never forgot the experience with Uncle Curt. It helped him understand the thinking behind conservation violations. While working undercover later in his career, he often thought about, but never told anyone, the story of his first deer tag. He waited in vain for someone to burst through a tavern door and blurt, "Does anyone want to buy a deer?"

THE DOGS OF MARCH

A pack of five dogs surrounds this doe near Wyocena in Columbia County. Dean Steele, a rural mail carrier snapped this picture in 1959. It was used to identify and dispose of all the dogs in the photo.

The cold winds of March howled into Wisconsin in the winter of 1959 and added more snow to the already knee deep white covering. Followed by several days of rain, the 30 to 40 inches of fresh, fluffy snow had became hard and crusted. Suddenly, wintering deer in south central Wisconsin were subjected to a disastrous condition. Conservation Warden Jim Chizek, at Portage, began receiving numerous calls complaining of dogs chasing and killing deer on the crust. Perfect for carrying the weight of dogs running on soft pads, the crust would not carry the weight of sharp-hoofed deer. The stage was set for a slaughter. Soon the endless whiteness was stained crimson by countless numbers of dead deer. The epic of the dogs of March had began.

Already in a weakened condition from the long winter, deer were quickly brought down by free roaming dogs. When deer broke through the crust, their long, spindly legs were trapped against the sharp crust and they couldn't free themselves. Dogs slashed at the deer's unprotected hind legs and jerked chunks of the deer's flesh from their hindquarters. Futile attempts to face their attackers failed. Hamstrung and unable to rise, deer were left to die a lingering death.

The adventure of the chase over, the dogs moved off in search of more lively prey. Ever vigilante flocks of crows soon swooped down in a raucous attack on the helpless sufferers. First arrivals tore at their eyes as their heads flopped helplessly in the morass of snow. Others joined in to feast on the open wounds in the hind quarters. Death became an agonizingly slow ritual being carried out on a large scale, their despair in death unknown to most mortals. Mortals who would not, in spite of almost daily news releases detailing the problem, confine their animals.

Frenzied hunting by single dogs or packs lasted for hours, days and sometimes a week or longer depending on the nature of the dogs involved. Dogs trailed to their home, were sometimes so starved and worn out they couldn't get to their feet. The size of the dog seemed not to matter. All loose running dogs regardless of size were involved. Dogs the size of beagles and smaller were just as guilty of killing.

Alarmed at the number of deer being killed, Chizek called upon his supervisor for help. Area Warden Louis "Pat" Oshesky authorized Jim Chizek to call upon other wardens for assistance. Responding were Wardens Leonard "Lennie" Tomczyk from Columbus, Frank "Franky" Adamske of Baraboo, Special Warden John "Jack" Allen and Warden Pilot Kenneth "Kenny" Beghin. Wisconsin law authorized only conservation wardens to kill dogs destroying deer. The statutes also gives other law enforcement officers the same authority."

To bolster their effort, Chizek called for volunteers. The response was outstanding. Members of the Columbia County Sheriff's Department included Wayne "Bud" Johnson, Ralph Hiller, Lavern Hugget, Oliver "Ollie" Jones, Armin Ohnesorge, Robert "Bob" Hamele. State Trooper Charles "Chuck" Foley and State Forest Ranger Frank Palenik, Poynette also joined the team. A mammoth dog hunt resulted with rifles and snowshoes the order of the day.

When reported by Department of Natural Resources Pilot Kenny Beghin or concerned citizens, areas of kill were systematically searched by groups of volunteers on snowshoes. When found, the predacious dogs were shot. Taking advantage of the hard crust, the dogs utilized the same advantage over the hunters as they had over the deer. They traveled mile after mile easily and swiftly as the hunters plodded behind at a snails pace on snowshoes. While civil actions could have been taken against the owners of offending dogs, the problem was so great that no time was left after the hunt to investigate, contact the district attorney or prosecute the cases. Follow-up investigations would wait until the spring break-up. All daylight hours were spent spotting, trailing and disposing of dogs, with follow-up interviews of their owners extending well into the night. Exhausted wardens and volunteers fell into their beds after a full day in the field.

The track of an errant pack was routinely taken early in the morning when the snow was the hardest and allowed for faster and easier movement on snowshoes. It was also a time when the deer could run on top of the crust and thus evade the marauders for a time. By noon, the sun had warmed and weakened the crust and reports of dogs killing deer began to come in. Trails were generally dropped in midafternoon when snowshoeing became too difficult.

During the next several weeks many strange incidents took place. Numerous dogs were killed by wardens and law enforcement volunteers. Other dogs were also meeting their doom whether guilty of killing deer or not. Vigilantes, often using the conditions as an excuse to kill their neighbors dog, often blamed the incident on the wardens. Chizek sat late into many evenings trying to convince someone his crews had not killed their dog.

Beghin reported to Chizek that he had spotted 60 deer carcasses in the Swan Lake Marsh bordering the city of Portage.

"I'm going in there tomorrow at daybreak. I'll get some of them," said Chizek angrily.

Striking out from county P as the eastern sky began to brighten, he snowshoed swiftly upon the hard frozen snow to take advantage of the early morning crust. Sweat drops formed on his forehead. Following two dog tracks he came upon a floundering deer. The gory sign visible in the snow revealed it had struggled in that lonely spot all night. The crack of the .30 carbine he had slung over his shoulder brought merciful relief to the suffering doe.

Suddenly the morning stillness was broken first by a hum and then a roar as Beghin buzzed overhead.

"C-A-5 to C-2-25."

"Go ahead 5."

"Is that you making all those marks in the snow?"

"I'm not leaving much of a track, snow's hard this morning."

"I don't mean tracks, I mean all those trampled down spots where someone wearing snowshoes has fallen down and couldn't get up. I know it couldn't be you. Must be someone else shoeing down there."

"You're right, It couldn't be me."

"Just checking."

Puffing hard, Chizek shifted the 30 pound portable radio to a more comfortable position on his shoulder.

"Put that thing on the ground and get your shoes on. See if you can keep up with me. I'll even allow you to carry this portable."

Beghin signed off, "KA 4570."

Continuing on the track, Chizek crossed numerous dog trails appearing to be from previous days. He found where the two dogs had bedded down. He began finding more dead and dying deer. The story of their bloody demise was brutally written in blood in the vast whiteness of the large marshy area. Reading sign, he deciphered each bloody scene as an ambush and a short chase. Then the deer broke through the crust and floundered in the deep snow as the dogs bored in, tearing at their hind quarters until they finally succumbed and lay still. At that point, the attack ceased and the dogs bloody tracks lead to the next chase. Dead and alive deer had hordes of voracious crows feeding on them. After dispatching one such pitiful animal, Chizek stood contemplating the horrible way its life had ended. *Those dogs must be all in. They've been out here several days now, yet they don't bother to feed. Just chase for the fun of the chase and move on. It must be a terrible feeling for the deer as they close in, ripping at their legs, falling time after time until they can no longer get up or move. It must be even worse when the crows begin lighting and tearing at their eyeballs. The eye must be a delicacy to crows. They always start there.* Suddenly he snapped out of his reverie. *I'm wasting time. The sun is coming out strong. Got to get a hustle on before I start to break through and the going gets tougher. Maybe I can still catch up with this pair today. I think I could recognize them from the glimpse I got of them earlier.*

Quickly picking up the bloody tracks he followed them north. The trail took him from one kill to another and another and through herds of deer preferring to stand and watch wide-eyed with ears pointing forward, rather then run on the crust. Again he found suffering deer being fed on by crows. Blood-soaked snow disclosed the drama of life and death played out in this unseen wild place. Chasing the crows off their hot meal he quickly ended their suffering.

As the day wore on he began to break through the crust deeper and deeper until walking was nearly impossible. Working his way out to highway 33 he called Lennie to pick him up.

"Hi Lennie am I glad to see you. I'm bushed. I gave up the track of two dogs about a half-mile back in the marsh. I will pick it up in the morning."

Picking up the trail at sunrise the next day Chizek pushed himself hoping he could finally trail the two dogs to their home. Suddenly the portable crackled, "C-A-5 to C-2-25, are you in the Swan Lake Marsh?"

"I'm on the trail of the same dogs I was trailing yesterday about a quarter-mile south of highway 33."

"I'll be there shortly. Oh...I see your dogs. They just ran out of the marsh. They crossed 33 and ran up to a farm where old Fort Winnebago stood."

"10-4-5, I'm on my way out. Call Baraboo and have Columbia County pick me up on 33."

At the jail, Chizek called Bud Johnson, "Bud I've located those dogs in the marsh. Would you help me pick them up?

"Soon they were talking to the farmer and gazing at a large gaunt German shepherd lying near his barn. Chizek pointed, "This is the dog I've been following. I got glimpses of him from time to time. Look at him. He's all in."

Wringing his hands the farmer countered, "I just can't believe he would kill deer."

"We'll check him out."

Grasping the animal's jaws Chizek forced them apart to reveal deer hair and clotted blood and tallow. "See this? There's no doubt he's been killing deer."

"Guess your right, take him. I don't want you to kill him here."

"How long has this dog been away from home?"

"About a week I guess. I was wondering where he was."

"O.K., where's the other dog?"

"We have no other dog. He does run with Suzy a lot. Maybe she was with him."

"What does she look like?"

"A medium-sized cur. Brown shaggy fur."

"Sounds like the dog I saw. Who does she belong to."

"Lyle Short. He lives in Portage."

"We know him. We'll check her out."

"Bud we'll have to carry this beast to the car. He can't get up." Loading the dog the two hurried to downtown Portage. At Lyle Short's home Suzy was laying on the front porch. She also had trouble getting up and stumbled around the yard weakly yapping in a futile attempt to chase off the intruders. Tired and gaunt she collapsed. After showing Lyle the deer hair and tallow in Suzy's jaws, he also surrendered her. The stillness of the Pine Island Wildlife Area was shattered by the ripple of gunfire as Johnson sent the two marauders to doggie hell. A total of 11 dogs were eventually killed after ravaging deer in the Swan Lake Marsh, a tiny percentage of the total number of marauders.

Early one sunny, wintry morning Chizek drove south out of Portage on state highway 51 leading four carloads of wardens and law enforcement volunteers. Near the radio station he spotted a dog harassing a deer on a wide expanse of marsh. Pulling over, he pointed out to the others the drama being played out before them. Gazing through binoculars he announced to the assembled group, "It's a Beagle."

Someone quipped, "Not much a little Beagle can do to a deer."

"Oh yes, countered Chizek, size don't make much difference on the crust. He'll kill her if we don't do something."

Quickly, the 14 people donned snowshoes and loaded their rifles and began to narrow the distance between themselves and the dog.

Taking the lead, he passed the word, "Hold your fire. We're way too far away to shoot." Slowly the line moved across the frozen marsh. With the distance slowly lessening the hunters could easily view the beagle circling the deer. Finally she fell, never to rise again. One of the hunters could no longer restrain himself. He raised his rifle and began to fire.

Swinging around Chizek yelled to no avail, "It's too far. Man your shooting over 700 yards."

In a scene resembling Gettysburg, rifle fire crackled across the open spaces as everyone in the skirmish line, accept Chizek, opened fire on the dog. Bullets threw up spurts of snow well short of the dog. Running easily over the crusted snow, the dog crossed the railroad grade putting him out of view and danger.

Approaching the exhausted deer laying on its side, many in the approaching ring of people expected her to arise and run off. Recognizing the baleful lost look in her eyes Chizek knew she was at the end of her life. The men gazed unbelievingly at the gaping holes in her hind quarters as he raised his rifle to end her suffering.

Several days later, Dean Steele, a rural mail carrier, called the sheriff's office to report six dogs holding a deer at bay a few miles west of Wyocena. Responding to the radio call, Chizek was on the scene within 10 minutes, but it wasn't fast enough. A large doe lay hamstrung along county G. Fortunately, Steele had taken a photograph of the scene and Chizek got a copy. Using the picture, he teamed up with Frank Palenik and visited the homes in the vicinity to identify and dispose of every dog. Chizek was not very popular in the neighborhood for some time. As luck would have it, it was his neighborhood.

The aircraft patrolling near Portage was quickly diverted to Badger Ordnance Works and Devils Lake State Park where a large hound was killing a deer. Beghin quickly spotted the dog chewing on the deer and directed the crew led by Warden Frankie Adamske to the spot. Staying in contact with the plane, the hunters proceeded slowly in an attempt to get close enough to the dog to shoot him. Suddenly the large, red bone hound bolted from the struggling animal, running toward the Badger Ordnance manproof fence. A volley of fire echoed through the slightly wooded area. The dog rolled once, recovered, and scooted into a thicket of prickly ash. Taking the blood trail, they followed him to where he squeezed under the fence heading east. It appeared he was not seriously wounded.

A farmer near Merrimac called about a week later and told Chizek he had found a wounded dog in his old silo foundation. The farmer led him to an 8-foot-high concrete foundation. Peering over the side he looked at red bone hound. He was limping about and jumping up on the walls in a futile attempt to escape the trap he had fallen into.

"That's the dog I told you about. The one we shot at Badger last week. Let's see if we can get him out of there."

"I have an old ladder behind the shed there. I'll get it."

Chizek slowly backed down the ladder, wary that the large dog may attack. He was greeted with a wagging tail and a slobbering tongue. Grasping the dog around the legs he slowly worked a short distance up the ladder to where the farmer could reach his collar and hoist him out. Examination revealed a swollen and infected front foot where a rifle bullet had passed through. Looking closely at the collar, he was surprised to find a metal plaque with the owners name inscribed.

"I know the owner of this dog. He owns a restaurant across Lake Wisconsin. This dog is about 12 miles from home."

"Will you return the dog to him?"
"I'll talk to him, but this dog has killed a deer and must be killed."
Later in the day, Chizek arrived at the owner's restaurant. He was greeted by Ted, "Set down Jim, coffee?"
"Not today Ted, I have your hound. He's been shot."
"How bad? Can I see him?"
"Not too bad. Shot in the foot. It's swollen up like a balloon. He's really lame. Come I'll show you."
"Well that's great, I was wondering what happened to him."
"How long has he been gone?"
"About a week. I've been worried. I just bought him about a month ago from a breeder in Missouri. I paid $300 for him. He comes from good breeding and coon hunting stock."
"I've got bad news for you. He's been chasing and killing deer. You know how the law applies to dogs running deer."
"Yeah, the law says he must be killed."
"There's no other way. I personally saw him kill a deer and shot at him. Others saw him and shot at him too. How would you like to handle this?"
Ted sighed, "Is there nothing else we can do? I mean...I sure don't want to lose a $300 dog."
"I know, but he was definitely killing deer."
"O.K., maybe I can get my money back. The dog was guaranteed to be broke off deer."
"Do you have it in writing?"
"Yeah, but the guy is hard to deal with."
"The dog has to go."
"O.K., I don't want you to shoot him though. Will you let me take him to a vet and have him put to sleep?"
"Sure, I don't care how we do this as long as the dog is disposed of."
Several weeks later, Chizek received a letter from an insurance company inquiring whether Ted's hound had been wounded by gunfire before it was disposed of. Unaware the dog had been insured, he called Ted.
"What's going on with your dog? I got a letter from an insurance company asking if your dog had been shot. I didn't know you had insurance on the dog. You said you were going to collect from the dog breeder on your guarantee."
"The breeder wouldn't repay me the money so I decided to try to collect on my insurance. I knew their rider disallowed payment on a dog who was shot. I gave them your name as a reference. All you need do is say the dog was not wounded and I will be paid the $300. Would you do that?"
"God Ted you know I can't lie to them."
"You stop at my restaurant all the time. I consider you a friend. The least you could do is certify the dog was not shot. No one will know the

difference. After all you were responsible for my loss."

Chizek pronounced firmly, "You know Ted I don't feel responsible for your loss. A lot of people have lost dogs this winter because they wouldn't keep them confined. Besides, I have a job of public trust. I must and will live up to their expectations. I will not lie for you."

The phone went dead.

Chizek walked away shaking his head. *What will people ask me to do next?* Several weeks later he found out that Ted had collected from the breeder before he made the insurance claim. He was trying to use him in a fraudulent scheme to collect twice on his dog.

A *Portage Daily Register* headline read, **AIR GROUND DOG HUNT IS FAILURE**

A coordinated air ground search by conservation wardens, seeking out deer-killing dogs, was staged here Friday without results.

Evidence of a continuing deer kill were noted when several members of the party witnessed a fleeting glimpse of a beagle attacking a deer just east of highways 51-16 south of Portage.

Eleven dogs were disposed of this week in the area south and east of Portage after heavy snows hampered the movements of deer and they were being attacked by roaming dogs. Ten positive deer kills by dogs are known in this area, Warden James Chizek said Friday. Pat Oshesky, area warden supervisor, said the total number of deer killed by dogs is expected to be much higher.

Oshesky directed Friday's effort as a conservation plane piloted by his assistant, Ken Beghin, crisscrossed the area in hopes of locating roaming dogs, meanwhile keeping radio contact with wardens cruising on the ground below. The ground team included wardens Oshesky, Chizek and Leonard Tomczyk and Sheriff's Deputies Wayne Johnson and Oliver Jones.

The project was primarily concerned with an area between highway 33 and county P from highways 51 to 16 east to Pardeeville. While heavier deer concentrations were noted in Sauk county, the dog-deer kill in this area is about the worst in the state.

Chizek and a smaller party of lawmen disposed of seven dogs on Thursday all definitely known to have attacked deer. In addition, four other dogs were disposed of earlier in the week.

Efforts to locate dogs were unsuccessful during the morning and the hunt was continued Friday afternoon. Meanwhile the plane was diverted for a time to the Badger Ordnance Works area in Sauk county where wardens held a similar air directed search with unreported results. Earlier reports told of three dog-killed deer and a deer population of about 150 in the immediate BOW area.

"People in the area are generally very cooperative but some

don't realize the seriousness of this situation," Oshesky said Friday, remarking that the whole problem could be eliminated if owners would simply keep their dogs confined during this period when heavy snows make it impossible for deer to ward off attacking dogs.

Dean Steele, a Pardeeville rural mail carrier, told of the situation where he viewed six dogs attacking one doe earlier this week.

Once a dog has drawn blood, it's almost impossible to stop the animal, Oshesky stated, explaining that wardens are empowered by law to kill any dog which has killed, injured or attacked a deer or other wildlife. A civil action may also be started, Oshesky said, to sue dog owners for damages.

Stopping at a night club south of Portage on highway 51 Chizek was greeted by Jimmy the Greek. "Hi Jim, what's your pleasure?"

"Guess this isn't a pleasure visit Jimmy. I'm here because your dogs are killing deer."

"I don't know if they kill deer. They just live here under my cabins."

"Are they your dogs?"

"The old bitch is my dog. She keeps having puppies."

"I've seen your dogs chasing deer. You have quite a bunch."

"Yeah, I think there are 11 pups."

"Not any longer. I shot two of them this morning. I saw the rest run across the fields to your business. Where are they?"

"As I said they live under my cabins. I don't want them. I don't even feed them. They keep coming back. You can kill them as far as I'm concerned. I don't want any deer killers around anyway."

"O.K., lets go see."

Surveying the area Chizek found 10 cabins built on blocks with a small space under each. The dogs lived under them comfortably and could come and go with ease.

"I don't see any dogs now. I'll check every time I go by and shoot them."

"O.K., be glad to get rid of them. In fact when I see them I'll call you."

As the winter wore on Chizek continued to hunt and shoot the Greek's dogs with his assistance. With the breakup in spring and the snow completely gone, all but one of the pups and the old female were dead. A medium-sized, very wise mongrel, she managed to slip away from him.

In mid-June, Chizek pursued a dog chasing a deer across county V in the Wisconsin River bottoms. He was struggling through downed trees and voracious swarms of mosquitoes when a noise stopped him in his tracks. Blaat-Ba-Blaaat! He immediately identified the sound as a fawn in distress. He turned and hurried toward the noise. He saw a fawn running for his life with the dog in close pursuit.

He heard a splash as the fawn jumped in the river. *It's doomed. He'll never out-swim the dog. Got to hurry. There he is. My God he's right on the fawn.* Swiftly raising his .30 carbine he attempted to get the dog in his sights. *Can't get a shot. Might hit the fawn.* Lowering the rifle, he sprinted around a small, deep slough toward the dramatic butchery. Several times he stopped to peer through the underbrush. He saw the dog swimming alongside the terrorized fawn and the fawn swimming in circles trying desperately to escape. He ran faster battling through the brush as he glimpsed the dog grabbing the luckless animal in the neck and head. At times, the fawn disappeared beneath the surface with the dog circling the area, waiting for him to surface. *He's drowning it. It's just a matter of time. Got to hurry. Think its already too late. If I could just get a shot.* After a long struggle, Chizek arrived puffing at river's edge. The dog, like a good retriever, swam with the fawn's neck in his mouth into the shallows. The dog dropped the fawn and looked up. In a second, Chizek's bullet entered the dog's brain. Dropping the rifle, he waded into the shallow water, grasped the 25-pound spotted animal and quickly carried him onto high ground. I*f he's not too badly injured I might be able to revive him.* He desperately administered artificial respiration by working the fawn's rib cage in and out. While the young buck convulsed several times, after 20 minutes he finally gave up. *Guess he's either too badly injured from the biting or he has drowned. Nothing more I can do.* Soaking wet from the river and sweat, he again began to notice the hordes of mosquitoes attacking him, Striking back at them with both arms, he shrugged his shoulders in disgust, picked up the rifle and walked off. The memory of watching the helpless fawn struggle and die haunted him for many years to come.

Several days later, Chizek was summoned by the Greek who said the female was at his business.

Arriving at the night club he was met by the Greek.

"She's under the end cabin."

"O.K., I've got my shotgun."

Sliding the gun from the case, Chizek reached inside his auto for the shells laying on the dashboard.

Suddenly there was a shout. "Look out Jim, here she comes."

Snapping around, Chizek was greeted by the specter of a brown, furry ball rushing toward him from the cabin. The female had decided to run no longer. She was attacking! Every hair on her body, including her tail, was standing on end. Flecks of foam were flying from her teeth. She swiftly closed the distance between them.

"What the?" Chizek stuttered, fumbling with the shells in his hand. Dropping all but one shell, he talked to himself. *Take your time. You only need one shell. Careful, just put it in the chamber and close the gun.* Jerking the gun to his shoulder he immediately fired. The dog took the full charge of buckshot in the face and buckled. She slid to a stop at his feet.

"My God she meant business. She almost got me."

"Yeah, I thought sure she would get you. I've never seen anything like that."

"Me either. She knew me. I've been chasing her so long she hated me. Just lucky I hit her under the circumstances. She would've put a real hurt on me."

Slowly the winter snows receded and the problem lessened. At first, Chizek thought the problem was over. But he was wrong. Although less urgent, he found a tremendous number of dogs still killing deer on the bare ground–a habit the dogs learned on the heavy snows of March was not forgotten because the snow left.

Chasing and killing deer continued as people relaxed, sure the problem had left with the snow, and again turned their dogs loose. A generation of deer killers would have to fade out of the picture before the problem would lessen.

ANDY

It was mid-morning on June 5, 1990 when Warden Andy Krakow, stationed at Montello, answered a call on his police radio from the Marquette County Sheriff's office. He was very close to the scene of a domestic abuse case they were investigating.and drove about 3 miles east of Montello where a young man was said to be threatening to kill his mother.

Entering the driveway, Krakow sighted the pickup truck described in the complaint parked near the garage. He braked his patrol truck about a car length behind it. Knowing Sheriff Steven Sell and Deputy Sheriff Kim Gaffney were also looking for the truck and were nearby, he picked up his mike.

"I have a Ford truck here Kim..."

Glancing to his left, his face blanched as he sighted a young man leaning a rifle on the corner of the garage and aiming it directly at him. Terrified by the menacing figure, he instinctively dropped the mike and reached for his hand gun. His truck window shattered as a bullet entered the cab and hit him in his left shoulder. Shards of glass covered him. In frantic terror he tried to rationalize what was happening. Seconds later, a second bullet crashed through the glass and pierced his neck, again showered him with slivers of glass. Half conscious and in a fearful daze, he struggled to turn his head to look at his aggressor. He didn't hear or feel the third, killing bullet strike him below the left eye.

Hearing Krakow's call, Gaffney speeded up and swung into the driveway where he slid to a halt behind Krakow's truck. They saw a young man run from the warden's truck, throw down a rifle and continue running behind the nearby house. Gaffney jumped from the squad in hot pursuit. After about 60 yards, the boy stopped and surrendered. Hustling the boy along toward the scene of the murder, Gaffney checked the scoped .22-caliber semi-automatic rifle. He found one unexpended round jammed in the firing chamber, in such a position the cartridge could not be fired.

Meanwhile, Sell rushed to Krakow's blood-soaked body sprawled on the front seat of his truck. Realizing he was in bad shape, he tried unsuccessfully to locate a pulse. Unable to believe what his startled senses were telling him, he tried twice more. Still no pulse. Frantically, he ran toward the squad. Slipping on the wet grass, he evaded a headlong fall by crashing heavily against his squad. He yelled into his mike, "Send an ambulance, Andy's been shot!"

It was obvious to Sell that Krakow was dead. In spite of his personal feelings toward his friend laying before him, he took his emotions in hand and carried on his responsibilities. Immediately, he called for Chief Deputy Phil Malsack to head up the case. Arriving in a matter of minutes, Malsack advised the young man of his Miranda rights and began questioning the 13-year-old youth.

"Did you shoot this officer?"

"I didn't want to kill him."

"You did shoot him then."

"Yeah."

"Why?"

"I thought he was the only officer coming. If I could get by him I could shoot my mom."

"Did you know Andy was dead?"

"Yeah, I saw blood coming from his head."

"Did you see a badge on Andy before you shot?"

"Yep, I knew he was an officer." As I said, I thought he would be the only one to come out here and I could still get my mom."

The questioning continued, with the young man freely admitting he had shot at Krakow a number of times.

Andy Krakow's death brought the inevitable question. Why? It seems the youth who shot him was a problem child for some time. Because he was unruly and in constant trouble in Chicago, his parents had moved to the Montello area to be near his grandfather who they felt would instill better principles in him and where they felt they could better watch and control him. However, troubles continued in their new environment and seemed to escalate and become more threatening. During the Memorial Day weekend, a family fight ensued with the boy threatening to kill his mother. After the sheriff intervened, they followed the grandfathers suggestion and removed all weapons from the family home. The day before the shooting, the boy received a detention notice from his school, prompting a violent argument between him and his mother and resulting in the youth jumping from her car and running away. County officers located him near Princeton and returned him the nine miles to his Montello home about midnight. The boy's father stayed awake all night to make sure he didn't do anything.

The day of the shooting the boy's left for work early and the boy argued with his mother during breakfast.

"You're dead," the boy said to his mother.

After eating a bowl of cereal he twice repeated his earlier threat.

"Aren't you scared?"

"No," replied his mother, not admitting she was afraid. She then went to call her husband.

Irritated, the boy jerked the phone jack out of the wall. After replacing the outlet she again tried to call but to no avail. He again removed the wall outlet. She then went to the bedroom to call, but the phone went dead as the boy had cut or jerked the other phone from the wall. Returning to the kitchen she found him wielding two large butcher knives. She struck him on the wrist with a large flashlight, knocking one of the knives to the floor.

Enraged he shouted, "Give me the keys to the truck, I'm leaving."

Uncertain what to do, she threw the keys to the floor where he scooped them up.

"I'm going to grandpa's house to get the .22 and when I get back you're gonna be dead," he said in a very quiet rough voice.

The mother ran to a neighbor's house as the boy drove the truck to his grandfathers mobile home. In a panic, she called the sheriffs office.

"My son pulled a knife on me, took our truck and went to his grandpa's house to get a .22 rifle. He's coming back to kill me. I see him right now at my neighbors house. He has the rifle!"

After walking around the neighbors house, the boy saw Krakow drive up and decided to kill him..

Andy Krakow was dead. A good father, husband and game warden had been murdered. His wife Jill was left to raise their children Angela and Travis alone.

A sunny, warm June day greeted countless mourners gathering at Montello to say a last good-bye to a good friend and faithful fellow worker. The small village of Montello was overwhelmed by the response. A large contingent of uniformed wardens from all over the state attended to honor him and provide support to his family. Uniformed officers from many jurisdictions joined the honor guard.

Unable to deal with Krakow's passing this letter was written by Michael S. Kitt, stationed at Marinette. Because he had no one to mail it to, he sent it to the International Game Warden Association. It was published in their magazine.

Dear Andy,

How ironic it is that I am writing you a letter. I'm the guy that hates writing letters. Remember? It was so much easier when I could just tell you what I was feeling. Andy, I'm having a hard time understanding this. Why did the Lord take you so soon? You had so much you wanted to do yet. I guess it's not my place to ask, since my reasons for knowing are selfish. Since you moved to a new station we haven't talked as much, but that doesn't mean I didn't think about you all the time. I think about when I was a recruit–and how you treated me as your equal and how you took time out to talk to me–to teach me. But mostly, I think about how you took time to be my friend. You taught me that this job is much more than just writing tickets. You showed me that education was the key. Sometimes I forget, but then I always remember what you taught me.

You have given me memories that I will never forget, both on and off the job. Remember the big sturgeon bust? Or how about the guys who spotlighted the buck behind their cabin? Or how about the time we took our kids fishing and let them catch all the fish. Remember how they felt? Remember how we felt? Or how about the time you and Jill and the kids stayed over at our house? It was cramped, but we sure had fun. Or how about the two of us sitting and talking until morning in the hallway of some motel whose name I forgot. But now you're gone and I'm mad as hell! Who's gong to be there for me when I really need the advice only you could give me? Why did this happen? Why am I having such a hard time dealing with this. Will I treat people differently now? Will my anger show? Will I forget what you taught me? I'm sorry. I'm being selfish. I haven't given any thought to your family or anyone else. Everyone was at the funeral. We all cried, each for our own reasons. We all vowed to take care of your family because we know that's what you would want. We will.

We'll all miss you. I'll miss you. I'll try to make the empty feeling go away because I know you would want me to. I'll raise a glass to you from time to time. I won't forget what you taught me. And I'll try to be the best damned game warden that I can be. I know that's what you would want. I'll miss you.

Your friend Mikey

The justice system was soon tested, especially in the area of juvenile crime. On June 4th, the day before the slaying, the youth's father had contacted the Marquette County Sheriff's Department. He asked that his son be put into secure detention because of his bizarre actions and threats to his mother. A psychologist and social worker were also contacted. They advised the father that they couldn't lock the boy up under provisions of juvenile statutory authority. Realizing the danger, they told the father to make the young man stay home, even if he had to knock him out.

After returning home at about 1 a.m. with the boy after he ran away from his mother, the father and mother decided to take all the safety precautions possible. After removing anything that could be used as a weapon, the father remained awake all night on guard. It was after the father left at dawn, that the altercation between the mother and her son took place.

The trial began with all the fanfare one would expect when a murder is committed in a small town, especially when the victim was as popular as Krakow.

Judge Mark Farnum ruled that certain people could not be present in the court room during the juvenile proceeding: Krakow's brothers and sisters and fellow game wardens. A second controversy arose as to whether the social worker who was called the night before the murder had acted properly in not placing the juvenile in jail.

In a letter to the *Portage Daily Register*, Marquette County Corporation counsel Richard O. Wright answered these concerns. His letter read in part:

> *Unfortunately, secure detention for the juvenile was not one of the options legally available to the social worker, Jack Schwartz, when he concerned himself with the situation the night before the murder. It is absolutely incorrect to say that Wisconsin statute 48.208 states that a child may be placed in secure detention if the intake (social) worker finds probable cause exists for the juvenile to cause physical harm to another or run away. "That statute provides no such option–maybe it should, but it doesn't and Mr. Schwartz had no choice in the matter that night...Wisconsin Juvenile code (Chapter 48) is a mess and it doesn't work. The murder of our Marquette County warden is one horrendous example of how it doesn't work and even though hindsight is 20:20, I do not doubt that had Jack Schwartz had the legal ability to place this particular juvenile in secure surroundings that night, he would have done so.*

In his opening remarks, District Attorney Dick Dufour told the jury, the boy had killed the warden so he would be free to also kill his mother. Noted staff pathologist Dr. Billy Bauman of St. Mary's Medical Center in Madison testified as to the macabre details surrounding the death. He stated the first and second shots entering the truck cab had not been fatal. They had hit Krakow in the shoulder and pierced his neck. The third shot had caused immediate unconsciousness and almost instantaneous death. It had entered his face about one-and-one-half inches below his left eye, passed through his brain and lodged in his head below his right ear.

It took the jury just over two hours to make a decision. They brought back a verdict of guilty on the juvenile equivalent of first degree murder, attempted murder, car theft, and a misdemeanor charge of destruction of property. Judge Farnum sentenced the boy to Lincoln Hills maximum-security juvenile facility for an indefinite period extending up to his 25th birthday.

Dissatisfied with the way juvenile court had been handled, a letter of protest was sent to the *Portage Daily Register* from Jill Krakow's father, Alan L Christensen:

To the Register:

On June 5, 1990, my son-in-law, State Conservation Warden Andy Krakow was murdered. Thus my daughter Jill, her two children, and all the members of the Krakow-Christensen family became victims for the first time. Over the next three months through September 28, 1990, we all became victims for a second time.

Through the hearings and trial we were treated as second class citizens. We found out that the criminal and family have more rights than the victim's family.

The so-called "public defender" used every legal means to have all of us prevented from attending the hearings and even the trial. At one hearing we were ordered out, except for our daughter Jill, who had to sit there alone. At the trial, no brothers or sisters of Andy or Jill and none of the game wardens (who wanted to be there) were allowed in the courtroom. The scale of justice is way over-balanced for the juvenile. Here are some examples. At the trial, on one side of the table sat the public defender and the private investigator. On the other side sat the district attorney and the chief deputy. The going rate for private investigators is $55 per hour and for the public defender is $60 per hour. For district attorneys it's half that and for the chief deputy way under half. Thus the scale is tipped. The title "public defender" is misnamed. The real public defender is the district attorney who is there to protect the public from the criminal by having him put away, while the criminal defender (which is a better title for someone who is defending a person who has admitted to the crime) is trying to have him released so he can do it again.

No pictures may be taken of the juvenile or his family (to protect them), but pictures may be taken and published of the victim's family. No names of the juvenile or his family may be printed or spoken out of court, which is wrong. The picture and name of the criminal should be public knowledge so the public may be forewarned as to the danger of any murderer, rapist and armed robber regardless of age.

The final tip of the scale is that the district attorney must convince all 12 members of the jury that the defendant is guilty, while the criminal defender must convince only one of them that there is reasonable doubt.

Changes must be made in the juvenile criminal code to make them more responsible for their criminal acts and to bring the scale of justice more in balance for crime victims.

Write your state and federal legislators to enact rougher criminal laws to give more rights to the crime victims. We must never forget that Andy had ALL his rights taken away by a senseless criminal act. Jill was left alone to raise her two young children who would not have the benefit of a wise father to advise and support them through their adolescence years when both a mother and father are a requisite in this complicated time.

Alan L. Christensen

He will also be missed by the State of Wisconsin and the warden family as summed up in an article written by Warden Cletus Alsteen and published in the *Wisconsin Conservation Wardens Association* magazine shortly after Krakow's death.

There is a brotherhood in all law enforcement. All game wardens are family and we support each other by nature. Warden Joel McOlash is my support now through one of the most difficult times that I will have as a conservation warden.

Andy Krakow, my fellow warden, my friend and my confident, you were a man's man, you had backbone, you had principles you stood by and you had character. A game warden's game warden. And yet I knew Andy in another light. He was a strong man who knew when to be gentle.

Yesterday morning I started to grieve you. Andy. And I cried until the uniform pants were tearfully steam pressed and I knew I would miss that Andy smile which always started with that little smirk and gently broadened across your face and lit up your whole face till your cheeks looked like a happy chipmunk with his cheeks full of pine cone seeds. It would sweep over you that smile, much like the first rays of dawn when we sat there in the duck marsh and there was frost on the cattails and it would gently warm like the morning sun until there was this big beautiful panoramic sunrise. I will miss that smile. And that Andy laugh. That laugh that was so uniquely Andy Krakow, much like the clarion call of the wild geese is so unique to the wild goose. I will miss that and I cried.

I reflect back to June 1981 when I was a young warden and I was back up in Lena, Wisconsin visiting my folks. I took the day off and went up into Marinette County to fish the upper inlet and as I came back through Wausaukee I saw Andy pulling out of a gas station and motioned to him and went down the road a ways and we pulled over and we sat on the trunk of the car and talked game warden talk. And you impressed upon me at that time that no matter how much stress a supervisor or strife placed on your personal life, you always must remain a professional. Andy, you were a professional. A true professional.

In fact, I could call you up to help me on a complaint in the Grand River Marsh, or Lake Puckaway and I'd tell you, Andy we're working undercover, it's plain clothes and Andy the professional that he was, would always show up with that tie on, uni-

form, full leather under his camo. And I often wondered how we'd ever catch a duck hunter with him looking like that. But we sure did. And good cases too. Oh, you were dedicated to the warden force and to your principles.

As I recall last fall, you were busy all week in Madison union bargaining and we would work a bow hunting complaint on Saturday evening that I had lined up in your county or mine. It didn't matter. And on the way to it I'd ask how the negotiations were going and you'd use me as a sounding board to vent your frustrations of the state's stalling tactics and the strain it was placing on your marriage and the family. Then we'd get out and we'd pinch a few bow hunters and Andy was a warden again. And being professional, on Monday he went back to Madison to the bargaining table and fought for the warden force another week. And you sacrificed your family until April, when the negotiations were done and the contract was settled. And I cried some more.

And I remember Andy coming home from those area and district meetings and we'd have a few cold quaffs and argue about the new department policy or guideline or rule they had set up that we knew we could not absolutely work with. And by the time we got into that jug of tonsil wetting solution we'd be laughing and joking and giggling and next day we'd be out there supporting department policy. I cried some more. I will miss that.

And then I thought about your death notification and the loss I felt immediately. And then I thought of Jill, Angela and Travis and I knew I had to be there with them and be that pillar of support they would so much need in this difficult time. And we grieved together trying to make some sense out of this tragedy. And I specifically remember how upset they were after a misguided news director put on a pro-gun control blitz after your death notice on the T. V. news and insulted everything that you stood for and worked for in youth in the hunter safety and education movement. And I thought how misguided the media is. And I also thought how smart Andy was. He had that unique ability when dealing with volunteers in the hunter safety profession. After class he would take off that uniform and sit down with the instructors and discuss some of their problems and relax and create that fellowship needed so much.

Deep down I know there has to be some good in this tragic death. Perhaps, Andy you are the martyr sacrificed to stimulate the long-awaited and much needed revamping of our children's code in the state statutes. Maybe the system failed, I don't know. Time will tell.

And then I thought of a friends comment. He confided in me about a duck hunter down on the lower end of this county who had confided in him and this is what the man said, "Andy was fair and firm. He was honest. He pinched me and I had it coming and I will always respect him." And I thought why does a warden never hear that when he's alive. And I shed more tears.

And I think about how you and Jill and Angela and Travis have touched each of us in the warden force and more broadly the warden family. Andy Krakow, a game warden's warden and a game warden's family. Jill, Angela, Travis, you are and always will be a part of the warden family.

Author's notes:

• On the morning of June 5, 1990, Andy Krakow became one of the heros of the Wisconsin warden force. He served his department and the citizens of the state with distinction. In 1998, a law enforcement memorial was dedicated at the State Capital in Madison. The ceremony and names etched in the memorial honor those who fell in the line of duty for the State of Wisconsin. Krakow's name was one of the seven wardens etched in stone. There his name will be honored and memorialized forever.

• Each year, the Wisconsin Conservation Wardens Association Limited, in consultation with Jill Krakow, awards a scholarship to a deserving student of conservation known as the "Andy Krakow Scholarship."

• Since the tragedy, juvenile laws have been tightened.

THAT'S BEEF!

On a bitterly cold January day in the 1940s, wardens Kenneth "Kenny" Beghin and Arthur "Bud" Knutson were exploring an area north of Bradley in Oneida County.

Driving into a rough, ice-caked logging road with deep snow banks, they came to a dilapidated log shanty used to house a logger during the winter months. A flurry of Canadian jays, often called "lumberjacks," retreated from a slop pile near the door as the two walked around the small clearing. The wardens noticed a wooden box sitting on the roof of the shack. This being a common way to store meat in this era, they investigated. Without moving the box, they gazed over the eaves of the shack where they could see chunks of frozen meat.

Beghin mused, "Looks like venison to me."

Moving into a better viewing position Knutson agreed, "Yep, I think its venison. Don't see any tags around. It's probably illegal."

They could hear the logger's axe ringing through the crisp, still winter air several hundred yards away in a clump of aspen.

Pointing toward the sound, Beghin voiced his thought, "Should we go down and talk to him Bud?"

"Maybe we should take another look at the meat and make sure its venison."

"It's venison. Most of these loggers kill them in their logging jobs. Let's just go down and talk to him."

The snow crunched and squeaked under their boots as they followed a skidway trough where wood had obviously been dragged by a team of horses to the shack for fuel. The horse trail led them directly to the logger, steam rolling off him like a lathered horse as he swiftly chopped the limbs from an aspen tree. Turning his head as the wardens approached, the giant of a man stopped mid-swing, his axe hanging like on a string in mid-air. In a surly voice, steam billowing out of his mouth he growled, "What the hell do you guys want?"

Beghin answered "We're game wardens and..."

"I know who you are, that's why I'm asking what the hell you're doing here?"

"We saw some meat in a box on your roof and..."

"That's beef, now get the hell out of here."

"If it's beef you have nothing to worry about."

"I don't have time to monkey around with a couple of keystone cops that can't tell the difference between venison and beef. Now beat it."

"It will only take a few minutes of your time to walk to your cabin."

"O.K. he shouted."

With one hand, he chopped the double-bitted axe into a newly-sawed stump. With a loud thump, the axe buried itself down to the eye. The two wardens looked on and wondered what nature of beast they were dealing with– a man of Paul Bunyan stature and strength, but without his docile demeanor. Brawn from toes up, the 7-foot-tall giant plowed his way toward them through knew deep snow, snow flying as high as his head. He stomped onto the skidway, boiling mad.

"I really should throw both of you off my land, but I'll show you that the meat is beef."

Following the mad giant, both wondered. *What would happen if the man who seemed demented decided to attack them.*

Constantly complaining and threatening, steam flying from his mouth in clouds, he continued to mumble, "I should tie these weasels in knots. I should break their legs like icicles."

Turning, he hurled a proclamation at them, "That's beef." He increased his pace. His swift, purposeful long-legged stride toward the shack kept the two wardens struggling in a half-trot to keep up. Glancing at each other in wonder, they spoke not a word, afraid they would push the berserk brute past the breaking point. He kept turning his head and looking at them in a threatening manner.

Reaching the shack, the man went immediately to the overhanging eaves, reached up and pulled the heavy box of meat down as if it was weightless. It was filled with a substantial number of rock hard pieces of frozen meat. Dropping it on the ground and glaring at the two, he bent down, grabbed a chunk weighing about 10 pounds with both hands and with a growl raised it to his mouth and tore a huge chunk out of the frozen block. Spitting it out he shouted, "That's beef!"

Beghin shouted, "That's beef!"

In a whisper he continued, "Lets go Bud."

In the car as they left the woods, Knutson murmured, "That's beef!"

DYN-O-MITE WARDENS

Arriving at the Portage station in the winter of 1956, newly appointed Conservation Warden Jim Chizek hardly had time to get his feet on the ground when the spring fire season blew in with a fury. Besieged by constant fire calls, he worked night and day feverishly fighting fire along with Forest Ranger Frank Palenik, stationed at Poynette.

The Columbia county board's request to include the county in an extensive fire control zone had recently been granted by the Wisconsin Conservation Department. With no previous fire control laws, fires burned out of control for generations in the county. Citizens were incensed when rangers and wardens entered their lands uninvited to fight fires they deliberately set to "green up the landscape." An era of conflagration was to die hard as rangers and wardens began a thankless job of fire prevention. In consultation with District Attorney Howard Latton they decided to issue warnings until people became accustomed to the new controls.

Defiance to the law and to prevention methods brought forth numerous incidents bordering on violence. They were threatened with shotguns, pitchforks and other items. They decided they would no longer take the abuse.

Discussing their problems with District Attorney Latton, Chizek told him of the many threats received and of their failure to educate and break the frontier tradition of "light a match, throw it in the dry grass, and go to town."

"Quite frankly, Howard, I'm not going to do it any more. If they're burning illegally I'm arresting them. Some of them should be charged with assault. I'm not going to be chased off a fire with a pitchfork or any other weapon."

"I agree Jim. By next spring they'll have had one whole year to become aware of the new law. Do as much education through the media as you can and next spring, go ahead and arrest them."

During the next winter and early spring, the newspapers carried many items further informing citizens of the new law and that arrests would follow if not obeyed.

The spring of 1957 came on with a rush as the snow disappeared under warm temperatures and strong April winds. Better prepared for the inevitable, Chizek now had a fire control pumper trunk and fire fighting tools.

Again the fires burned throughout the county and blackened the spring skies. Arrests were made in aggravated cases. The battles began anew, but the violators were now channeled through the courts. A backlash to strong enforcement began as some people fought back with arson. Most arson fires were started at night and by daybreak, April winds whipped small fires into conflagrations.

Chizek and Palenik were working closely with local fire departments. Talking to the fire chief from Pardeeville who was concerned about a rash of nighttime fires, Chizek asked the chief to have his department write down anything suspicious upon arriving at fire scenes. To preserve evidence, he also asked the chief to block off the roads where vehicles may have been driven.

Several days later, Chizek was roused from a deep sleep at 3 a.m. Jack Tessman of the sheriff's department told him about a fire near Pardeeville. Arriving at the scene, Chizek was elated when he spotted a fenced-off road. *Ah ha, looks like we've finally got some evidence. Must be something behind that fence to help me identify the firebug.* The chief told him that a witness saw a car speed from the pine plantation where several fires were set. He asked the witness to stay long enough to relay the information to the warden. The man described the vehicle as an old Chevrolet, probably a 1952 model, dark in color. He said it contained about six young men, that he couldn't identify. Chizek pondered. *I think I know that car. I've seen it around the area. I think it's Carl Jones'.* Jones was a young lad of about 19-years-of-age who frequently drove around with a number of men his age. Several complaints of the bunch hunting illegally were related to him.

As the fire department was leaving, Chizek began preparing plaster casts of the tire imprints left behind in the protected area. He took his time, carefully pouring the plaster as recently demonstrated by his new training officer Harold Hettrick. The sun was peeking over the horizon, when proud as a peacock, he loaded the 3-foot casts into his truck. *Man I wish Harold could see these. He would be proud of me. Pretty good for my first try.*

Investigation time was limited as the firefighters often stayed on fires most of the night in an effort to extinguish them along the perimeter before the morning winds fanned them back into fast-moving infernos. Several trips to the Jones house found no one at home.

As the spring wore on, more fires were reported. Firefighters continued to battle each blaze until the immediate threat to plantations and buildings was contained. Chizek and Palenik were left to monitor and mop up the site, which often went well into the night.

Grabbing a nap when ever possible, they continued to fight fires and investigate when time allowed. Palenik became so exhausted he collapsed near dawn one morning while mopping up on a fire near Swan Lake. Chizek half-carried him out of the huge marshy area or rather floated him out as they were fighting fire in water up to their armpits. On their way out, he stumbled upon a deer that had been burned to death on a small highland island in the marsh. While Palenik rested, Chizek inspected the island. He found 12 more dead deer. He envisioned them being trapped, not wanting to cross open water while the fire raced through the long, dry grass extending above the water and encircling and closing in on them. Heavy lethal smoke took their last bit of breath as one-by-one they sank to the ground on what they perceived as a haven. Thousands of planted pine trees went up in smoke along the fringes of the huge marsh.

The spring could be considered a disaster with fire wiping out tremendous numbers of valuable trees and game areas. One fire burned 20,000, 20-year-old Norway and white pine trees on a private plantation and 20,000 on the adjacent French Creek State Public Hunting Ground. Crowning in the tops of the pines, fire raced across county and town roads in spite of back fires and valiant efforts of the Conservation Department, the Portage and Pardeeville Fire Departments and a large number of volunteers.

Using a swat to knock down flames at the edge of a pine plantation, Chizek heard the repeated roar of an engine. He rushed through the low-hanging limbs bursting into an open marsh where a state-owned caterpillar had tipped over in a drainage ditch. The operator, Donavan Gabbei, was attempting to free it by rocking it forward and back, not realizing that gasoline was spewing from the gas tank and ominously spreading over the water in the marshy area.

"Don, get out of there."

Glancing at Chizek he reversed the engine and gave it gas.

"What? I think I can get it out."

"No you don't have time. The fire is too close. Get off the machine and come on up here." Glancing at the ever-widening gas film on the water, sudden fear crossed Gabbei's face. He quickly shut the machine down, jumped to the ditch bank and ran splashing toward Chizek. Clearing the oil slick he turned to see an area the size of a football field explode with a loud whoosh. There was nothing more they could do but watch the machine burn up.

An eyewitness saw a man light the fire and leave. Chizek charged the man with burning without a permit and starting a fire and allowing it to escape. In a trial before Justice of the Peace Frank Ladenberger, the six person jury found the man not guilty. When asked where their case was weak, several jurors stated, "We believed the man who saw Donald set the fire. After all, he lived just across the road. He made no mistake. He knew him personally. There's no doubt Donald started the fire and deserved to be fined, but if we found him guilty, the state would then come after him for the loss of the trees."

They hadn't listened when District Attorney Howard Latton explained that the outcome of a criminal case didn't have any bearing on the evidence of a civil case and vice versa. Feeling he couldn't afford to pay for the loss of the trees they simply ruled, "Not guilty."

Chizek and Latton continued to discuss the possibility of raising a civil suit against the man for the lost trees on the public hunting ground. As fate would have it, the man murdered his wife and committed suicide.

With the fire hazard remaining high, Chizek asked Warden Leonard Tomczyk of Columbus to help him. With the wind whipping, the two set out from Portage in the fire-control-truck. Immediately, Pilot Mary Green announced several fires from her fire control aircraft. In radio contact with Palenik, the two wardens responded to several small fires near Portage while Palenik suppressed several in the southern part of the county.

The two wardens then were directed to a fire in a 80-acre grassy field between Portage and Wyocena. Entering on a fieldroad, they drove past a huge hollow oak tree spewing fire about 30 feet into the air. The fire roared up through the hollow center. Loudly snapping and crackling, the hot fire threw huge chunks of burning debris into the air where the wind scattered them haphazardly around the burning grassland.

Maneuvering to avoid the heat Chizek commented, "That's what I call a real roman candle Len. It will take some doing to cool it down."

"Yeah, I've set hollow trees on fire in the north during the deer season, but only when there's snow on the ground. They're almost impossible to put out."

They started with the easy part. Since the grass field was surrounded by oak highlands and a marsh, they cut the fire off before it could enter the dry marsh where the wind would have carried the fire several miles. This accomplished, they decided they could extinguish the rest of the fire without calling for assistance. Enduring several sweaty hours in the hot sun, they used the pump mounted on the truck, swats and shovels. They were elated when the flame along the perimeter was finally suppressed and cooled. They then concentrated their efforts on the center of the field where the huge dead oak was still furiously burning and shooting flames skyward like a huge blowtorch. Roaring furiously, the fierce flame funneled its way up the hollow center, creating its own draft. Pumping furiously on the hollow tree, they soon were without water. Luckily only the rotted litter scattered about the base of the tree continued to burn. Chizek unloaded the shovels.

"We've got to get all this burning dead wood away from the tree or it will chimney again. With this wind, we're too close to the perimeter to let it burn itself out. If it funnels up the tree again it may throw fire beyond the burned over area. Then we'll have another fire."

Tomczyk replied, "Yeah I'll start shoveling some of this stuff away from the trunk. Looks like the fire was started from this tree."

"I think our arsonists are at it again. I maybe know who set the fire over near West Lake. Just haven't had a chance to talk to him. I have a hunch all these fires have been set by the same people."

"Who's the guy you suspect?"

"You know the young man I was telling you about, Carl Jones."

"Yeah, sounds like a good one. Boy this stuff is sure hot up near the trunk."

Shoveling mightily, Tomczyk continued to throw tinder away from the trunk. He furiously pounded the glowing coals left on the ground with the short-handled shovel.

"Come on over here, Jim. If we don't get this out soon it'll burn like a blowtorch again."

Joining Tomczyk at the base of the tree, Chizek shoveled and pounded the fiery embers in a attempt to extinguish them.

"Boy my feet feel like they're on fire. By the time we're done here I'll need a new pair of hipboots. Wonder what Pat would say if I put them on my expense account? Ha!"

"Don't try it Len chuckled. He'll have your hide."

"Yeah I know, but I may tell him I'm going to do it just to see what he says. I burn up at least one pair of hip boots each spring. I think it's time the state starts buying them for us. Let's get this damn thing out so we can get something to eat."

With the burning tinder shoveled back about 15-feet in all directions of the trunk, they hammered at the remaining coals around the base of the tree. They shoveled dirt on the area between the tree and the burned area and covered the rest of the coals.

Satisfied, they left, only to have the spy in the sky direct them to another fire.

Chizek chuckled. "There's Miss Green again." Eating was just a passing thought.

Several days later, he drove up to Carl Jones' home. His father greeted him at the door.

"I don't think Carl set any fires, but you can talk to him if you'd like," said the boy's dad.

Turning his head to the interior of the house he yelled, "Carl come out here, the game warden wants to talk to you."

Greeting Carl outside and gesturing toward the old Chevrolet, Chizek said, "Is that your car?"

"Yeah," Carl said shyly. Have I done something with it I shouldn't have?"

"I think so. Were you on that old road leading to West Lake about a week ago? The night of the fire over there."

"No, I've been on that road, but not the night of the fire."

"I've been led to believe you were on that road. The firefighters described a car just like yours. I believe it was yours. It really doesn't matter what you say anyway, cause I took plaster casts of the tire prints from the old road. I can place your car there. Come, I'll show you the casts."

Opening the tailgate he gestured grandly toward the perfect prints he had collected. Look at these. Don't you think I can match them to your tires?"

Gulping, his body suddenly tense, Carl replied, "I don't know, they may not match."

Reading his body language, Chizek was sure he had his man.

"I think they'll match. Lets take a look. You're sure you weren't over at the West lake fire? These tire casts will place you there. You may as well tell me the truth."

His voice barely audible Carl croaked, "Well O.K., I was on that road the night of the fire."

"Speak up, I can hardly hear you. Did you help start the fires in the pines?"

"Yeah, we were just having fun. We meant no harm."

"Meant no harm. You must realize someone planted those trees to harvest some day? About 15-years of growth has been lost plus the cost of planting and replanting. Not to mention the fire department's costs. We all must contribute to their effort. Who was with you that night?"

Reluctantly he named eight other young men.

"Now Carl, I would like you to put all this down on paper. Would you give me a statement on your activities the night of the West Lake fire?"

"Guess I might as well. I've told you most of it anyway."

Handing Carl a piece of paper, Chizek guided him in writing the statement.

"Just begin at the beginning and write things out in the order they happened and who did what. O.K.?"

"Guess so. Should I include the other fires too?"

"What? There were other fires?"

"Well yeah, a few."

After several hours, the statement was complete. Carl confessed to being a part of a group of young men who had set 52 fires! He also named several other young men who took part in setting the fires.

"Now is this all the fires you helped set?"

"Yep, all I can remember."

"What about the fire near Wyocena where the large, grassy field burned. Were you involved in setting that?"

Excitement showed in his voice, revealing a slight stutter.

"Not really, I didn't help start it. But, But...I...I was there."

"You were? Why didn't you tell me about it when you told me of the other fires?"

"C...cause, that one was st..st..started differently."

"Differently? How was it started?"

"Well...Ji...Ji-ohn had a few sti...icks of dynamite, a cap and a fuse. He thought it would be fu...fu...fun to blast that old dead oak in the field."

"Did you blast it?"

"N...not really. We tried, but the ch...ch...charge didn't go off."

"What started the fire then?"

"Th...the fuse started it while it was bu...burning. We stood by the s...side of the field and watched a while. The field and t...tree began to burn, but the dynamite never did go off."

Suddenly Chizek's heart was in his throat.

"The dynamite never went off? Do you realize Len Tomczyk and I fought that fire and put it out? We could have been blown to kingdom come. You and your buddies could have killed both of us."

"G...guess we weren't th...thinking. I'm sorry."

"Sorry don't cut it. Just add the incident to your statement. You as well as your buddies will answer for all these crimes. I don't look for the courts to look favorable on such shenanigans."

"Where did you place the dynamite charge?"

"We just buried it in the rotten wood at the base of the tree."

"We shoveled and pounded the fire at its base. I can hardly believe we didn't set it off."

After the statement was signed, Chizek, proud as a peacock at his first effort at lifting tire prints said, "I'm going to show you how these tire casts match your tires. Carrying them to Carl's car he said, "See how they match."

"What do you mean match? They're completely different."

Looking closer he groaned, "My god they are different."

Crestfallen, Carl said, "You tricked me. I wouldn't have told you anything if you didn't convince me you had my tire tracks. I will never live down squealing on my buddies."

"I really didn't intend to trick you. I thought the prints would match. It doesn't matter now though. With your statement, all of you are going to court."

The next day Tomczyk, Chizek and Palenik returned to the old burned-out stump where they gingerly removed the sticks of dynamite. The blasting cap was still in place.

Palenik, an expert blaster was at a loss for words.

"Did you guys hammer around the base of the stump here where the dynamite was?"

Tomczyk answered, "Yeah, that's where most of the fire was. The dead wood falling from inside the tree must have been a foot thick there. I know both of us shoveled and hammered around it."

"I'm here to tell you that both of you were very lucky. As hot as that fire was it's unbelievable it didn't detonate the cap. Not only that but it doesn't take much of a blow with a shovel to detonate the charge. Caps are very unstable and will go with very little shock. You're both very lucky to be here. Better thank your maker before bed tonight."

All of the suspects were prosecuted as a result of Carl's statement. Prosecution of the nine men brought about a change in attitude in Columbia County. Even citizens holding the "burn and let burn" frontier mentality thought these young men had gone too far.

For years Tomczyk and Chizek suffered the spears of their peers. How do you put out a fire? Pound the dynamite charge with a shovel! The title DYN-O-MITE WARDENS echoed across the state to the chagrin of the wardens.

The lawmen were only too glad to be able to laugh with their comrades. They knew that by the grace of God, they had escaped injury or death.

FISH WAR TUG RIDE

Joe Clamp's confiscated boat, the Susie Q. Photo courtesy of Don Euers.

In the 1860s, conflicts between Wisconsin residents and commercial fishermen were brought to the attention of the state legislature. Convinced that there was indiscriminate harvesting of fish on the Great Lakes, the legislature appointed Rolla Baker as the first fish warden in Wisconsin in 1879. Assigned to the city of Bayfield, he enforced the newly established regulations governing the taking of fish on Lake Superior. In 1885 two more fish wardens were assigned to patrol Lake Michigan and Green Bay. In later years, the title and responsibilities of fish and game wardens were combined and henceforth they were called game wardens, and finally conservation wardens.

Through the years, the people in the commercial fishing industry developed a theory. They felt that the state had no authority to regulate their fishing activities because federal laws governing navigation and interstate commerce applied to the Great Lakes. Working hard to persuade the state that this was the case, they also tried to influence the legislature to enact laws that subjugated the state to federal regulation. State representatives attempted to do this.

As enforcement began and additional regulations were added, people who for generations had lived off the bounty of the lakes, found their livelihood threatened. Laws limited the number of fish they could take and sell, and regulated the size of nets and mesh. Problems continued as wardens kept pressure on the commercial fishing industry in spite of having little manpower and very poor equipment. Fishermen resisted through the courts and occasionally through physical confrontations. At the start of the 1930s, the relationship between the State Conservation Department, as represented by the wardens, and commercial fishermen was tenuous at best.

In 1936, the fishermen's theory was dispelled. The state attorney general wrote an opinion stating that conservation wardens could enter boats on outlying waters to check for contraband and fishing gear in Wisconsin's jurisdiction. It also declared that these laws did not interfere with federal regulations.

Even though this confirmed what had been law for years, the fishermen still would not accept this edict and continued their defiance. They were further reined in as the attorney general spoke strongly in an opinion in 1943 further clarifying existing law:

1) Fishing nets that are legal for use in certain waters, but are illegal for use in waters where found, are a public nuisance. (2) If part of a fishing net is composed of illegal mesh and part of legal mesh, the entire net is illegal. (3) Where a fishing net of an unknown owner constitutes a public nuisance, it may be seized and destroyed without a court proceeding. (4) Where the known owner of an illegal fishing net is not prosecuted criminally so as to result in an order for confiscation, the net may be confiscated in a forfeiture action.

With these opinions ringing in their ears, the fishermen stuck to their theory that only the federal government could control their fishing activities. They continued attempts to change state law. With the knowledge of the past, wardens proceeded cautiously, as did the crew of the fish tug Barney Devine.

The Barney was commissioned in 1941. Originally named the Albert J., it was renamed the Barney Devine after late Chief Warden Barney Devine. It was affectionately called the Barney by the people who rode and knew her.

The Barney was a strongly constructed tug. It was 50-feet in length, 14.5-feet wide, and had a draft of 6 feet. Its configuration compared favorably to most of the oil-powered tugs fishing the Great Lakes. An enclosed insulated pilothouse allowed the crew to operate in cold weather and on the often stormy Great Lakes. Built completely of steel, it was capable of breaking a foot of hard, blue ice and had a cruising speed of 10 m.p.h. It had a modern radio compass to facilitate accurate navigation and a ship-to-shore telephone. The Barney slept four and included a galley.

Finally, wardens had a viable means of patrolling the mighty Lake Michigan fishery.

On this foggy, December day in 1947, the Barney crew included Supervisor of Commercial Fishing, Donald Euers (stationed at Sturgeon Bay), Captain Orville Weborg, and Engineer Walter Zerbes of Kewaunee. All had varied experiences with the fishing industry.

Weborg, a skilled and experienced pilot, worked the Barney past the sharp ice bordering the shoreline to the breakwater. He moved the throttle ahead, slowly gaining speed as they reached the open lake. He set a course easterly from Two Rivers, which harbored the largest fleet of commercial fishing boats on the lake. The annual catch surpassed any freshwater port in the nation.

A lively discussion ensued of past clashes with fishermen as they made their way toward the center of the lake where they knew commercial fishing would be taking place. The conversation became serious as they discussed recent complaints. The latest controversy centered around the mesh size of gillnets allowed for taking chubs. State law required that nets used for taking chubs be no less than 2.5 inches by flexible-rule measure. Decreasing the mesh by just one-eighth inch would allow the taking of chubs of an earlier-year class. The conservation department felt this would injure the fishery. It was also illegal to use a net more than 35-meshes deep.

The wardens arrived at an area approximately 25-miles east of Two Rivers where they knew there were substantial numbers of chubs. Weborg throttled the tug back, slowly searching for spot buoys placed by violators as a means of laying nets hidden to all but the offending boat. After the buoy is placed, the boat runs a known course at a known speed for a known period of time before the illegal net is placed with anchor stones only. No markers are visible on the surface of the water. When pulling the net, the procedure is repeated. After the net is grappled up, it's attached to the net lifter. It would be nearly impossible for anyone else to find such a net in this inland sea without prior knowledge.

Nosing through the fog, the crew of the Barney suddenly closed in on a fish tug busily lifting a net. Checking back the motor, Weborg crept slowly alongside the craft. Visually inspecting the net as it was spread to its maximum, it was immediately obvious to Euers' practiced eye that the net was far too deep.

Very familiar with all the boats fishing the lake he whispered, "It's the Susie Q."

The admonition carried a warning. They all knew the boat was owned by John Clamp of Two Rivers. Clamp, overlord of the commercial fishing community in the Two Rivers area, had long battled conservation department control of commercial fishing activities. Verbal and at times physical resistance had erupted as conservation wardens enforced unpopular laws. This resistance was encouraged and abetted by his brother, State Assemblyman Ted Clamp and another commercial fishing ally, State Senator Marion "Chuck" Prieve. Skirmishes had ensued in the past with John Clamp and his crew involved in prior apprehensions for illegal fishing activities. Hailing from Quebec, Canada, the Clamp and Prieve families had immigrated to the Two

Rivers area in the 1840s. They had begun taking fish commercially before any significant regulatory acts or wardens were in place.

The adrenaline began to flow as the crew of the Susie Q spotted the warden boat. The boat swung hard to port as John Clamp, large knife in hand, scampered to the net lifter, where he began hacking desperately at the net where it lay on the roller and lifter. In a matter of minutes, the large net fell behind the Susie Q, sinking in its roiling wake slowly to the bottom. He stood transfixed, watching the net disappear, hoping he would never see it again. *Now what will we do with the rest of the net? There must be a way to get rid of it!* Dismissing this thought, he hurried back to the pilothouse. His immediate need was to escape the Barney and stop the wardens from recovering the net.

Seeing Clamp cut the net, Euers yelled, "Swing her around, we've got to get that net."

Weborg skillfully swung the boat, jumping a wall of water spewing from the Susie's wake, which threw Zerbes and Euers off balance. They were preparing the large grappling hook they always carried for recovery of illegal nets. Regaining their balance, they swiftly dropped a marker buoy to mark the spot where the net had been dropped. As Weborg completed another turn to put them in position to grapple, the Susie Q came boiling through the water in an attempt to deter them from dropping the grapple. Forced to turn to prevent a collision, the Barney again made a circle, bearing down on the marker buoy. The wardens were again confronted with the violator's boat coming at them in a collision course. Forced to change course to avoid ramming, the Barney circled to try again. Far enough ahead of the Susie this time, the warden boat passed very near the marker buoy. In this favorable position, the grapple line was dropped. It grew taut and trembled as it straightened under the pressure of hooking the giant net.

The crew of the Susie saw this, pulled away and laid off to one side, preparing for the next move. They'd come prepared for doing battle. They always carried a special grapple designed and constructed by the fishing fraternity for cutting the nets that the wardens attempted to recover. The grapple was large with a razor-sharp upper edge. Knowing that the wardens needed physical evidence to convict them, they had many times cut nets being grappled up and won cases in court when wardens could not produce the illegal nets. Neither side was giving an inch in this fish war!

Knowing the battle that would result, the wardens were reluctant to begin lifting the net while the Susie was in the area. Standing off, the Barney's crew waited for the violators to leave. With daylight fast waning, the wind picking up, and the handling of their craft becoming difficult to the point of pulling their grapple loose from the net, they decided to begin lifting, fully aware that the violator's boat would interfere with their operation.

Seeing the Barney lifting their net, the crew of the Susie swung dangerously close to the Barney, expertly dropping their grapple in an attempt to hook and cut the net. Hooked to the net, the Barney was now less maneuverable and was forced to maintain a constant speed and course, allowing the other boat a better chance at hooking the net. After several passes, the Susie's rope tightened. It had hooked the net and both boats squatted in the water, propellers spewing frothy water in a tug of war. Suddenly, the Susie squirted ahead as its heavy grapple line broke. It was clear now that the wardens had won. They had the net hooked and would soon lift it for evidence.

Seemingly defeated, the crew of the Susie laid off to the side temporarily while Clamp considered how he could get out of this pickle. Desperate, he sent the Susie on a head-on course aimed directly at the Barney. On deck, Euers saw the elevated bow of the Susie bearing down on them. *Damn it, they're going to ram. I've had enough of this foolishness. I'm going aboard to get the other end of their net. We never have enough evidence. We will this time. I'll stop this once and for all.* He waited for the expected collision. As the Susie banged into the Barney, they momentarily stood motionless in the water. Euers jumped nimbly to the deck of the other tug. As soon as he was safely aboard he began to second-guess his split-second decision. Watching the distance widen between the Susie and his haven aboard the Barney he wondered. *What am I doing alone on this boat? Left my gun and life preserver on the Barney. Can't stand much of this weather. Got to get inside.*

Moving swiftly across the foredeck he grasped the pilothouse railing and began pounding on a window immediately beside the captain. He glanced at Clamp, who turned and grinned at him, fully ignoring his order.

"Let me in, let me in!"

Going from one window to another, his order became a plea as he realized the jeopardy he was in if the crew chose to use the boat and the weather against him. Approaching the window directly in front of Clamp, Euers motioned and shouted to let him in. Clamp smirked and walked away as though he didn't hear or understand. Angered at the disregard of his orders, Euers kicked at one of the heavy glass windows until it broke with a crash, throwing slivers of glass around the pilothouse and onto the crew.

"There, can you hear me now? Damn it, let me in. You're all under arrest for using undersize nets and will soon be charged with obstructing a warden," said Euers.

With a smirk on his face Clamp shouted, "Get off my boat, You're not getting in here."

Temporarily defeated, Euers wandered around the open deck wondering what to do. *The pilothouse window is too small for me to get through. They wouldn't let me through it anyway.* A quickening easterly wind, swiftly dropping temperatures and dissipating fog rang an alarm in his mind. *This could get awful uncomfortable out here. Got to think of some way to stop this boat. The stack! Wonder if I can get to it? I may be able to shut this thing down.* Climbing gingerly to the top of the pilothouse, he removed his coat and jammed it unceremoniously down the stack. With a loud blast, an eruption of fire belched from the stack, throwing burning scraps of his incinerated coat into the air. *Oh-oh! It burned my coat to a crisp. Now I've done it. The weather is getting colder and I don't even have a coat.* Looking longingly aft for the Barney, he was disappointed to see that it was nowhere in sight.

Meanwhile, the Barney, after an hour of frantic lifting, finally retrieved 4,000 to 5,000 feet of gillnet. Attached to it was the Clamp grapple and about 100 feet of heavy rope. In a frenzy, the men threw the gillnet in a pile on the deck.

Weborg said, "Lets go. We can straighten the net out later, We've got to catch that boat. Can't tell what's happened to Don."

Darkness and the temperature fell simultaneously as they turned back toward the shore. Worried about Euer's welfare, the Barney's crew noticed that the boat began to violently shake as Weborg pushed the tug to its maximum.

With the wind picking up and the temperature swiftly dropping, darkness seemed even darker to Euers. He hunkered down shivering beside the pilothouse. Suddenly a light appeared on the horizon. *The Barney. At last they're coming. They'll be here soon.* His spirits soared at the thought of his friends coming to help him.

His enthusiasm quickly turned to despondency as the Susie Q made a turn into the oncoming sea. The cold water cascaded across the open deck and drenched him. He scrambled behind the pilothouse to avoid some of the water and to keep from being washed overboard. *What are they up to now? Are they trying to freeze me or wash me off the boat or are they heading toward Michigan and out of our jurisdiction? Man, that would be a long, hard, ride tonight. They're probably cutting up the rest of their net and throwing it overboard. I hope they hurry and head back to Wisconsin. They may let me inside once the nets are gone. I hope so!*

Shivering and suffering from exposure, Euers suddenly felt the boat shift and turn out of the wind and back to the west. Creeping to the open window, he shouted, "Let me in! It's freezing out here."

Smiling, the captain diverted his gaze to Clamp for guidance.

Clamp said nothing as he turned his back to Euers who said, "Come on, John, what do you have to gain by keeping me out here any longer? The Barney is right behind us now. Besides, I'll bet you've disposed of all your nets."

After a long silence, while Clamp seemed to be considering some distant thought, he said, "O.K. Don. Go to the stern. The side door will be open and you can swing down inside."

As Euers approached the side door he wondered...*Should I trust John? The door may not be open. They could push me overboard when I swing down. Oh well, got to take a chance!* He signaled to the Barney that he was dropping to the lower deck. They confirmed the message. He walked resolutely to the edge of the deck. With a final glance back, he firmly grasped the hand rail at the top of the deck and lowered himself over the side, feeling for the opening with his feet. Relieved, he found the door open. Quickly he swung his body inward and let loose, landing on the lower inside deck with relief.

Now what? I'm not going into the pilothouse begging. Damn it, they've put me through enough. Charging into the pilot house, he firmly announced, "You are under arrest for using nets deeper than 35-meshes." Stomping around he searched for illegal nets. He found only weights and floats cut from the net and fish boxes containing 300 to 400 pounds of chubs.

Pointing a trembling finger at Clamp, he charged, "Looks like you threw all your nets overboard. That's why you ran into the seas after dark. Oh well, the Barney will have the net you cut anyway and you'll be charged with obstructing a warden. Now let's head for Two Rivers."

"Are you telling me what to do on my boat?"

"This boat is seized and will be held for evidence. It may no longer be your boat. Head her in. Now!"

An awkward silence pervaded as they cruised the remaining miles to port.

Following close behind the Susie, Weborg skillfully steered the Barney into a position where they could possibly pick up Euers, should he be pushed overboard. Relieved to see Euers safely aboard he thought...*pushing Euers off their boat would be akin to murder. We would never get him aboard in this rolling sea. He would not last long in this cold water. We maybe would have one chance to grab him.*

"Whew, glad that's over. Walt did you call Herbie?" (Herbert Vander Bloemen was the warden at Manitowoc)

"Yeah, and I'm also calling the Two Rivers police and the Coast Guard. We're sure to have a welcoming committee at the dock."

Following closely as they entered the harbor, the Barney suddenly began to churn up muddy water.

"Damn it," shouted Weborg. "We're running aground."

He desperately reversed the boat and watched the Susie nose into her berth.

"Can't dock by the Clamp shanty. We'll have to land back-a-ways."

Concerned about the loss of time, he threw the throttle forward, pushing into the first open berth. Scrambling off the boat they hurried up the shore to assist Euers.

A large crowd greeted the Susie Q as it docked. Scrambling from the boat, Euers spotted Warden Herbert Vander Bloemen at the end of the dock trying to restrain a large crowd. Quickly jumping off the boat as it docked, Euers ran shouting up the dock,

"Stand back. We want no trouble."

Catcalls and shouts came from the throng.

"What right do you have to interfere with John's fishing?" Evidently the crowd was convinced of the fishermen's position and it was contrary to the state's.

"John's in violation here of the net sizes and he's under arrest. Please do not interfere."

Vander Bloemen attempted to control the crowd who were getting more unruly by the minute.

"You're interfering with conservation wardens in the performance of their duties. Please stay back."

As the crew unloaded the fish, Vander Bloemen roared above the crowd, "These fish are confiscated. They're illegal and are seized in the name of the state."

Euers joined in, "These items are seized as evidence. Please don't interfere."

Barely able to hold the crowd at bay, they were joined by Senator Chuck Prieve and Assemblyman Ted Clamp. Pushing through the crowd and seething with anger, they demanded to know why the wardens were interfering with John's fishing. Noting their status as community leaders, Euers tried patiently to explain that John Clamp was under arrest for using illegal gillnets and that the remaining floats and leads on his boat, along with the fish, were seized subject to the order of a court.

Told by the state lawmakers to let John go, Euers politely refused.

Glaring at Euers, Chuck Prieve turned to John Clamp, "Do you want them to have your fish?"

"Hell no!"

Turning to the crowd Prieve shouted at the top of his voice, "Come on boys, lets take em."

Waiting for a sign from their leaders, the crowd now surged forward as one.

Carrying one of the boxes of chubs toward his car, Vander Bloemen was physically blocked by Prieve. Prieve grasped the box and attempted to wrestle it from him.

"Let go, I'm taking these fish," said Prieve.

"No way, these fish are seized," yelled Vander Bloemen at the top of his voice.

"You know better than this Chuck. You could be charged with interfering with a warden performing his duties!"

The crowd closed even tighter around him, willing hands clutching and trying to wrench the box from him. Overpowered, Vander Bloemen soon lost his grip and watched as the group carried the box into a nearby net shed.

Emerging from the boat with a box of sinkers and floats, Euers was accosted by a horde led by Ted Clamp.

"Set 'em down Don, you're not leaving with John's equipment."

"Get out of the way Ted or you'll be arrested along with John."

"Not by a damn sight," replied Ted, "You're outnumbered here, get out of the way."

Gazing around, Euers spotted two officers from the Two Rivers Police Department in the crowd waiting for instructions. One of them yelled above the turmoil, "What do you want us to do?"

"Nothing anyone can do I guess. This is like an ant going against a tornado."

Realizing the futility of trying to stop the now determined mob, Euers held up his hands to draw attention and said, "O.K., take the stuff, but remember you'll be charged with obstruction!"

Swarming over the dock like a bunch of ants, they picked up the sinkers, floats and fish and disappeared with them into the same net shed where the chubs had been taken.

Warrants were sworn out for State Senator Marion Prieve and State Assemblyman Ted Clamp charging both with resisting and obstructing conservation wardens. John Clamp was charged with fishing with nets more than 35-meshes deep, having a mesh of less than 2.5-inches flexible rule and with resisting and obstructing conservation wardens. The Susie Q was seized, pulled out of the water and held for evidence at Manitowoc.

The two state representatives went to the press to defend their stand on commercial fishing as reported in part in a local paper:

Fishermen denounce wardens attitude *The "anti-commercial fishing attitude" of state conservation authorities was roundly denounced yesterday by three Two Rivers commercial fishermen who have been involved in rows with state wardens for many years.*

State Senator Marion (Chuck) Prieve, Assemblyman Ted Clamp and his brother, John, said their families had been commercial fishermen for four generations.

Throughout that time they said the state had favored those who fish for sport against those who fish for a living.

Prieve charged, "The state's whole policy is to issue a license, collect the fee, then let them fish but not catch any fish.

"If the Conservation Commission had its way, there'd be little or no commercial fishing in Lake Michigan and a natural resource could not be used to supply a legitimate source of income to hundreds of families."

The fishermen contacted the *Wisconsin State Journal* who interviewed them and reported:

Charge State Tug Hit Boat-Fishermen Study Suit

Two Rivers, Wis.—Three Two Rivers fishermen were arrested

after a fight with state game wardens over fish nets here early this week were considering bringing federal action against the wardens, charging them with ramming a fish tug with the state tug Barney Devine.

Assemblyman Marion Prieve, one of the fishermen, said that pieces of net seized as evidence by state wardens were not those of his brother, John, and that his brother's boat, the Susie Q, had been rammed by the Barney Devine. Wardens had charged that the Susie Q had rammed the Devine.

The two Clamps and State Senator Marion (Chuck) Prieve are facing trial on charges of obstructing and resisting conservation wardens. John Clamp also is to be tried on two counts of using illegal fishing nets.

"Propaganda," says Clamp

Assemblyman Clamp said Friday, "There's a lot of false propaganda floating around about John Clamp's illegal nets. They haven't got any of John's nets, as John says the nets they pulled out of the lake weren't his.

"He says he thought that they might be pulling his nets so he stuck around. And that's how this ramming took place."

And the facts are that the Barney Devine did the ramming –not John Clamp.

"The marks on John's boat will prove that to be true. The coast guard captain says that it's very obvious that John could not have rammed the Barney Devine because of the markings on John's boat.

"So that puts the shoe on the other foot and we're considering very seriously taking action against the Barney Devine in federal court to determine just what our rights are on federal waters."

Statement Draws Blast

Clamp's statement drew an immediate blast from Thomas Daley, skipper of the Two Rivers Coast Guard Unit.

"Why, I didn't even know Clamp," Daley said. "I certainly never said anything like that. I know nothing about the case and if I did, how could you tell which boat rammed which by looking at scratches?"

Clamp, after an angry telephone call by Daley, withdrew his statement that Daley had said that the Susie Q could not have rammed the state boat;

"I probably got my facts wrong," Clamp said.

The *Milwaukee Journal* printed the following in its, "On Wisconsin" column;

Fishermen Who Promote Lawlessness unfit as Legislators

It will be up to the courts to decide whether Senator Marion

Prieve, more descriptively known as "Chuck" and Assemblyman Ted Clamp are technically guilty of obstructing justice in the most recent affair of the Two Rivers fishermen's nets. That is not our concern here.

This last affair is but one of a long series of fracases in the Two Rivers area in which officers of the law, carrying out their duty, have encountered violent resistance from fishermen. In 1943, "Chuck" Prieve himself was convicted and sternly lectured by the court for a physical assault on a warden.

This newest fracas was of the old pattern, except that here were now two members of the legislature, sworn to uphold the law, who were at least encouraging a group that was using force to prevent wardens from doing their official duty. The legislators were promoting violent lawlessness whether they actually broke the law themselves or not. At this time we pass no judgment on their act as defined by the statutes.

Their general behavior, however, should make it clear, if it wasn't clear before, that Messrs. Prieve and Clamp are not men who should be sitting in any legislative body sharing the power to enact laws which others must enforce and obey. Previous attitudes and acts should have disqualified these two. Their most recent effrontery, in which they assumed that they were the governor, the police and the courts, should settle the matter.

No matter how these representatives of a lawless minority of Two Rivers fishermen got into the legislature, their tenure should be terminated just as soon as that is possible. It is inconceivable that these two represent the attitude of the majority of good citizens of Two Rivers, or the majority of decent fishermen. And the citizens of Wisconsin shouldn't be compelled for long to tolerate this pair as lawmakers.

Upon hearing the warden's story, District Attorney Fred Dicke presented arrest warrants for the three to Judge Osuld T. Bredsen who signed them. The district attorney announced that the warrants would be served immediately.

In January of 1948, John Clamp was convicted of using illegal nets and resisting and obstructing conservation wardens. He was fined $700 and his commercial fishing license was revoked for one year. The fine was later reduced to $400 in a circuit court appeal and the fishing tug Susie Q was returned to him allowing him to resume fishing after his revocation. Marion Prieve was fined $100 or 30 days in jail on a charge of resisting and obstructing conservation wardens. Ted Clamp was found not guilty of resisting and obstructing conservation wardens. The judge said, "It is the opinion of this court that neither Prieve nor Clamp went to the docks to preserve the peace as they have testified in their defense. There is no evidence, that either of them told anyone to be quiet or not to cause a disturbance and neither acted wisely in their positions as community leaders."

In finding Ted Clamp innocent, he pointed out that he had interfered no more than other men gathered at the docks who were not arrested.

RUNNING-DROP

The "running-drop" has always been a stock-in-trade used by wardens. Young wardens were automatically expected to know this productive, but dangerous procedure, even though it wasn't taught in warden training. Their experiences often left them with bruises, cuts, scratches or serious injuries.

The drop is performed in a moving patrol car travelling between 5 to 10 m.p.h. Warden Jim Chizek put it this way.

"We'd run up on them without lights. That's when the action started."

At the right moment, the warden on the passenger side would jump from the car and run and catch up to the violator's car, hopefully in time to see the occupants putting a gun in its case or tossing the gun or furs out the window. Sometimes, wardens had to hold the car door closed to keep a violator from running away.

Even when performed to perfection at low speeds, running-drop was very dangerous. It requires the timing and speed of a white-tail and the courage of a timber wolf to successfully pull it off. If not done perfectly, one is lucky to only lose skin. Despite the danger, wardens performed the running-drop for one reason only–to get the evidence they needed to prosecute violators. This is one story about running-drop.

In 1951, Ed Thompson returned from the Korean War to his station at Friendship in Adams County. There he found a young, entrepreneurial warden named Harold Hettrick, who was filling in at his station. Hettrick was soon to experience the hazards of the "running-drop."

On a cold October night, while working deer-shiners, Thompson and Hettrick spotted a perpetrator's car travelling at about 10 m.ph. With their headlights off, they got up close behind the auto before Thompson flashed the car's red light and siren. When the car didn't stop immediately, they saw a passenger struggle with a gun. Thompson yelled, "Get out Harold. Get out. Get up there!"

Opening his door to make the leap, Hettrick's right foot met the road with a jar that jerked him out of the car. His left foot didn't follow and got stuck between the seat of the car and the door post, causing his body to twist and turn. His face slammed hard on to the road. Unaware of Hettrick's dilemma, Thompson continued the pursuit.

When the car finally stopped, Hettrick had been dragged several hundred feet. Limping around in a stupor, blood streaming down his face, Hettrick assisted as well as he could in making the arrest. Despite the botched running-drop, the wardens still got the uncased gun for evidence.

Aching and sore, Hettrick began analyzing the methods utilized in the running-drop. He reasoned that he and Thompson were not a properly-matched team. Thompson was a short-legged man with small feet and had adjusted the car seat up close behind the steering wheel, not giving him enough room to get his long legs and big feet out of the car. It was obvious that a lot of study was needed to perfect the running-drop maneuver.

A year later, while working with Harley Peterson and another warden out of Appleton, Hettrick had his next bad experience with running-drop. With Peterson driving, Hettrick bailed-out of a moving patrol car to catch up with some illegal fish spearers. Hettrick was running alongside the patrol car, when the warden sitting in the back seat opened his door and inadvertently knocked him down. Hettrick rolled under the door and down the gravel road. Again, it took weeks to recover and grow back the lost skin.

Hettrick vowed there had to be a better, safer way to make the running-drop. Mulling it over, he experimented on how to get out of a moving auto without injury.

Five years after his first bad experience with the drop, Hettrick had transferred to Hortonville where he worked with Kenneth "Ken" Corbett, stationed at Clintonville. Both had entrepreneurial spirits. Surely two inquiring minds could solve the problem that so sorely had bothered Hettrick for the last 5 years. How do you get out of a moving car without breaking bones and losing skin?

They researched the problem for some time and felt the whole warden force would benefit when they solved it.

Then came the need for the drop. They needed to get into a farm yard on a dead end road where they had complaints of illegal deer shining. They decided the only way to get into the area unseen was to use the running-drop at night. During the daylight, there was no place to hide a car, to stop, or even use running-drop without being seen. The men, Clyde Strum and George Plum, were as cagey and alert as coyotes. They were aware of any strange vehicles in the area. It was vital that they always knew when a game warden was in their vicinity. They depended heavily on the party telephone line, an older version of the neighborhood watch.

They increased the intensity of their research and put together a plan similar to a military operation. County Warden Ralph Kleist assisted. They focused carefully and critically on the problem. Since they couldn't get out the side, front door safely, they worked on jumping off the open tailgate of the station wagon. With the criterion set, they tested their design for effectiveness.

With Kleist driving, Hettrick tested his grandiose theory–that he could safely get off the tailgate with the vehicle moving. He sat on a boat cushion on the tailgate with his legs pointing forward toward the driver. He then boosted himself up a bit and with a push let the tailgate run from under him. He landed backwards on his butt on the cushion. Ken found more success by simply tangling his feet off the tailgate and running off it. Clearly, the speed of the vehicle was the difference between success and scabs–15 m.p.h. was the maximum speed of the drop. Making several successful drops, they were satisfied they had mastered the technique and perhaps had pioneered an era in game warden effectiveness. They were ready to implement the new and improved "running-drop."

Their strategy was to "drop" Hettrick and Corbett near the farmhouse just after dark near the fields where the two violators were reported to have shined and shot deer.Just after sunset, Kleist drove the car past the suspects house at 15 m.p.h. with Hettrick and Corbett sitting in their respective positions, one looking forward the other looking backward on the tailgate. At the last minute, Hettrick decided to abandon the use of the boat cushion. He found he couldn't hold on to it along with all the other equipment–a portable radio weighing about 25 pounds, a lunch bag, thermos bottle, binoculars and other necessary gear. As they neared the "drop-off" spot, Kleist accelerated slightly for fear that their slow moving vehicle would be noticed. At the same time, Hettrick boosted himself off the tailgate and landed with a thump on his rear where he slid and rolled over backwards.

"Too fast," he gasped, as he tumbled heels-over-head. Heaving heavily, he gathered himself, glanced back and saw the car–Corbett was still on the tailgate.

Corbett, also overloaded with equipment, saw Hettrick take his disastrous tumble and decided the best part of courage was cowardice. He decided he wouldn't subject himself to the danger.

"Turn around Ralph, we've got to pick Harold up. I'm sure he hurt himself bad," said Corbett.

Bedraggled and bleeding, Hettrick lay along side the road dabbling at his wounds. He was still gasping to regain his breath as the station wagon returned.

"Are you all right Harold," asked Corbett?

"Yeah, I guess so, knocked the wind out of me. Help me pick up this gear. I sure hate to give up on those potlickers. But guess that'll have to wait for another day."

Gathering up their equipment, Corbett noticed Hettrick's trousers were worn through and both buttocks dripped with blood.

"Ha ha Harold, looks like you applied the wrong end to the acquisition of knowledge in our experiment."

It took Hettrick a much longer time to heal after this adventure. He later was heard to say, "How do you grow skin on hamburger?"

He never did perfect the running-drop, but he kept the trousers with the large holes for many years as a reminder of his entrepreneur years. When Hettrick became a training officer many years later, he often mentioned this story as an example of how to be innovative, but he never taught the "drop."

Today, the running-drop is used less often in part because of its danger and in part because a warden's job includes more investigative work.

BLACKY

Blacky's cave along the Dells of the Wisconsin River. The grapevine he grew in front of the cave for privacy has since died out. Jim Chizek photo

Wardens have numerous encounters with strange people. Some of these people leave a lasting impression and a never ending wonder of what makes them tick. One such person was Thomas "Blacky" Cline.

When first stationed at Portage in 1956, Warden Jim Chizek was told about a strange character who lived in a cave along the Wisconsin River at Wisconsin Dells.. Curious, one of the first places he scouted was the Wisconsin River. Sure enough there he was fishing below the Wisconsin Dells hydro dam in an old wooden, leaky, flat-bottomed boat. His first visit with Blacky aroused more curiosity and raised more questions than he had imagined. Chizek watched him beach his boat and then asked the slim, middle-aged man for his license. He complied with a smile, belaying his reputation as a bad fish violator.

"So you're the new game warden. I suppose we'll be seeing a lot of each other."

"I don't know. What makes you think that?"

"You mean you're not here to acquaint yourself with where I live and fish? You've certainly heard of me."

"I won't lie to you, that's why I'm here."

"Won't you step into my palace. I'll give you the $10 tour."

In a very friendly manner, he pointed to his home, a depression in the rock canyon wall of the lower dells. The depression was about 30-feet long, 8- to 9-feet deep and about 5.5-feet in height. At about 5-foot 8-inches tall, Blacky had to stoop slightly to walk around.

The cave contained an old spring bed with a ragged mattress that was neatly made up with a tattered quilt. In a section of the cave he called a kitchen, he neatly stacked a few kettles, a frying pan and several chipped plates. The front of the cave was open to the weather except for a wild grape vine he had planted and trained to provide some privacy from the many fishermen wandering within several feet of his front door! Rubbernecking boaters, fishermen, and tourists on cruise boats, strained to catch a glimpse of Blacky. Everyone told stories of this puzzling, legendary loner.

Asked about how he survived, Blacky said he lived mostly on fish taken from the river. He also mentioned how he hated the long walk and climb into Wisconsin Dells via the dam. To shorten his trip, he chopped hand-and foot-holds into the perilously-steep, sandstone cliff above his cave, and inserted poles into crevices, which allowed him to climb straight up and into town.

Asked why he lived under such harsh conditions he replied, "I like it here and will live here till I die."

"Do you live here in the winter?"

"Absolutely."

Gazing downstream, Chizek spotted a flow of water carrying white items into the river–items that could only be toilet paper. Returning his attention to Blacky he mused, "Even though the city sewer outfall is only a short distance from here?"

"It doesn't bother me...very little smell."

"It isn't where I would want to live, but if you like it here, I guess, to each his own."

Returning to Portage, Chizek checked old arrest cards on Blacky. He found numerous arrest records dating from the early 1940s. Arrests began with Warden Louis "Pat" Oshesky and were followed by Warden Allan Galston in the 40s and 50s. Most recent arrests were made one year before Chizek arrived by wardens Edward "Ed" Thompsen and Joseph "Joe" Rubesch with assistance from Wilham "Bill" Hiebing. Working undercover, Thompsen and Rubesch had charged Blacky with 14 various counts of selling fish including the sale of walleyes and sturgeon.

So began Chizek's odyssey with Blacky Cline. *Where did this strange man come from? Why did he live in a cave. How did he man-*

age to acquire food? What brought him to the point of living like this? Is there something in his past that made him isolate himself? A woman, a lost love perhaps, or a crime committed in some far off place he wasn't disposed to pay for, or some deep, foreboding psychological reason? Isolation wasn't his only motive, as he spent much of his time walking the streets of Wisconsin Dells visiting and mixing with people. He spent a considerable amount of time commiserating at the Sportsmen's Bar.

Checking with the Wisconsin Dells police, Chizek learned that Blacky had rode the rails into Wisconsin Dells in the 1930s at the age of about 35 and had lived in the cave below the dam since. The police reported having no trouble with him except that he occasionally got drunk at the Sportsmen's Bar. Several times he had fallen off the 60-foot perpendicular cliff above his cave while attempting to negotiate his steep ladder while drunk. These incidents always took place in the middle of the night when returning to his cave from the Sportsmen's Bar. Despite breaking his arm several times, he somehow managed to survive each fall.

Blacky puzzled Chizek. He was a conundrum. Chizek often found himself wondering about this strange man, unable to shake the probability of anyone living the way he did. Blacky was highly educated and had beautiful scroll handwriting, like a monk of old. He was very religious and loved to talk about the Bible. Although Chizek never saw a Bible among his possessions, all laying open to public inspection, he quoted it scripture and verse. He was also very knowledgeable about current happenings and loved to discuss world events. He acknowledged that he kept up with current events by reading the newspapers at the Sportsmen's Bar. When the subject of whether he had relatives in other places arose, he clammed up. Through years of making numerous inquiries, Chizek never found anyone who knew his history. He was convinced that Blacky was running from someone or something, perhaps something very ominous or serious.

Although Chizek enjoyed talking with him, a foreboding feeling often came over him while in his presence. He never completely trusted him especially along the lonely Wisconsin River at night or while arresting him. Oh yes, Chizek did arrest Blacky many times while stationed at Portage. Most arrests were for selling fish, as Blacky had no other means of income. Yet, unbelievably, he always seemed to come up with enough money to pay his fines.

Chizek got to know his every move. Many people complained that he was peddling fish on the streets of Wisconsin Dells. Blacky was an expert fisherman and used an old rod with no reel that he cast out like a fly fisherman. He piled the line in the bottom of the boat and hand-lined it in. Several times, Chizek tried to give him a reel, but was unceremoniously turned down. Blacky said he had no use for it, preferring to fish without one.

At a group check on the river, Chizek put his boat in several miles below the dam and motored upstream toward the dam. He was within radio contact with wardens Frank Adamske and Jim Flanigan, who were observing from a high bluff overlooking the anglers. Chizek slowed the boat when he received an incoming call advising him that Blacky had just caught a large rock sturgeon, put it in a gunny sack and tied it to his boat. Wondering how he could get near him, Chizek realized the half-mile of open river from the first curve below the dam to Blacky almost made it impossible. Alone in a small aluminum boat with a new 33 horsepower Mercury gave him confidence, a commodity Chizek had a surplus of at the tender age of 27. Carrying one person the rig could fly. I was sure I could cover the half-mile so fast that Blacky wouldn't have time to release the fish. He asked Adamske and Flanigan to keep a sharp eye on him as he highballed it upstream, staying close to shore to utilize all the tree cover available. Studying him closely and seeing no untoward activity, Chizek felt he had it made. So much for the unbridled confidence of a young warden! Too close to shore, the motor struck a rock and threw him heavily to the deck of the boat. Dazed, Chizek held the broken tiller in his hand as the boat spun about. Just enough of the skeg and prop stayed in the water to continue the movement. Centrifugal force made it almost impossible to reach the kill switch. None-the-less, Chizek inched his way along the gunnel and finally hit the switch. He slowed the dizzying spin and regained control of the boat. Head spinning, he gazed upriver to see if Blacky had seen his performance or heard the ungodly roar of the motor when it popped out of the water. Blacky sat quietly in his boat as if nothing had happened. This reassured Chizek. With the fortitude of an eternal optimist, he threw the tiller on the deck and grabbed the oars. *I'll still get him!* Dipping his oars deep, he rowed desperately against the strong current of the river. Sweating and puffing, he finally he arrived at the boat.

Blacky greeted him cordially, "Well Jim, what're you up to today?

Without answering, Chizek pulled the gunny sack into his boat, opened it and was surprised to find only walleyes. Dropping the sack with a splash, Chizek pulled himself hand-over-hand around the boat looking for the second sack he knew had to exist, but to no avail. Disgusted, he sat back with a sigh.

Blackie's face broke into a huge smile. "The way you're looking me over one would think you were looking for an old blue sturgeon or something."

Noticing the severed rope hanging over the gunnel Jim blasted, "You know damn well what I'm looking for. See those guys standing on the top of the Dells docks? They're wardens and they saw you catch a sturgeon!"

"You know what they say Jim, possession is nine-tenths of the law. I have no sturgeon."

Drifting away from the boat, Chizek called Adamske and asked what happened.

"What do you mean what happened? Everybody on the river saw and heard you hit that rock. Blacky took one look at you and cut the sturgeon, sack and all loose."

Now Chizek had two problems. First, he had to explain the incident to a rough and tough supervisor Louis "Pat" Oshesky. Chizek's file still retains a copy of the long, detailed letter explaining how and why he had destroyed a new motor and why he deserved another new one. Second, never make a mistake in front of other wardens. They will tell! Soon the tale circulated among wardens far and wide, each adding their personal touch and glorifying it.

As the years went by, Chizek continued prosecuting Blacky for infractions of fish laws. He always pled not guilty and defended himself in court without an attorney. He did a respectable job and used the language of a learned and polished lawyer to the point of embarrassing the justice of the peace. After justice court was abolished, County Judge James Daley incarcerated Blacky for six months. Chizek was pleased, feeling that with winter fast approaching, Blacky would at least have warm shelter. He would also be out of his hair for a time. Often talking to him in the jail, he learned that Blacky couldn't stand to be locked up. He told Chizek that he hated him for this indignity and swore he had put a curse on him. He said he missed his cave, even with the severe weather.

After about half the sentence was served, Chizek approached District Attorney David Bennett who accompanied him to a proceeding before Judge Daley. They asked that Cline be released. Judge Daley agreed and released him.

After that, Blacky claimed he didn't feel well. He blamed Chizek and his stay in jail for his malady, not considering several more serious falls off his improvised stairway. Despite his claim of ill health, he continued to live in his cave through the bitter winter months. One bitter cold day, with temperatures hovering at about 20 below, Chizek hiked down to the cave to check on Blacky. To his surprise, he was out in his dinky boat, the wind whipping it dangerously back and forth in the dangerously fast current created just below the dam.

Chizek watched him catch three nice walleyes and shake his fist at a bald eagle that scooped up a small walleye from the river. Blacky struggled with his oars that didn't fit the locks well, and rowed into shore. He beached his old row boat, and with a deft movement, wisely tipped it over. Water gushed out onto the frozen sandy shore. Quickly, he gathered some driftwood. While the fire flickered to life, he stood and he literally jerked the guts out of the fish and put them into a frying pan. In about 15 minutes he had finished eating, washed the pan in the river with an old rag and river sand. Dipping water from the river he swiftly dashed the fire out, carefully stashed the pan and stretched out on his old bed inside his cave.

As Chizek approached, Blacky turned his head to see who the intruder may be. He sat up as Chizek inquired about his health.

"About the same," he replied. "You know I've never felt good since that time you put me in jail."

"But Blacky, why do you stay out here in the cold like this? Couldn't you find a place to stay for the winter?"

"I guess I could, but I like it out here."

"That old boat is going to be the death of you one of these days. It leaks like a sieve and is too small for the kind of current out there."

"Naw, I've been on this river for over 25 years and never tipped over yet."

"The least you could do is wear a life preserver."

"Don't need no life preserver. I'm not going to tip over, and if I ever did, a preserver would do me no good in that cold water anyway."

"At least your body would be easier to find if you were wearing one."

"I'll leave that job up to you. Would you look for my body or leave me for the catfish and crows to nibble on?"

"You know I would, but I don't care too. Looks like an eagle got one of your walleyes."

"Yeah damn fish eater. I hate 'em. I would kill 'em if I had a gun."

"You know they're protected."

"Yeah, but that never stopped me from doing what I want to do anyway."

"You may have to spend more time in the county jail for that."

"I doubt that. The judge let me out early the last time."

"Don't bet it'll happen again though. That eagle didn't hurt your fishing. The fish he took was probably injured in the dam. It was just a little one anyway. I was watching you. Why did you put your fire out right away? I would think you would at least warm yourself with it for a while."

"No, the cold don't bother me. That stinking jail did though. Look what it did to me. I'll never be the same."

"Yeah I know Tom, do you have enough clothing to stand this cold? I could perhaps fix you up with some."

"No thanks. You've already done enough and my curse will soon start to take effect."

"O.K. Blacky, I guess I can take a hint. See you later."

Chizek arrested Blacky several more times during the mid-1960s. Blacky became even easier to catch because the judge had revoked his fishing privileges. However, he became more and more reluctant to arrest him because it did absolutely no good and was a waste of time and state dollars. He also admitted to feeling sorry for him, though he never voiced it to anyone except his wife. He was torn between his feelings of fruitlessness and his responsibility as a public servant. Yet he always responded to the public he represented.

In 1966, shortly after taking a promotion to become district warden in Park Falls, Chizek learned that Blacky had died. He immediately called Bernie Olson, the police chief in Wisconsin Dells. He said that Blacky had passed away at the age of 65 in the Sportsmen's Bar. One night at closing time, the bartender found him in rigormortis still setting in his chair.

Chizek and Olson shared their curiosity about Blacky, so when Chizek asked him to check his criminal record, Olson took his fingerprints at the morgue and ran checks on him throughout the United States and Canada. Olson received one response. Tom Cline had been incarcerated once in Canada and booked under an alias as Thomas King for vagrancy.

What's the rest of the story!? Chizek would always wonder.

GET EVEN!?—NOT! GET AHEAD!

Conservation Warden Jim Chizek was closing the door of his Lake George home near Portage at 5 a.m. on the opening day of deer season in November of 1962, when the phone rang. Quickly and quietly he tiptoed to the phone so not to awake his family.

"Yes, this is Jim Chizek. How can I help you?"

"This is Eli Vinegar. I have a problem. I've lost my hunting license."

"Well Eli, a duplicate can be issued by the county clerk."

"Yeah, I know that, but I would like to get out at starting time. Could you issue it?"

"I could, but you would be required to get an application from me and get it notarized before I can issue it. I was just leaving to go to work. I will drop the application off at your home."

"But I want to hunt right away. If I get it notarized right away could you issue it?"

"I hate to have my wife bothered but if you're lucky enough to find a notary at this time of day, she could issue it. The duplicate will cost you 50 cents," Chizek replied, knowing full well it would be impossible to find a notary at that time of day on a Saturday.

He briefed his wife about Vinegar's story and she went back to bed, thinking it would be impossible to rouse a notary this early. A short while later, she was awakened by the incessant ringing of the door bell. Wiping the sleep from her eyes, for the second time that morning, she opened the door to be greeted by Vinegar with a notarized application in his hand.

With hopes of still getting a little more sleep before getting the children up, she quickly issued the license so Vinegar could get out to hunt the early hours of deer season. Handing him the license she said, "That will be 50 cents"

"What do you mean 50 cents? I already paid the notary 50 cents."

"Yes, that was for notarization, but the duplicate license fee is 50 cents and I know Jim told you that."

"Yeah he told me it could cost 50 cents and damn it I already paid the notary 50 cents and I'm not paying you anything more."

"You know Eli I wouldn't have had to get up and issue this license.

I'm doing you a favor. Now you thank me by acting like this. The license costs 50 cents as marked on the license."

The conversation began to get out of hand and Vinegar became more belligerent and began to swear and downgrade her. She then turned and saw 5-year-old Frankie toddling down the hall, awakened by the disruption. Baby Donny began to cry in the bedroom and Mrs. Chizek snapped, "Eli we don't talk that way in our home and I won't stand for it. Give me the 50 cents and leave."

"I don't have to. This is Jim's office and you better just shut up."

"Eli this is my home and I'm calling the sheriff if you don't pay up and leave."

"O.K.," he shouted with an oath and fired a fifty cent piece across the floor. "I'll get even for this. I'll just go out and kill the first doe I see."

The house rang as he slammed the door. Hollow silence followed.

Later that day, Chizek comforted his wife as she told the story, "I will talk to him tomorrow."

The next morning, a sleepy-eyed and cranky Chizek met with trainee Warden Jim Flanigan. He had spent much of the night thinking about what Vinegar had done and didn't sleep much. As they checked hunters that day, he told Flanigan what happened. The more Chizek thought about it and talked about the incident, the madder he became.

"Damn it! I'm going to have it out with Eli before this day is out," he said.

"In the early afternoon, the two wardens stopped at Vinegar's house to find only his wife at home. Chizek advised her that he would like to talk to Vinegar. As they left, a neighbor flagged them down and reported that Vinegar had in fact killed an illegal doe just as he had threatened, but he didn't know where he put it. The two wardens began an investigation with zeal and urgency, mainly because the case was more personal than usual.

"The wardens questioned Vinegar's friends and acquaintances and it soon became apparent that the illegal deer was in Vinegar's house. With the vague information they had uncovered, the wardens approached District Attorney David Bennett in an attempt to obtain a search warrant for Vinegar's house. Dave said he didn't feel there was enough evidence to issue a warrant and instructed the two to gather more information.

"As the day progressed they occasionally called Dave advising him of every little scrap of information they had obtained, but in the end, it wasn't enough to merit issuance of a search warrant.

"At 4 p.m., Chizek realized he would never apprehend Vinegar unless something unusual took place. He knew as soon as Vinegar arrived at home and was told the warden had stopped there that he would take steps to get rid of the illegal meat. Desperate, he called

Bennett a last time.

"I have talked to almost everyone in the first ward and can't get any more information about Vinegar's illegal deer, but I've just got to get him. I know he has the deer." He went on to tell Bennett of the episode with Shirley. "I've just got to get him Dave. I've got a plan that I believe would flush him out."

"What do you have in mind Jim?"

"I thought we would call him and tell him the game warden is coming to search for illegal venison. Jim Flanigan and I would be laying outside his house when he brings the meat out. Would you go along with that?"

"Who would you get to call him?"

"I thought maybe you would."

There was a long pregnant silence on the phone as Bennett mulled over the consequences of this action. Finally with a sigh and a chuckle he replied, "Yeah I guess I would do that."

"Good, now when you call, tell him the warden is on his way to his place right now. Tell him to get the deer out of the house right away. The more you scare him the better chance he'll panic and run outside with the venison. We'll be at his house at 5 p.m. Call then. Be sure to plant the thought in his mind that he must get the venison out of his house quickly. Don't give him too much time to think."

"O.K. Jim, be ready."

Darkness was gathering as the two wardens slunk like lobo wolves into the area around Vinegar's house. Getting near was difficult as Vinegar had a menagerie of cur dogs running loose, all of which were barking at the two wardens.

Chizek got within about 150 feet of the front door and hid behind a row of shrubs when one of the more vicious of the pack growled and snarled at him. Man they're sure to know something's going on out here with all this ruckus. Surprises me no one has checked out what the dogs are barking at. Flanigan was able to get past the dogs and work his way within 20 feet of the back of the residence. Hiding behind several small trees he heard the telephone ring through the paper thin walls of the house and hear a woman answer.

"Eli's not home. What?"

The woman spoke loudly and despite the distance, Flanigan heard her screech into the mouthpiece. "I don't know what to do. Maybe I can call him."

Shortly after she hung up Flanigan could again hear her talking. *Ah ha, she's calling Vinegar.*

"Someone just called. He's on his way here now. The game warden. You get home here right now."

Chizek was becoming impatient. *I know Dave's called by now, what's going on? Getting awful dark, Maybe this thing has fizzled.* The putt-putt-putt sound of a scooter distracted him away from this thought. It spun into the yard past a hedge which concealed the operator from him. The dark shadow of a slight man abandoned the scooter and ran into the house.

Holding his breath Chizek thought, *don't know if that's Vinegar, about his build, something should happen soon.* Suddenly the front door slammed open and the slight man jettisoned himself off the porch in a stooped position with a bundle in his arms. He scooted around the corner of the house toward the edge of the clearing behind the house.

Pushing through the hedge, Chizek chased after the man in the dark. Suddenly his body catapulted through the air as his foot caught a protective wire around a small tree. He hit the ground with a thud, the wind partially knocked out of him. Gasping for breath he scampered to his feet. Throwing caution to the wind, he turned on his powerful flashlight to avoid hitting any more obstacles. He had the advantage of chasing a man in the dark with a light and swiftly closed the distance between the running man and himself. When only a few feet from him, the fleeing man stopped and threw a bundle wrapped in store paper into the brush at the edge of the clearing.

"What do you have there Eli?"

"You've got me."

"Let's go pick it up snapped Jim. And then I want to talk to you about that incident at my house yesterday with Shirley."

Flanigan joined the two as they were picking up the scattered pieces of venison in the underbrush. He heard Chizek's stern voice reprimanding Vinegar about the issuance of the duplicate license and how he had mistreated his wife.

He tried to cool the situation by changing the subject, "Why don't we talk about that later Jim. Let's get the facts about how this deer was taken."

Temporarily deterred by Flanigan's intervention Chizek snapped. "Eli this isn't the whole deer.

Where's the rest of it?"

"I don't know."

"Cut the crap Eli you know where it is and we're going to get it. After what you put Shirley through you're not getting any breaks in this neighborhood. Now where's the rest of it?"

"You wouldn't do anything about it anyway."

"Why."

"Because he's your neighbor."

"Try me. Where is it?

"Clarence DeVille has it."

Turning to Flanigan he said, "Lets go Jim."

The three men swiftly drove to the Lake George area where DeVille lived. Knocking on the door they were told to enter by a man's voice inside. As the door opened Clarence asked, "What're you doing here Chizek?"

"Perhaps Eli can tell you."

DeVille paled, "What's going on Eli?"

"They got me so they might as well get you too."

"O.K., it's in the deep freeze, I'll get it out."

After picking up the frozen venison, Chizek continued to reprimand Vinegar in a calmer but determined voice about the issuance of the license.

"You know Eli, Shirley doesn't work for the state. She only issued the license as a favor to you. What right do you have to harass her or disturb my family?"

Finally Vinegar apologized for his behavior.

"Eli I don't want your apology. But I know someone who does and she damn better well get one or I'll be coming to call on you."

"O.K. Jim. I'll make a trip out to your place tomorrow and apologize to your wife."

"Make it good Eli or else."

"Yeah, I understand. I'll do it."

The following morning, the two wardens contacted David Bennett and brought him up to date on the status of the case. Chizek was still smarting over the whole affair as the two wardens went over the evidence they had seized. Chizek pawed through the pieces of meat and said, "You know what Jim we don't have the whole deer yet. Those guys are not going to get away with an ounce of this deer. There must be someone else involved in this. We're going to get every damn one of them. Maybe they won't have any respect for me, but they better start showing some for Shirley."

At court that morning, Vinegar and DeVille plead guilty to charges of possession of untagged venison and were each fined $100 and costs, plus the loss of all hunting and fishing privileges for one year.

They were about to leave when Chizek asked County Judge Daniel O'Conner if he could speak.

At the judges nod, Chizek began.

"Your honor this has been a difficult case because Eli gave my wife a hard time while doing him a favor of issuing a duplicate license. I know I'm not to be vindictive while carrying out my duties, but I also have a responsibility to stand up for her and the well being of my family. There are some parts of the illegal deer still missing and I'm not in a mood to let people of Vinegar's ilk get away with anything. Would you ask Eli who has the rest of the venison?"

Judge O'Conner turned to Vinegar, "Tell him who has the venison."

"I can't your honor."

"You can't or won't?"

"Won't I guess."

"Your honor," broke in Chizek, "Would you put him under oath and ask him?"

"Raise your right hand Eli."

After issuing the oath, the judge again asked him who had the remainder of the deer.

"I hate to do this but I guess I have no choice. It's my son Erick."

The judge nodded his head and said, "Normally Jim, I would issue a search warrant but instead I am issuing an arrest warrant for Erick, which will also give you the authority to search for the contraband."

After Erick was apprehended, Chizek again looked at the evidence and found there was still some of the deer missing. Still determined to get it all, the two wardens went to Vinegar's home.

"Eli there's still some of that venison missing. As I told you before, don't expect any breaks from me. There isn't much missing but I want every scrape. You lied to Judge O'Conner and if you don't tell me who has it you will face him again. Do you understand?"

With a resigned sigh he replied, "Yeah, I'll tell. My mother has it."

"Where does she live?"

"Just down the street. Are you going to arrest her?"

"How old is your mother?"

"She just turned 87."

"You're getting your first and last break Eli. We won't arrest your mother."

After apologizing to Shirley, Vinegar always addressed her in a very polite manner whenever they met on the street.

BEAR, BEAR WHERE'S THE BEAR?

A recruit game warden, John Benedict, stationed near Bruce in Rusk County, had received a number of bear damage complaints. It was a year in the 1940s when late spring frosts and dry weather produced a very poor crop of berries and nuts in wild northern Wisconsin. Bear were plentiful and without sustenance in the woodlands, they pillaged area bee hives, killed livestock and broke into cabins and homes. They were especially destructive to apiaries.

Cliff Freeman, stationed at Birchwood in Washburn County, was a very colorful warden known for his mischievous sense of humor and for often pulling pranks on other wardens. He also had a legendary reputation for his ability to handle bears. An excellent bear trapper, he had trapped many a marauder in his years in the north.

Receiving complaints of a bear smashing bee hives, the new warden having no experience with bear damage, and at a loss as to how to respond to the complaints called Freeman.

"This is John and I need help. Down in the southern part of my county a bear is tearing up a farmer's bee hives. I've never handled bear damage before. Could you give me a hand?"

"I sure could. The only way to take care of an animal like that is to trap him."

"I've never set a bear trap and know nothing of how to do it."

"I'll be over tomorrow morning bright and early to show you how. Do you have a bear trap?"

"Yeah, it's down at the ranger station."

"I will meet you there at 8 a.m."

"Meeting the next morning they picked up the trap and journeyed to the complaint area.

The two left their autos in a small clearing where the woods road ended. The rookie pointed out the group of hives, several of which were tipped over. Others lay hither, thither, splintered and scattered across the clearing. Walking among the havoc Freeman suddenly yelled at the top of his voice, "LOST IN THE WOODS! Ha Ha, this is what it's like to be a game warden. Is this what you want to be? Hunt, fish and a cabin in the woods."

Bewildered and unfamiliar with Freeman's unorthodox sense of humor, the young warden stared at him and slowly broke into a bashful smile.

"Yeah I guess so," he said. He had just been introduced to the playful side of Cliff Freeman.

"Enough of this foolishness," quipped Freeman," Let's get on with the bear trapping."

Having many years of experience in trapping nuisance bears, Freeman took charge. "See this trail. This is where the bear is coming into the apiary. Bring the trap over here and I'll show you how to make a set. These tracks are huge. This is a big HE bear and he feels he owns the area. This trail is so well used he'll come in without a care in the world. He's king here and fears nothing, especially humans. He's one to be careful with...a boss bear if I've ever seen one," he said with a twinkle in his eye.

The young man didn't realize more than one trap was being set this day.

Handing the young warden an axe, swede saw, hammer and nails, Freeman continued to elaborate on the danger of such a ferocious animal.

"I had a big one that got out of a trap once. Almost got me. Once they're mad they don't run away. They run toward you. Shot him at the last minute. He dropped at my feet. I was so damned scared I was lucky to get a shot off. His mouth was wide open, looked like a washtub coming after me."

He continued with wild bear stories as he supervised the building of a pen that would fence off an area where the trap was to be set. He nailed a large warning sign to the enclosure proclaiming, "BEAR TRAP." He bragged, "We'll have Mister Bruin come the dawn. I guarantee it."

He tied a large chunk of bacon to the back of the enclosure and explained, "Bears love bacon. It takes them by the nose and leads them into trouble. The bear will enter here in this opening and be forced into this narrow entryway to get to the bait. He'll step over the log I've placed here and be forced to put his foot in this narrow area where we'll place the trap. Get the trap and those clamps I brought along and I'll show you how to set and place it."

He proceeded to set the large trap, explaining the operation to the lad step by step. "Now screw this c-clamp down on this spring. When all the way down, slip this holding clamp on the spring like this. Then remove the c-clamp and screw the other spring down the same way. Now let's place the trap while it's still safe."

Firmly bedding the trap by digging into and leveling the ground in the placement area, he attached the trap chain to the step log.

"This log serves two purposes. First as a step log and second as a drag or clog to slow him down, tangle him up, and eventually stop him. Opening the jaws he continued,"Now we bring the pan trigger into place and unscrew the c-clamp. This will hold the trigger in place and hold the jaws open."

Moving the c-clamp to the other jaw, he tightened it enough to allow the holding clamp to be removed. Tossing the c-clamp out of the enclosure he proclaimed,"The trap is set. Be careful not to go near it."

Freeman placed several more stumps and logs in place and stepped back. He pointed to the set with a gleam in his eye and said,"I've left him only one spot to step over the log to reach the bait. We'll have him by the left foot in the morning."

All during the setting of the trap, Freeman continually related past harrowing tales of bear trapping experiences, all enhanced to intimidate the inexperienced young warden.

"Remember when you get near a bear in a trap, he's dangerous. As I told you, I've had bears pull free of the trap or loosen the clog and they were on me in a flash. I was always able to shoot fast enough and straight enough to stop them before they got to me. Are you a good shot?"

"Pretty good, but I've never shot a bear. In fact I've never seen one."

"You've got to hit them good or they won't go down. Just be careful when you're tracking that you don't stumble onto him without warning. Oh well you'll be O.K.."

"Tracking?"

"Yeah, he won't be here, he'll be hiding out in the brush somewhere. Don't worry, you'll have no trouble following the track."

After listening for hours of the dangers of bears, John apprehensively asked. "Will you come with me tomorrow to check the trap?"

"No, I have a court case tomorrow, but there's nothing to taking care of this beast. Just be awful careful when you approach. You'll see this whole area torn apart and a drag trail where the log and trap knocked down the brush, small trees and all. You'll have no trouble trailing him with the trap on his leg. Just follow him down the drag trail to where he's tangled up and shoot him. Be awful careful though, there's nothing more dangerous than a trapped bear at bay. If he should get out of the trap or his clog comes loose, he'll probably charge. Sneak in here very carefully and follow out the trail with your guard up. You won't have any trouble."

As the two men walked toward their vehicles, the young man suddenly realized, Freeman was going to leave him. He had a feeling of being deserted. *I'll have to face the bear alone in the morning.*

"Are you sure I can handle this by myself? I would feel a lot better if you were along."

Noticing the sickly pallor on his face, Freeman had difficulty holding back a smile of satisfaction. He had the rookie hooked but good and wasn't going to give him any slack.

"Don't worry about it. Be careful and things will be fine. Shoot straight. There's nothing more dangerous than a crippled bear."

Satisfied that he had instilled in the young warden a fear of every thing that could possibly go wrong, plus a few extra things his mischievous mind had conjured up, he waved to leave. "Call me tomorrow when you get him."

Freeman grinned all the way home with only one small pang of regret. He'll have a hard time living down what is about to happen to him when the rest of the wardens find out about this!

That evening the young man answered his phone. It was Freeman. In a husky voice he said, "Got to thinking about that trap and worrying about you going in there all alone. Wish I could be there to make sure you don't get hurt. Bears are unpredictable and can be very dangerous. You're after a big one. Be very careful."

"I know, you told me so. Are you sure you can't come over?"

"Can't make it, but I just called to make sure you take your time and be very careful. I know you'll have him. Be careful and call me when you get him so I won't worry. Satisfied that he had his victim scared out of his wits, he hung up. Smirking he shouted, "Got him! Got him good."

After a sleepless night, the young warden imagined what it would be like to face a ferocious bear in his trap. He drove to where the trap was set, wistfully wishing Freeman could be there to lend both moral and physical support. Carefully he loaded his rifle to capacity. *Can't be too careful!* He walked gingerly into the wooded area surrounding the hives. With bated breath he approached the trap enclosure. Just as Cliff had described, the enclosure was torn apart, the trap gone! *Oh oh, now what do I do? I've got him!* Suddenly he seemed more alone than at any time in his life. He was in the wildest, most desolate wilderness in the world. Turning he saw the drag trail. *My God, he must be a big one, look at the brush he's broken off. Wonder how far he'll go before he gets tangled up and can't go any further?* His heart in his throat, he stood very still listening, struggling to hear over his pounding heart. *Something seems funny. I can't hear him struggling!* With the rifle held even higher, his blood thundering in his ears, he forced himself to proceed. *You wanted to be a warden, now's the time to prove yourself, get the bear and have it over with.* He stopped where the trail ended in a thick bramble. *He must be in there.* Circling around the tangle, he looked apprehensively at it and satisfied himself that nothing had left the clump of brush. *Well this is it. He's in there. Got to go in after him!* Completing the circle around the bramble, he approached the opening where the bear had obviously entered. Slowly creeping forward, his rifle at his shoulder, his body tense, he carefully peeked around some small balsam trees. Protruding from a thicket of hazelnut, he saw a small part of the trap spring. Nothing else was visible. *Why can't I see the bear? I'm only 15 feet from the trap. Have to go closer.* Bucking up his courage, he slowly crept closer.

Peering intently into the thick brush he hesitated. *There's something in the trap. I can see the fur. It's too small. What's going on here?* Stepping hesitantly forward, he finally saw what was grasped in the giant jaws. A black furry TEDDY BEAR!

Author's note: John Benedict is not the real name of the young warden in this story. The real name of the warden was not confirmed.

Warden Clifford Freeman was a perennial joker and used this mocked up photo to shock people. He used to say, "The second worst pain–when he hit the end of the chain."

AN AGGRAVATED CASE

In the spring of 1933, Chief Warden Harley W. "Mac" MacKenzie became concerned with the violating activities of Mr. Jesse Bilford. Although wardens R. A. "Bob" Nixon of Florence, Harley T. McKeague of Rhinelander and Stuart Hayner of Eagle River had arrested him several times, Bilford continued to kill and sell deer illegally. MacKenzie constantly received information relating to Bilford's errant ways, and in his hands on way of supervising," he communicated his opinion to the wardens in a letter, "You haven't charged Bilford properly on earlier occasions. I'm sure the district attorney would have approved your use of the repeater act in such an aggravated case."

MacKenzie was a tough task master and ruthlessly drove the three to increase their law enforcement efforts to not only apprehend Bilford, but to penalize him to a degree that would force him to stop violating.

"You men must put this guy out of business. Get on him. This is an aggravated case."

On March 8, 1933, MacKenzie sent a letter to R. A. Nixon:

> *Dear Bob,*
>
> *I am enclosing a copy of a letter I have today sent to Warden McKeague who, with other wardens, has been responsible for procuring evidence against one Jesse Bilford for wholesale violations of game laws, particularly of killing deer.*
>
> *I want you, with these wardens, to put forth every effort to see that this man is properly prosecuted. It appears from the records and complaints that he has been a destroyer of large quantities of game over a period of time.*
>
> *I would appreciate hearing from you promptly as to what action is being taken relative to the prosecution of this man.*

Incited to action by MacKenzie's latest letter, the three wardens met the day after receiving it. They discussed MacKenzie's concern, the dressing down they had received from him, and how he constantly referred to the situation as an 'aggravated case.' During the conversation, it became apparent to McKeague and Nixon that Hayner did not completely understand the meaning of the word, 'aggravated.'

As all wardens do when a weakness is revealed in one of their group, they attack the weak member just like a pack animal attacks a weak littermate. Hayner suffered through the day, as a deer might suffer from the onslaught of a wolf pack. Hayner knew the attack would continue at their next meeting, where he would probably be hamstrung and left for the crows to pick out his eyes. Aggravated, he decided to temper the attack by writing a letter to Nixon.

Dear Bob,

I grabbed my little book when I got home and started to look up agitate with one "g," but instead I unconsciously turned to the word that bothered me all afternoon–aggravated. To me the letters I've had from Mac asking for help have certainly been aggravating to me so an "aggravated case" covers the situation to my satisfaction.

Mac's orders call for an accounting from me so I'm asking you to forward his letter when you're done with it. I'm keeping the carbon copy.

I suspect you may feel that we didn't try too hard to charge Bilford with the repeater act as Mac suggested. However, I doubt if Mac would have done the job any better than this. I'm not going to worry too much about it just now anyhow.

Agitate? No and it's not irritate, but it's an adjective covering the condition. Why didn't you birds tell me what it was? That damned word sure aggravated me all afternoon.

Here's to you, Stuart.

RESERVATION OR NOT

In 1974, Wardens Larry "Freight Train" Miller and Milton "Milt" Dieckman arrested two Indians who were spearing fish through the ice of Chief Lake in Sawyer County. The Chippewa Band quietly sued the Department of Natural Resources claiming they had retained hunting, fishing and gathering rights on lands ceded to the United States by the treaty of 1854.

In 1976, U. S. District Judge James Doyle ruled against the tribe. This ruling was appealed by the Chippewa to the 7th U.S. Circuit Court of Appeals. In 1983, nine years after the arrests, the 7th Circuit Court of Appeals ruled that the Lake Superior Chippewa had in fact retained hunting, fishing and gathering rights on all lands ceded to the United States by the treaty of 1854. The Department of Natural Resources appealed the ruling and the U. S. Supreme Court declined to hear the case. Thus, the Chippewa's rights became the law of the land. In 1985, the Chippewa exercised their rights to off-reservation spear fishing for the first time.

With this decision, it became very difficult to explain the law under ordinary circumstances and nearly impossible under trying field conditions. Indians and non-Indians commonly hunted, fished and violated game laws together. In a mixed group of this kind, identifying Indians is impossible. The warden had no way of knowing to which of the party he can and cannot apply the law. This type of enforcement problem in no way resembles Indians assembled at a boat landing spearing as a group while exercising their right to do so.

This put the warden in a very precarious position, requiring him to screen people at a moments notice. Their split-second decision is always under review of the courts, who can mull over their decision for months or years. If the violating group is uncooperative, belligerent or pugilistic, the warden is forced to make decisions on what he sees and hears. This created situations that could and did put wardens in physical and legal jeopardy. When participants are also drunk or high on drugs, the degree of animosity toward law enforcement increases and the chance of violence and assault are heightened.

Can an Indian resist an illegal arrest by a warden on the ceded area? If wardens do not know the boundaries upon which they made the arrest, the incident may come back to haunt a warden if the court, after months of deliberation, determines an incident took place within its boundaries.

These problems are not new. Before the court case granting Indians off-reservation hunting and fishing rights, Indians could already hunt and fish without state control on their reservations. While off their reservations, they were required to comply with state law as it applied to all citizens regarding hunting, fishing or trapping. Simple? Not quite.

It was a cool October night in 1938 when young Warden Stanley "Stan" Swenson paced around his vehicle mulling over complaints he had received of illegal hunting near the Lac du Flambeau Indian Reservation. Warden Harley McKeague of Rhinelander indicated large numbers of deer were being shined along roads near the reservation. Swenson was now watching a roadway outside the reservation, reported to be one of many where deer had been poached, transported and sold to roadhouses in Wisconsin and Illinois. Orders were filled for as many as 20 deer at a time with the price being as high as $20 per animal. McKeague's informant said the ring was run by several men from the Wausau area who were being guided by several Indians of the Lac Du Flambeau Chippewa. Because he was aware that Indians could legally kill deer on the reservation Swenson parked several miles outside of it. Hidden behind a screen of white pine trees where automobiles lights could not penetrate, he paced impatiently about, afraid that if he sat in the car he may doze off or not hear a shot in his vicinity.

Suddenly he became tense as a car light appeared on the dirt road behind him. Any car on the road at 10 p.m. was suspect as only one car would travel this road in a week. Watching closely, he saw a bright spotlight swing back and forth illuminating the road edge as the car drove slowly toward him. The car stopped 100 yards away. A shot and a flash of fire stabbed through the pitch blackness of the night. Quickly, several men exited the car jabbering among themselves. They ran to the ditch edge, grabbed the still kicking deer and dragged it to the rear of the car. Swenson heard a thud as the deer landed in the trunk of the car and the trunk slammed shut. Hearing the car doors slam shut, Swenson listened as the tires crunched over the gravel. The large motor purred its way very slowly toward him.

Swenson drew a quick breath as he recognized the 1938 black Packard sedan described in the complaints. *Oh oh. these are the guys, guess I'll follow them a ways and see if they quit with one deer or continue to hunt. This is not the best spot to stop them alone anyway. Looks like there are four of them in the car.* Pulling out behind the car with his lights out, he followed them several miles as they continued to search the roadsides with a large flashlight. Studying the foursome closely to see what he was up against he thought, *got to get close so I can see through this dust.* Creeping cautiously up to 10 or 15 feet behind the vehicle so the dust from the road wouldn't hinder his vision, he observed two men wrestling over a bottle of what appeared to be liquor in the back seat. *Looks like I've got trouble here, they're drunk. No telling what they'll do when I stop them.* Crossing a highway, Swenson wondered briefly where he was. *Oh oh, that was highway 70, I'm on the reservation. These guys are probably Indians. They'll claim they killed the deer on the res.* Unsure how to proceed he continued to follow the car. Swenson was still considering his next move when he realized he was in the Indian village. When the car stopped he gazed around for recognizable landmarks. *Good spot to corral these guys. I could get help here. I know this house. It's Carl Thompson's house and he's just been appointed as a federal warden. Whew what a relief.*

As Swenson got out of his car it was obvious the men in the car knew they were being followed. They casually greeted him as he approached their car. Looking in the window he said "I'm a state game warden and you're under arrest for hunting deer during the closed season and shining deer. Get out of the car."

"The hell with you," the driver responded.

"Give me the keys to your car. I'm seizing it for evidence," demanded Swenson.

Suddenly the rear door slammed open and out stepped Carl Thompson brandishing a hand axe, "Get outta here Schwenson. Ya got no authority on the reshervasion."

Stunned at seeing his only hope of assistance drunk and on the other side, Swenson stood wondering what his next move should be. *Maybe I can talk Carl out of this. Not much chance. He's really drunk.*

"Carl put that axe down! You're only going to get yourself into a lot of trouble. As a federal warden you should know better than to get involved in illegal hunting."

"The hell ya say," replied Thompson striding toward Swenson the axe raised threateningly. Emboldened by Thompson's actions, the other three scrambled out of the car, one holding a Winchester lever action rifle. The four began moving toward Swenson. Back peddling now and frightened, Swenson drew his revolver and pointed it at the four.

"Hold it right there men. This thing is getting out of hand and damn it you're not laying a hand on me. One more step and there will be blood spilled tonight."

Three of them hesitated glaring momentarily at the steady muzzle of the hand gun. Swenson directed the gun directly at the man with the rifle.

"Just slowly reach that rifle into the car and drop it."

Jerking the gun up and down several times to reinforce his command he growled, "Do it, drop that gun."

Swenson breathed a sigh of relief when he heard the click of the hammer being let down as the man reluctantly laid the rifle on the back seat of the car.

"Whadja do that fer John?" yelled Thompson as he raised the axe higher and stepped unsteadily forward, his booze-befuddled mind making him stumble several times, muttering, "Come on boys, he can't get us all."

Swinging the gun directly at Thompson, Swenson shouted, "Stop or I'll shoot." He thought. *Hold the muzzle steady or they'll know how damn scared I am. I'm in a mess. Have to work my way out of it!*

Realizing he would be the first to be shot, Thompson hesitated.

Swenson was a sturdy six-footer who had played football in high school and wasn't afraid of physical contact. He took advantage of Thompson's hesitation. Moving stealthily forward like a cat he knocked the axe aside and grappled with Thompson. Surprised by Swenson's bold action, the other three stood like statues, bewildered as the two well-matched men wrestled over the deadly axe. As physical action usually does, Swenson's mind was cleansed of fear. *He's drunk. All I have to do is hang on longer then him.* Slowly, Swenson took charge as the booze took its toll. He could feel Thompson weaken. With a final mighty heave he twisted the axe from his hand.

"O.K., all of you line up next to the car over here," he panted gesturing with the handgun.

"I'm going to search you." Cowed for the moment, they allowed the search. Relieving them of several hunting and jack knives he marched them at gun point behind the car. "Now what're your names?"

"Tell 'em to go ta hell," shouted Thompson. "Ya don't hafta tell 'em nuthin."

The three stood silent. They glared at Swenson, daring him with their posture and gaze to try to force them to tell their names.

"Stand back," he commanded. "I'm going to look in your trunk. I know you have a deer in there because I saw you shoot it." Pointing the gun at them he reached down, turned the handle and lifted the trunk lid. Surprised he stared at two deer. "Looks like you were lucky earlier tonight. Two deer. They're seized and will be held as evidence."

Thompson sputtered, "Ya can't take those deer. You're on the res."

"They were shot off the reservation and are seized."

"Damn it Sti-an. I'm the federal woden here and I haf the ah-thority of a sov-er...sovereign nation and ya ain't t...aking those deer."

Distracted by the argument, Swenson suddenly realized one of the men had disappeared in the dark. *Now I've got to move fast or he'll have the whole gang after me. I'm outmanned here and need help. Got to have the evidence though.*

"Get out of the way Carl I'm taking the deer. Holding the three at gun point, Swenson, who was very strong, unloaded the two large, undressed does with one hand and dragged them the short distance to his car and loaded them in his trunk. "O.K. Carl give me your car keys. I'm going to lock your car up and leave. I'll be back with help for the car."

"I ain't got 'em Stan. thisss is Bob's car, he has the keys."

"Is Bob the one who skipped out?"

"Yeah, you'll never catch up with him."

"I'll get him later, right now I'm leaving with the deer."

"Sobering up somewhat, Thompson now began to bargain, "Leave the deer and I'll testify against these guys."

"Carl you're all in this together and as far as I'm concerned you'll all be prosecuted. I believe you may lose your job over this little fracas."

"Come on Schtan, John and I are Indians. You can't prosecute us. We kin kill deer off the res. They won't fire me. I'm just protectin' Indian rights." His voice suddenly more clear he continued, "We can hunt on all the land ceded to the United States during the 1854 treaty."

Surprised at his knowledge of the treaties in spite of his drunkenness, Swenson snapped, "Carl that's not what our statutes and our legal staff say. I'll discuss this with the district attorney and I'll bet you'll be prosecuted."

"I don't think so, but leave at least one of those deer and I'll tell you where these guys are selling 'em. Yeah, that's right, they've been selln' alotta deer from this area and I'll tell ya all about it. Just leave one deer."

Gesturing with his hand gun Swenson pointed at the man standing to one side, "Is this man an Indian?"

"Hell no, he's from Wausau."

"Tell me his name."

"Go ta hell. No deer, no name."

"Can't leave a deer Carl." Pointing at the non-Indian he asked, "What's your name?"

"You know what you can do to a hanging rope, I don't have to tell you my name."

"O.K., you may not have to tell me your name, but you can damn well bet we'll find out who you are when I lock you up in the Vilas County jail."

Voice stern, Swenson pointed his gun at the non-Indian and spat, "Get in my car."

Intimidated, the man hung his head and slunk into Swenson's car.

As he passed the large sedan, Swenson reached inside the open rear door and grasped the .30.30-caliber rifle. Holstering his handgun he carefully jacked the lever action, tipping it with each motion dumping the shell into his hand so as not to put one in the barrel. *Can't be too careful, sure don't want one to go off under these conditions.* Swenson swiftly drove to the jail at Eagle River and locked the man up without knowing his name.

Swenson called Wardens Louis "Pat" Oshesky and Hartley "Dutch" Paul from Three Lakes and Harley McKeague from Rhinelander for assistance. The four proceeded back to the reservation and found the sedan was gone. Telephoning district headquarters at Wausau, they asked that a road block be set up on highway 51. Wardens Wayne Giese and Bernolt "Bernie" Palas set up a road block at a stop sign in Merrill. About 3 a.m. the Packard came roaring through Merrill's main street at 90 m.p.h., never slowing for the stop sign and swerving dangerously to miss the warden's car setting crosswise in the road with the red light flashing. In hot pursuit, the two wardens began a dangerous, high speed chase southbound on highway 51.

Though out-powered by the large automobile, the wardens got lucky when the Packard hit slow moving traffic and couldn't pass. Forced into the ditch, the driver was identified as Thomas Watson from Wausau. He told the wardens that the man in jail was Bob Wright, also from Wausau.

Arraigned before Eagle River Municipal Judge George E. O'Connor, Watson plead guilty to unlawfully possessing the carcasses of two deer during the closed season and to transporting them. On the first charge, he was sentenced to pay a fine of $50 and serve 30 days in the county jail. On the second, he was ordered to pay a fine of $100 and serve 60 days in jail. In default of the fine, he was ordered to serve an additional ninety days in jail. His 1938 Packard was ordered confiscated.

In Vilas County court, Justice of the Peace Fred Hatch at Sayner arraigned Watson and sentenced him to 90 days in jail and an additional 90 days for failure to pay fines of $150 and costs. After court, the two admitted they had killed seven deer in the past few weeks. They implicated five cohorts who were later arrested on similar charges.

When Swenson returned to the reservation with warrants for Carl Thompson they found him at the John Johnson residence who they also had a warrant for. There they found a room full of deer carcasses plus deer heads and hearts.

In court, their counsel produced old treaties supporting the Indians contention that they were legally entitled to hunt off-reservation at any time. The court ruled against them and they were each fined $50 and costs.

As was the custom during that era, no charges of resisting arrest or assault were brought against anyone.

STURGEON # 7S2884

It was cold and windy on April 29, 1983 when Warden Dick Streng took position in the brush along the Wolf River. Shivering noticeable, he snuggled into his sleeping bag intending to spend most of the night, if necessary, to apprehend the culprit that people had reported taking illegal sturgeon.

He focused his attention on a fishing raft about 100 yards across the river. Fishing rafts of this type were anchored haphazardly along the Wolf River and mainly used for walleye fishing. Many had cabins on them. Streng suspected that this one was used to capture illegal sturgeon. Flashing a tiny pen light under the top of his sleeping bag, he snuggled even deeper into it. He noted the time at 9.15 p.m. It was early and he expected a long, cold wait.

A veteran warden of 18 years, he always let his special respect and concern for sturgeon at this time of year run his life, to the point of exhaustion. Stationed at Chilton, Streng had worked many years protecting sturgeon as they worked their way up the Wolf each spring on their spawning runs. His experience had taught him to be patient when dealing with sturgeon poachers. He also developed a love for this prehistoric fish, a fish normally very hard to catch. During the spring spawning run, their biological urges make them vulnerable to hook and line, the snag hook and snag line.

Streng called on his counterpart, Warden Tom Krsnich stationed at Black Creek for assistance. Knowing that the suspect was a convicted felon, Krsnich enlisted the help of Warden Joe Ryder of Winneconne. Their strategy included how they would handle the apprehension given the suspect's record and that he was apt to resist arrest. Both Krsnich and Ryder had worked many years and hours on the Wolf River during the sturgeon spawning run and shared Streng's deep concern for the prehistoric relic. They were now carrying out their plans–Streng would observe the suspected area in his sleeping bag along the riverbank and would stay in contact with Krsnich and Ryder by radio who were stationed in the catch car across the river near the raft.

The night silence was shattered by the resounding splash of a sturgeon leaping. Shivering as gusts of wind wafted across the river, Streng tucked the sleeping bag tighter, pulling it close up under his chin, contemplating why these prehistoric monsters performed in this spectacular manner–leaping completely out of the water, dancing on their tail and landing heavily on their sides. Could it be to shake off lampreys as some fish experts theorize, or some habit from their prehistoric past done instinctively that once may have provided a maneuver to save its life from some prehistoric predator? Or was it done for pure pleasure?

Letting his thoughts wander further, he wondered why Wisconsin seemed blessed with such an abundant number of the rare rock sturgeon. He was certain it was because of his efforts and the tremendous effort of wardens past and present. He inwardly wondered how more recognition could be given to "Sturgeon for Tomorrow," an organization dedicated to preserving sturgeon in Wisconsin. The organization annually funds meals and lodging for "Sturgeon Watch." Volunteers from all over gather to watch the numerous rock piles, curves and other areas where sturgeon gather, freeing up wardens to watch areas where violators are more apt to take fish. Scores of volunteers are lodged and fed at "Sturgeon Camp," a camp maintained by the Department of Natural Resources and "Sturgeon for Tomorrow."

At the camp, volunteer retired wardens wearing hats with "scrambled eggs" on them are known as "Sturgeon Generals." They assist wardens working the Wolf and Embarrass rivers with the coordination and placement of volunteer sturgeon watchers from all over the state and sometimes beyond the state's border.

Streng's reverie was broken as another large fish slapped the water. Binoculars to his face, he focused on the bright light emitting from the shanty aboard the fishing raft. Using night gathering binoculars and a spotting scope, he could see that the fishing equipment being used by a large man wasn't typical walleye fishing gear. It was large and heavy, more suited for trolling for very large trout or salmon on Lake Michigan. *Looks like I've got myself a taker, if he catches a fish!*

At 11:07 p.m., the large fisherman lunged back, bending the heavy trolling rod in half. He had set the hook in a very large fish and was methodically rocking back and forth slowly playing him toward the raft. *Ah ha, he's got a sturgeon, let's see what he does with it.* Streng carefully used his pen light inside his sleeping bag to note the time and actions of the suspect.

Keying the mike on his portable he whispered, "Tom we've got action. Looks like this guy has a sturgeon on."

"Ten-four, Dick keep us posted."

After several minutes of fighting with the fish, the light in the shanty went out, making it easier for him to penetrate the inky blackness. After many hours and years of keenly observing and interpreting night movements, many wardens could see more than the average person could at night, especially when using binoculars and scopes. He used these skills now to good advantage, as he watched the struggle between man and fish. Noting every minute detail, he heard the sound of the fish wildly thrashing in the water and saw a huge sturgeon slide onto the raft.

He again keyed the mike, "Stand by Tom he's got a sturgeon and it's a good one. Let's see what he does with him."

"Ten-four Dick. We're ready."

Observing very carefully, Streng watched as the man carried the fish ashore and down the shoreline where he boarded another raft. He proceeded to tie the fish in a bow by tying a rope around the head and gills, bowing the fish into a "U"-shape and tying the rope to the tail. In this position, a fish would be kept alive, but it couldn't swim away. This is a very old method of violators holding fish. It allows the violator to get rid of incriminating evidence by cutting the fish loose and releasing it quickly upon the approach of a warden. The fish can be left behind in the water unable to swim away for hours or days and recovered alive when the poacher is absolutely sure the coast is clear. As the fish was being tied, Streng called on his radio, "Tom this guy took the fish downstream to the next raft and is bowing it. It's time to take him."

Krsnich and Ryder exited their vehicle and swiftly walked the short distance to the raft where they silently walked up to the man busily tying the last knot in the rope.

"We're state game wardens. Hold it right there. You're under arrest for taking a sturgeon during the closed season."

Stunned, the man sat back on his haunches. "I can't believe it. How did you get here!?"

"It doesn't matter how we got here, John."

"You called me John. Do you know me?"

"Yeah we know you, but I still want some identification, a drivers license or fishing license will do. Scanning the several items handed him, he said, "O.K. John, you're under arrest and will have to come with us to the county jail. Put your hands up on the side of the raft and spread your legs."

Kicking John's legs apart to keep him off-balance, he proceeded to make a frisk search. "Joe put the cuffs on him."

"How did you know I caught this fish? I didn't see you guys."

"We had an observer. Dick Streng was watching you take this fish. We'll pick him up on our way out. Joe you take the fish. Lets go."

At the pickup point, the three wardens closely inspected the bowed sturgeon.

"What do you think. Could this fish live?"

"I don't know replied Streng, they'll stay alive for a long time tied like that, but he may be injured from the rope cutting its gills. The cartilage in his tail may also be broken. If that's the case he may never be able to swim again. Why don't you two take John to jail while I mark the fish for evidence and see if I can get him to swim again over at Tim's private trout pond."

Wardens Dick Streng, left and Tom Krsnich with the bowed sturgeon number 7S2884.

"O.K., we will come over to Tim's as soon as I get John taken care of." Without further discussion they set forth on their assignments.

Arriving at the trout pond, Streng freed the sturgeon and inserted a small metal tag numbered 7S2884 to identify it in court if needed. Placing the fish in shallow water along the shoreline, he slowly straightened the fish out by massaging his tail section. Slowly the fish began to breath more normally and wiggle his tail, a good sign.

By the time Krsnich and Ryder arrived two hours later, the fish lay fanning his fins. "How's he doing Dick?"

"Not too bad, there's some damage where the rope wore into his hide near the head and on the tail, but I think he'll be able to swim. Can't really tell at this point whether there's cartilage damage or not. He was bowed awful tight."

"Guess we'll just have to wait and see if he makes it," said Krsnich, slowly massaging the resting fish. A smile creased his face as the sturgeon swam slowly away disappearing into the dark pool. Stepping back he said, "Let's go home. I feel good about this, maybe we can save his life."

Uncertain if the fish would live or die, they had it picked up by a fisheries truck several days later and delivered it to the department hatchery at Wild Rose where it could be watched more closely. The wardens often stopped at the hatchery to check on the fish's health. Slowly the fish seemed to get more vigorous.

The court case was disposed of when John entered a plea of no contest and was found guilty in Judge Nick Schaefer's court. He was fined $100 and costs totaling $210, with the judge adding another $100 to the fine because the violator had delayed entering a plea for such a long time. He also sentenced him to 30 days in the county jail and revoked his hunting, fishing and trapping licenses for three years.

Tom Krsnich told the *Appleton Post-Crescent*,

> *"We rely on the public for a lot of our tips and information about violators. If this case deters just one individual from doing this sort of thing, we have to look at it as a success."*

Finally the great day in August arrived when the fish truck stopped at Asylum Bay bearing the sturgeon for release. The three wardens were present to see their dream come true. Most conservation cases are developed after the animal or fish is dead. This was a rare opportunity for the wardens to successfully prosecute a case and keep a valuable fish alive. They inspected the fish in the truck. It looked quite healthy. The scars had almost disappeared from around his head and tail and he swam normally.

Sturgeon number 7S2884 slashed the water with his powerful tail, free at last. He dove into the dark depths never to be seen again. What? Never to be seen again? Wrong! Sturgeon number 7S2884 was speared and identified by his tag in 1986, fully 5 years after being caught and bowed almost to the point of death

The following spring, Krsnich, accompanied by Dale Morey, boating safety administrator stationed at the Madison bureau of law enforcement, made another contact with John. He was fishing a short distance down river from where he had caught the sturgeon one year ago. He was again surprised to see the wardens.

His license revoked, Krsnich said, "John got another free ride to the county jail."

BUMPER CLAMP

On a cool, crisp October night in 1936, two game wardens, Charles "Chuck" Lawrence and Willard "Bill" Leasch, sat in their car north of Park Falls on Highway 13. Their were waiting for a car driven by someone suspected of running and selling loads of illegal deer from northern Wisconsin to the St. Paul area in Minnesota.

As the waiting grew tedious, the wardens discussed past cases and experiences. As usually happens, the conversation leans toward the more exciting incidents, like high-speed chases. Lawrence brought up the subject of how to stop a speeding automobile.

"You know Bill, I'm tired of chasing these cars especially on the dirt roads we have around here."

"Yeah," agreed Leasch, "It's really dangerous driving through a blinding dust cloud. You have to get awful close to see the car in front of you. Too close for safety."

"Yeah mused Lawrence, you're taking your life in your hands trying to penetrate the dust to get within the vortex immediately behind the car. You're not only driving blind, but you're being pelted with gravel rock. I've had several windshields broken by the rocks."

"I had my windshield knocked out about a month ago," complained Leasch. "It cost me a bundle to replace it."

"Really, the state should pick up the bill when something like that happens," Lawrence reasoned.

"Why do you think they prefer us to drive our own vehicles?" said Leach.

"Yeah I know we're getting rich driving our own cars for the state."

"Well Bill, my mother never raised any dummies. I figured out a way to stop a guy from running."

"How? Shoot out his tires?"

"No. Something so simple I can't imagine why no one had thought of it before. I had a local mechanic rig up an apparatus on my front bumper. It's a spring-loaded clamp. When they start to run, I take my chance to get past the vortex of dust. Once I'm through it, I simple ram them. The clamp closes on their bumper and locks. All I need to do then is put on the brakes and stop them."

"Sounds good, but what happens if the car you're clamped to is heavier and has more power?"

"I've never had a problem so far. I've stopped about a half dozen that way. No problem."

"Here comes a car Chuck. Could be our boy."

The two wardens were at attention as the car neared. Lawrence whispered.

"A Packard...Minnesota license...that's the number...that's him."

Lawrence threw the Model-A Ford into gear and lurched onto the highway behind the speeding vehicle.

"He's moving right along. We'll catch him when he reaches town. He'll have to slow down then."

Entering Park Falls, it was soon evident that the car wasn't about to stop. The driver picked up speed and exceeded 50 m.p.h. through the city.

"He's not going to stop, use your clamp," Leasch shouted.

Gaining on the vehicle, Lawrence murmured, "Hang on Bill, I'm going to ram him."

With a loud thump, the two cars locked solidly together. Lawrence, smiled and said, "Gottcha."

He applied the brakes, only nothing happened. With brakes squealing Lawrence breathed, "God, I can't stop him."

Without slowing down, the suspect drove the larger, more powerful car forward. As it rounded the block, the wheels of Lawrence's car locked in a cocked position and squealed loudly as it was dragged around the city. The violator took several turns and circled several blocks in an attempt to dislodge the warden's car. He finally succeeded and Lawrence's front tire blew with a loud bang. The violator headed north on highway 13.

Unable to follow, they thumped down the street on the blown tire to Leasch's car, parked on a nearby street. Knowing the violator had driven north, they drove in that direction. They surmised that the man would leave the main highway and turn west a short distance north of the city on a road that circled Butternut Lake. Spotting a car making a turn east, they speeded up and identified it as the same car. Again they directed the vehicle to stop, but it had the same effect as before–the violator gunned the motor and careened around corners until they were again heading south on highway 13 toward Park Falls.

Entering Park Falls, the speeding vehicle again began circling blocks trying to lose them. Both cars careened dangerously down the road for blocks, wheels squealing. Finally the car skidded onto highway 13 south.

"Bill," asked Lawrence, "Can you stay with him?"

"I don't think so. His car has more speed then this Ford."

"Then I'm going to shoot. He's not going to get away again."

Leaning out the right window he began shooting, fire belching from the muzzle as he aimed at the fleeing vehicle's tires.

Suddenly the car slowed to a stop. Angrily the wardens ran to the offender's auto and ordered the man out of the car.

They found five dressed-out deer in the back seat of the sedan.

Appearing before a justice of the peace representing Price County in Park Falls the offender was fined $150 and sentenced to six months in the county jail. His gun and automobile were confiscated.

Later Leasch said, "You sure are an innovative fellow Chuck! We never would have got that guy without your bumper clamp! Ha!"

For many years the story of this chase was handed down from father to son. Many said it should have been made into a movie as it certainly equaled the "shoot 'em up cowboy movies" of that era.

Author's note: At the time of this event, wardens drove their personal vehicles on the job and were paid mileage from the state. This is no longer the case.

EXECUTION

The title special conservation warden appears on the credentials of a lot of people who have assisted regular conservation wardens from the early 1900s forward. Through the years, special wardens have harnessed horses, laced on snowshoes, patrolled in flivvers, paddled canoes, and operated snowmobiles and high powered boats while assisting conservation wardens. Their duties sometimes are dull and boring like picking up car-killed deer, skinning animals and even such drudgery as washing the regular warden's car. They often end up at the front line when the going gets tough.

Special wardens have always been important to regular wardens and come from many walks of life. Many served as part-time wardens while employed full time as law enforcement officers from other agencies. Others are bankers, jewelers, farmers, woodsmen, and a host of other professions. Often, the pay was very low, and sometimes they toiled without pay because of their friendship with the regular warden. A special warden often became the warden's truest compatriot and confidant. At times, their lives depended on each other.

Injured on the job were some of the finest. Some made the final sacrifice. Jim Golomb was seriously injured in an automobile accident while working deer shiners for District Warden Jim Chizek on the Price and Lincoln County line in 1968. Leo Stecker was severely injured in a car accident while working fish spearers in 1966 near Bass Lake in Price County. District Warden Robert "Bob" Markle was killed in that accident. Bob Born was injured when a pickup truck hit and dragged him under it on the ice of Beaver Dam Lake in 1977. He was working with Warden Mike Dressen, who was also seriously injured in the incident. In 1972, Neil LaFave was shot to death. His story is described in *Butchery at Senisiba Wildlife Area.* In 1942, Albert Emil "Al" Reif was shot to death. This is Reif's story.

Full-time department personnel often carried special warden credentials and assisted regular wardens during peak work periods. Such was the case for Al Reif, even though it wasn't required. Reif was the supervisor of the Kettle Moraine State Forest at Mauthe Lake Forest Headquarters and had carried special warden credentials during most of his 10 years of service in the conservation department.

Since the warden force was down due to World War II, Reif felt a civic responsibility to serve and stepped forward to fill the need during the deer season of 1942. Two weeks before the deer season, he left his wife and three children at his Mauthe Lake home to drive north. He reported to Field Warden Robert Nixon at the Florence Ranger Station. It was here he met and worked with young Floyd Sanders, a 24-year-old special warden hailing from Superior.

Nixon put the more experienced and level-headed Reif in charge and sent them out to patrol for illegal deer hunting. In several days, the two became good friends, often discussing the terrible war and the looming draft call for Sanders, who at age 24 was eligible.

On Wednesday, just two days before deer season, the two patrolled along highway 2, a few miles northwest of Iron Mountain, Michigan in what was known as the cut-over area. Seeing a car parked in an abandoned logging road, the two investigated. As they left their auto, they heard several gunshots rang out to the north along the Brule River, which formed the boundary between Wisconsin and Michigan. The two separated to better cover the area and walked slowly toward the river. Not finding anyone, they worked their way back to the suspect car. Examining the car closely and peering through the windows, Reif remarked, "Hmm, Michigan plates, looks like someone has been hauling something in here. The rear seats have been removed and replaced with boards. Feel the hood to see how long this car has been parked here."

"The hood is cold, it's now 11 o'clock, been here quite a while. Maybe even all night."

"Hmm, this is an Oldsmobile. What year do you make it, Floyd?"

"I make it a '30."

Reif asked, "Do you think those shots came from Wisconsin or Michigan. The river is close here. The deer hunting season is open in Michigan."

"Too close, Al. I think someone from this car is shooting."

"Take a look here, Floyd. Doesn't that look like muskrat or mink hair on those boards laid out in the back?"

"Yeah, with the seats removed he could haul quite a load. Looks like someone may have slept here last night. Wonder what's under those blankets?"

Upon hearing the crunch of a breaking branch, both turned to see a dark, bushy-haired man walking swiftly through the brush toward them. As he neared them, Floyd said, "We're state conservation wardens. How are you today?"

"Never mind how I am. What the hell are you guys doing with my car?"

"We heard shots and we're wondering what you're doing here? Have you been hunting?"

"Hunting? Hell no. What business is it of yours?"

"Well we were sent out here by Warden Robert Nixon to see if anyone was hunting deer during the closed season. People in Wisconsin sometimes hunt illegally when the Michigan deer season opens because it's hard to tell from which state shots come from."

"Well, you can just pack up and leave cause I'm not hunting and I don't like people monkeying around my car."

Reif broke in, "Just a minute, mister. We have the authority to check you and I would like to see some identification."

"Identification? What for, I'm not hunting."

"Maybe not, but we heard some shooting back here. What are those hairs in the back of your car? They look like mink or muskrat hair. Have you been hauling fur?"

"No fur. Now beat it and leave me alone."

"Just what're you doing back here anyway?"

"It's none of your business, but I'm camping here. Is there something wrong with that?"

"Camping here," mused Reif, "I see by your license plate you're from Michigan. Where in Michigan?"

"Pentoga."

"And you're just camping here?"

"I'm on my way to Iron Mountain to buy groceries if it's any of your damn business."

"Well, I know fur hair when I see it. Floyd, take a look in the car. If there's nothing illegal in there, you can go buy your groceries."

Entering the rear seat of the vehicle, Sanders spoke loudly, "There's an uncased-.32-special rifle in here. It's unloaded."

"O.K.," said Reif, "We're going to hold you responsible for the uncased gun in the car."

Continuing his search, Sanders pulled a blanket aside when he heard Reif ask, "What's your name?" A pregnant silence was broken by the deafening roar of a gun. Startled, Sanders bumped his head on the roof of the sedan. Looking out the back window he saw Reif sag and crumple to the ground.

My god, he's shot Al, I can't get out fast enough. He's going to shoot me too. Got to get out quick! Scrambling to get out of the car, Sanders glanced toward the man. He was backing away, pistol in hand, his eyes riveted on the stricken man in front of him. *He's leaving, I'm OK. Can't let him get away. He's shot Reif.* At last free from the auto, he desperately drew his .22-caliber revolver. Glancing briefly at the magazine to insure himself it was loaded, he caught sight of the man running through the heavy brush of the cut-over area. He raised the revolver and fired two shots. Seeing that they had no effect, he glanced briefly at Reif and saw the hole in his temple. *I think Al's dead. Got to catch this guy.* Throwing off the bizarre thought that Reif could possibly be dead, he began to run to catch up with the assailant. A sudden shot from the underbrush brought him to a halt. *God, he's shooting at me. Better be careful. Can't let him get away though after shooting Al.* Bolstering his courage, he again began to run after the murderer.

Catching sight of Sanders running toward him, the man ducked behind one of the few large trees remaining in the cut over and leaned his handgun against the tree to steady it for a killing shot. His shot went astray. Sanders, running hard, was not to be deterred even as the shot toppled a bush a few feet in front of him. Like a mad man, he continued the pursuit, stopping occasionally to shoot. Finally his hammer dropped on an empty cartridge. Realizing he was defenseless against the gunman, he stopped to assess his situation. Peering through the brush, he spotted the man running toward him. *My God, he must have counted my shots. He knows my gun is empty. Got to get out of here.* He raced back to Reif and saw blood spurting grotesquely from his head in an ever-widening pool. He saw the hole in his temple and knew for sure he was dead. Mad at the injustice of the macabre scene, he reached down and drew Reif's automatic handgun.

"I'll get him for you, Al," Sanders proclaimed.

Turning, he spotted the man fearlessly approaching. Snapping off the safety, Sanders snapped a shot at him. The aggressor turned into a second fast retreat. Again guns blazed as Sanders chased the killer through the woods. Suddenly, Sanders realized that the man had stopped breaking brush and that he was once again coming toward him. Raising his automatic, he took slow deliberate aim at the man who seemed no longer afraid. The gun clicked. Empty. *Oh oh, I'm in trouble again. Got to get out of here. He will kill me if he can.* With the killer's gun booming ever louder, lead flying around him, Sanders ran north like Satan was on his heels until there was no more shooting and he could not see the assailant. He slowly circled his way south to highway 2. He hailed the first car coming from the east. Quickly he told the driver what had transpired and ask for a ride to take him out of harms way. The driver obligingly dropped him off at Chainey's, a resort at Spread Eagle. Sanders called the ranger station and told Nixon of the murder.

While intent on killing the only witness, the murderer realized he couldn't catch the young man scampering through the heavy cut-over underbrush. So, he stopped and watched Sanders hit the river and run north. Shrugging his shoulders, he returned to his vehicle and surveyed his handiwork. He dragged Reif about 100 feet into the woods before realizing he couldn't drag the body far enough to hide it. He panicked. Escape was his only thought. *Got to get out of here before that other warden gets help.* Running to his auto, he cranked the motor into life and drove swiftly away.

In the meantime, Sanders talked a man at the resort into driving him back to the crime scene. The killer's car was gone. He was studying the tracks to determine which way the car had turned out of the tote road, when Robert Nixon arrived with Sheriff, Anthony Grell.

"Where is Al?" asked Nixon.

"A ways down this old logging road, I'll show you," said Sanders.

They viewed Reif in what appeared to be a sacred grotto formed by the dry ferns. The wind seemed to wane as they talked in hushed tones so as not to disturb the moment. They examined the area and picked up visible evidence of the crime.

The reverie was broken by Nixon who shouted, "Damn it. This is completely uncalled for. We'll get the S.O.B. who did this and he'll burn in hell for what he's done."

Soon, other sheriff's officers began arriving along with the coroner and district attorney.

Before leaving the ranger station, Nixon called the sheriff's office and related to them the killing and the description of where it took place. He also called the Dickenson County Michigan State Police Barracks at Iron River. Meeting with Florence County Sheriff Arnold Grell, they put out messages to all conservation wardens in that part of Wisconsin and Michigan. All were instructed to assist in the apprehension of the automobile Sanders described as a 1930 blue Oldsmobile sedan. All sent squads. Meanwhile, they began blocking roads in all directions in both states. An almost immediate description of the killer was communicated to all persons assisting. Sanders described the murderer as about 35-years-of-age, 5-feet 10- or 11-inches tall, weighing between 160 to 170 pounds, and wearing a winter cap, blue flannel shirt, and whipcord breeches. He told the officers that the killer had told him he was from Pentoga, Michigan, a small settlement between Iron River and Alpha.

There was a two-hour lapse between the shooting and notification of officials. The assailant had plenty of time for escape.

Conservation Department Director E. J. Vanderwall made a statement: "We will do everything we can to bring in the slayer of Albert E. Reif, conservation department supervisor slain Wednesday by an unidentified man in Florence County."

He sent Chief Warden Al Robinson of Madison to join H. M. Hosford, supervisor of enforcement of the northeast district of Trout Lake, to coordinate the warden's efforts in assisting the sheriff's department.

For the next 10 days, about 100 officers, including Michigan State Police, Florence and Marinette County Sheriff's officers, and about 20 conservation wardens from each state, combed the area. Many leads were checked out, but none produced a thing.

On Thursday, a coroners jury was held in Florence. They viewed a .38-caliber bullet removed from the victim's head. Their verdict was that Albert E. Reif had been murdered by an unknown man. They issued a John Doe warrant for the murderer.

From the beginning, Michigan State Police suspected a Michigan trapper named Emil Schroeder from Sagola, Michigan. Although he lived in Dickenson County, a long ways from Pentoga, in Iron County, he seemed to fit Sander's description. He was known to be a trapper. His shack was under surveillance, but he wasn't at home. Finally, on November 28 near Sagola, Michigan, Conservation Warden George Helga spotted Schroeder walking on a highway. He immediately called the police barracks at Iron Mountain. Responding was Detective Jack Miller who picked up Fire Warden Helgsen Channing for support. They met Helga on the highway.

Schroeder offered no resistance when arrested. Upon searching him they found a .38-caliber revolver in his pocket, the same caliber Al Reif had been shot with. They hustled him off to Iron Mountain and incarcerated him.

Sheriff Grell contacted Nixon and told him of the good news.

"Get Sanders up there right away. I want to be sure we have the right guy."

Arriving at Iron Mountain, Sanders met with Sergeant James Smith of the Michigan State Police and Ed Corey, a Michigan fire warden. Brought from his cell, Schroeder, paled upon recognizing Sanders.

As he continued to gaze at him he blurted, "You've got the right man."

Sergeant Jim Smith, Detective Jack Miller, and John Bauschek, a detective from Milwaukee hired by the conservation department to assist in the investigation, witnessed the signing of the confession. Schroeder admitted he had shot Al Reif, but said it was in self defense. He thought the warden was drawing a gun. Soon, Sheriff Grell and Warden Nixon were en route to Iron Mountain to pick up Schroeder. who had signed extradition papers so he could be brought to Wisconsin for trial.

On Monday, November 31, Emil Schroeder was arraigned before Florence County Judge Irving Smith. He pled not guilty to the slaying of Albert E. Reif. Judge Smith remanded Schroeder to the county jail at Marinette where he was held without bond. Schroeder's gun, along with the bullet removed from Reif's head, and expended shells found at the murder scene, were submitted to a Federal Bureau of Investigation laboratory. They all matched.

In Marinette, Schroeder pleaded not guilty again, without the advice of an attorney. Circuit Judge Arnold Murphy, upon District Attorney's Allen C. Wittkopf's petition, committed Schroeder to the Winnebago State Hospital for a 30-day observation period to determine his sanity. He was delivered to the institution by Marinette County Sheriff Marriner Kohlman. The head of the institution, Dr. Byron Hughes, found him sane and the trial proceeded.

On Feb. 18, 1943, Marinette County Judge Arnold F. Murphy presided over the criminal trial of Emil Schroeder. Convening at 10 a.m., a jury was sworn in before noon. At 1 p.m., District Attorney Allen C. Wittkopf presented the state's case, with the defendant being represented by Attorney E.B. Martineau of Marinette.

Floyd Sanders told the story of how the incident had transpired. He told of the car search and the sudden shot and how he had seen Reif fall in death. He described the ensuing gun battle as well.

Bauschek read a question and answer statement given to Schroeder resulting in a confession to the crime.

"The other man (Reif) came back and talked rough to me again. He told me in a hard way that he heard me talking to somebody else. I talked back to him and told him to come in white; that I didn't know who he was. He said in an awful hard way something like, 'I'm going to show you. I'll show you I'm coming in white.' And he put his right hand on his gun and turned it toward me. With his left hand he reached in his left shirt pocket and pulled it back again and then he ran his hand under his right shoulder of his coat. I thought he was going to pull another gun and put it on me. I thought he was going to shoot first, but I guess I beat him."

Doctor J. P. Edwards told how he had removed the bullet from the victim's head and turned it over to the district attorney.

Sergeant Smith described the investigation leading to Schroeder's arrest.

Trooper Nowland identified and explained photographs he had taken of Reif's body, the shooting scene, and tire prints left there.

The state rested its case Wednesday evening and Schroeder took the stand in his defense the following day. He swore the officers did not identify themselves as conservation wardens. He said Reif had covered him with his holstered gun. Under cross-examination, Wittkopf had Schroeder attach Reif's gun and holster to himself and attach the thigh strap. He was asked to demonstrate how Reif had pointed the gun at him. Unable to do so, he testified that the thigh strap was not tied. The district attorney then recalled Trooper Milton Nowland, who described the picture of the body with the strap securely tied.

Further testimony revealed that Schroeder had driven to the old tote road the night before where he met with an Oshkosh fur buyer to sell some illicit muskrat and mink pelts. His testimony was that the fur buyer would not buy his skins in Michigan where they were illegally taken. He was paid $98.

Testimony for the defense culminated at noon when several of Schroeder's neighbor's testified to his good reputation in his community.

The judge instructed the jury.

"One of four verdicts must be reached by the jury: first or second degree murder, third degree manslaughter, or not guilty."

The jury retired at 2:45 p.m. to begin deliberations. At 5:45 p.m. they announced they had reached a verdict–guilty as charged with second degree murder. Judge Murphy announced the sentence to be from 15 to 25 years in the state prison. He went on in part to say:

"Members of the jury—I feel it is my duty to tell you I fully appreciate the serious problem which confronted you in this case. You're not only justified in doing what you did, but I candidly, honestly and sincerely say, that that is exactly the verdict I would have returned. That is what this defendant is guilty of. He was technically and theoretically guilty of first degree murder, but there were enough circumstances in favor of the defendant that easily could have impelled a conscientious jury to hesitate and refuse finally to find him guilty of first degree murder. I want to congratulate you. That was good work and don't have any misgivings with reference to it."

In a packed court room, sat a lone, dejected woman of 33-years-of-age. Cunera Reif sat grieving her lost lover. She wondered if justice would be done for this terrible, uncalled for, arbitrary act. She also wondered how she would manage to raise her three children–Albert Jr. 10, Robert, 9 and Donna, 4–without the love and direction of a devoted father. Was justice done? She thought not. She felt Schroeder should have been found guilty of first-degree murder and locked away for life. The statement made by the judge justifying the decision deeply troubled her. How could there be any circumstances favoring Schroeder who had cold-bloodedly executed her life's companion?

Reif's mother and father, Lena and Albert, and older sister Lena, were devastated by his murder. Many felt that Albert died one year later of a broken heart.

The next day a newspaper said in part:

> Allen C. Wittkopf, Florence County district attorney, asked the jury to return a verdict of first degree murder. Schroeder, he said, planned to kill Reif in order to avoid arrest for game violations and drove toward Florence after the killing in an effort to overtake and kill Sanders. Defense Attorney E.B. Martineau asserted that Reif and Sanders had not identified themselves as conservation officers. Schroeder, he held, shot Reif in the belief that he was a holdup man intent on robbing him of $98 he received the night before for the illicit sale of mink and muskrat skins. Schroeder testified that he had met a fur buyer by rearrangement on the side road to make the sale.

The *Milwaukee Journal* carried the following: **On Wisconsin—Al Reif—Muffled shots sounded in the woods of Florence County.**

> *Al Reif and Floyd Sanders of the conservation department investigated. It was their job to check illegal deer hunting before the opening of the season. They found a car parked on a tote road and waited there.*
>
> *A man shuffled out of the brush. They questioned him. He seemed to be unarmed, but he pulled a gun and let Al have it in the temple. Al slumped to the ground, dead; He never had a*

chance.

This then is an incidence of conservation—practical conservation in the field, far removed from politics. Men drive the roads and beat the brush and get killed, if need be, to uphold protective ideals and enforce the law.

H.W. MacKenzie once did that. He too was attacked by punks with guns, but he escaped death. Bruised and bleeding, he dragged himself to safety. Later he gave many years of his life to conservation work. Not long ago, politicians fired him.

Al Reif's regular work was supervisor of the Kettle Moraine State forest. It was his regular job to plant trees, build trails, develop picnic grounds, provide fireplaces, campsites,and parking areas for the people in the congested southeastern section of this state.

He and others made an attractive recreational area around Mauthe Lake, northeast of Kewaskum. Hundreds of city folks made use of it. Al was there over weekends and on holidays to see to their comfort. They will miss him.

He went north into the deer country voluntarily to aid the wardens before and during the deer season when many good hunters and a few punks with hidden guns go into the woods. That's where career men with conservation knowledge and courage are needed.

Al Reif was acutely concerned about land acquisition and worked very hard toward this endeavor. A stone memorial stands near the entrance road of the Mauthe Lake Headquarters:

This Stand of Trees is Dedicated to the Memory of—**ALBERT E. REIF—1909-1942—FIRST STATE FOREST SUPERVISOR OF THE KETTLE MORAINE STATE FOREST, WHOSE LOVE FOR THIS LAND AND WHOSE VISION FOR ITS PRESERVATION LIVE ON IN ITS ENDURING BEAUTY.**

On the morning of November 18, 1942, Al Reif became one of the martyred heroes of Wisconsin wardens. Reif was known as a loyal public servant who served his department with distinction. Al Reif junior's fondest memories of his father are his words, "I treat all I meet, rich or poor, farmer or banker, saint or sinner, with respect and alike."

Author's notes: In 1998 a law enforcement memorial was dedicated at the state capitol in Madison, Wisconsin. The memorial honors those who fell in the line of duty for the state of Wisconsin. Al Reif's name is one of seven wardens etched in its stone. There his name will be honored and memorialized for all time.

Emil Schroeder served seven years in Waupun and was released on parole. Several years later he resisted arrest on a parole violation. He was shot and killed in a police shoot out.

A GOOD JOKE

In 1959, the deer season caused enforcement problems. North of highways 70, 53 and 8, the season ran November 14 to November 29. South of that line, the season ran November 21 to November 29.

The early-season-opener in the north made warden Jim Chizek wonder. Watching all these southbound vehicles with their back-ends sagging made him suspect that an awful lot of illegal deer was being transported right past his front door at Portage.

He asked District Attorney David Bennett if he could set up a road block to check these hunters. Bennett's said he would back the stopping of vehicles containing elements of a hunt, meaning people obviously wearing hunting clothing or with any game showing.

Calling Warden Owen Anderson at Sauk City, Chizek asked him to assist him in his endeavor. Together they laid out a very simple plan. Anderson was to park by the levy along southbound highway 51 several blocks north of the Robbers Roost, an 18-year-old beer bar, to observe and advise Chizek about which cars to stop. As each suspect vehicle approached Chizek, who was parked across the highway from the Robbers Roost several blocks further south, he turned on his red light stepped out of his car and motioned them over. He then examined the items of game they were carrying. It worked so well that the two were hard pressed running violators to the county jail, where they were locked up or posted bail. They seized untagged deer or parts of deer and other types of illegal game, including a Lynx tied and frozen in a standing position to the top of a car.

This road block continued for several days.

Finally, Chizek was surprised to see a car go by with a nicely-antlered buck deer hanging out of the trunk. Grabbing his mike he called Anderson.

"C-215. Didn't you see that car go by with the buck in the trunk?"

"No deer went by me. I was watching."

"Well a deer did go by me. I'm leaving to run them down."

Moving slowly, the car had just cleared the city limits of Portage and was heading south when Chizek finally caught up. Responding to the red light and siren, the car immediately pulled onto the shoulder of the road. All five of the young men immediately got out of the car. One man said, "What's wrong officer?"

"I really don't know if anything's wrong, but I'm a conservation warden, and I would like to check your buck."

Watching them closely, Chizek noticed that they seemed very nervous.

"This buck is tagged, is it not?" he asked.

"Well, he's legal," replied the man.

The young men becoming more alarmed and Chizek looked closer at them. *A couple of these guys look familiar. Could they be from around here?*

"How far did you fellows come? Where did you take the buck?"

They muttered several answers all at the same time, with none agreeing.

Looks like I've got a good one here. They don't even know where they got the buck. Something's goofy.

"O.K. fellows open the trunk. Let's have a look."

Suddenly their features grew strained. Several looked very pale.

Approaching the trunk he pointed, "Let's get it open and see what you've got here."

One of them fumbled a pocket knife out of his jeans, leaned over and cut the cord holding the trunk cover down. As the trunk popped up, a mounted deer head rolled out of the trunk landing on the road shoulder.

Staring unbelievingly at the deer head, Chizek muttered, "So that's why you guys were so nervous. Where did the deer head come from?"

One of the young men who suddenly looked more familiar than ever explained.

"We were watching you stop those cars from the Robbers Roost. We kept talking about it while we drank beer. Finally the temptation was too great. We took this deer head off the wall and tied the trunk down to hold it in. You're not going to do anything to us are you?"

Playing along Chizek asked, "Do you think I should?"

"It was only meant to be a joke."

Grinning he agreed, "Yeah I know it's only a joke and I have to admit it's a damn good joke. Take your deer head and go on back to the roost."

Amid the now smiling faces, he interjected, "No more today fellows, O.K?"

"O.K., thanks for taking this as a joke."

"We've got to have some levity in life and I guess it doesn't hurt to laugh at yourself once in a while. I have to admit you fooled me. It was a good joke. Now get out of here."

OAT CAKES

As chief warden in the late 1920s and early and mid 1930s, Harley W. "Mac" MacKenzie retained contact with many acquaintances in the state from his stint as a field warden between 1917 and 1925.

Respected by the citizenry as well as the wardens under him, he often revealed his mischievous demeanor by carrying on a constant banter. Often he used the pen to continue his good humored jests. Mischievous behavior begets mischievous reactions as demonstrated by a letter found in the archives of the warden's museum being developed at the MacKenzie Environmental Education Center at Poynette. The center is named after and dedicated to MacKenzie who was a former chief warden and director of the conservation department.

This epistle, written by "Chaunce" and addressed to MacKenzie, is a tongue in cheek way of reporting on the activities of Conservation Warden Harley T. McKeague and exchanging pleasantries.

Wilderness Lake
Iron River, Wis.
Dec. 3rd 1931

Friend Mac.

"Mac" I'm going to tell you a little story, so get all set for a few shocks! Here goes–Today being my wedding anniversary–well–I had to celebrate. Naturally we had to have a real feed. Now then, being a poor, simple woodsman–we'll put it this way–what sort of feed is proper for such a great occasion? Venison–yep you hit it right off. All right, I had to get me a steak. So taking down my trusty Savage off the wall and wiping off the DUST! (Fact, it did gather dust and you don't need to grin). I hied me into the forest. Stalked a nice fat three-year-old and well Babm–"A Miss" you say? Mac look at me: a MISTER!!!

Then I skinned it, but first rolled up my sleeves (to the elbows), slipped one hand inside with a knife, did a few twists with it and turned MISTER over–out plopped the innards–well and good–then I hunted the dry spots on the way home with a liver heart and one leg on my back (hind leg) and made a circuit–stopped looked and listened!! Nary a sign of tracks!! Good I said and slipped up in back of the garage and–DAMN! Black coach! A flivver! Well Mac–now was that nice to have this McKeague park his car there the one day in the year when I am wicked????

All right–all right–we'll let it go–he wasn't in at the time–heard a shot off to the southwest and went scouting so when he got back I had a little color and stopped puffing–also had a chance to straighten out my face–phew but that was a close one!!!!

I'm trying to tell you that I have met McKeague and he seems like the real type of warden we need here–young–on the job and as I say seems like real goods–So I hope you keep him on this district here.

Now then next time you have any of your blood hounds stop in to see me have them whistle "Annie Rooney" and if they don't know that–why any other will do (as long as it's loud).

Having summer up here again now–the snows are going fast and the ground is almost bare again–am expecting the spring migration now any time!!

Well, old warrior I have used up two ribbons on you trying to have you drop in here and I feel that you should at least make good to the extent of one anyway!! And remember the password–OAT CAKES.

Chaunce

Author's note: This letter was found in the archives of the MacKenzie Environmental Center. The full name of the author was never revealed nor was the humor behind the password–oat cakes.

BUFFALO JIM

On a beautiful September morning in 1963, Conservation Warden Jim Chizek stopped to discuss a fire case with Forest Ranger Frank Palenik at the conservation education center near Poynette.

Palenik told Chizek the news of the day, "The center crew is unloading a couple of buffalo. The truck just arrived. The game farm guys are helping."

"You mean we're going to display buffalo here now?"

"Yep, Grange up at Sandhill gave them to the state when we took over management of his area."

"Oh, you mean the Sandhill Refuge?"

"Yeah, I understand we have a female and a bull."

"How big are they?"

"Not too big, I guess. They're two- or three-years-old."

"Let's run down and take a look at them."

"O.K., let me mail this fire report, I'll be right with you."

"Go ahead, meet me there. I want to see this operation."

As the truck backed into the open gate of the high woven wire fence for unloading, Chizek arrived. He was greeted by a large gathering of department personnel for this grandiose occasion: Game Manager Kenneth "Kenny" Mills, game farm employees Tony Rinzel, Marvin "Koke" Kaukl, Ernie Mallard, Cal Tomlinson, Bob Davis and Ted Cregeski, and Exhibit Specialist Johnny Thomas. Chizek joined the crowd, pushing in close to the high-racked truck for a peek.

Meanwhile Darlene Lukins, the center's secretary was left alone and was informed by a concerned citizen that the baby raccoons at the center had escaped. After desperately attempting to locate someone to catch them, she gave up. She left the office and was hazing them toward their pen when Palenik drove by in his fire-fighting truck. Waving him down, she enlisted his help in driving the wayward coons inside the enclosure. Finally successful, Palenik unceremoniously dropped the pin in the cage hatch and drove off to file his report, leaving Lukin's locked in the cage with her crying charges.

"Frank, Frank," she shouted as the truck disappeared past the old barn. *Darn them buffalo. Here I am stuck in the coon pen with no one around to let me out.* Reaching her fingers through the crack between the cage door and the casing, she became frustrated. The pin was just out of her reach. Resigned and with a sigh, her hands on her hips, she waited for someone to let her out. After a short wait, she saw Palenik's truck returning. Frantically she waved her arms crying out, "Frank, Frank!" She sighed as he looked her way, and slowed the truck to a stop at the cage.

"Well, well, what do we have here? A new exotic exhibit!? Ha, ha, now how did you lock yourself in with the coons?"

"You know darn well how I got locked in here. Those dumb buffalo will be the death of all of us. Just let me out."

Releasing Lukins, Palenik drove to the animal pen where the buffalo were to be unloaded–just in time to see Rinzel struggle with the latch on the truck rack.

As he dropped the tailgate-ramp for unloading, Palenik asked, "Have any of you ever handled buffalo before?"

Rinzel scoffed, "Naw, but shouldn't be any different than unloading beef cattle."

Securing the gate against the ramp, Rinzel and Kaukl walked back to survey their handiwork.

"All we have to do is shoo them out."

They pounded on the sides with their fists, pacing back and forth and peering through cracks in the rack at the two dark mangy beasts. Finally, the female walked hesitantly toward the open door at the rear and walked unsteadily down the ramp into the pen. She turned and studied the activity at the truck.

Someone yelled, "Let's chase her away."

Kaukl replied, "No, don't do that, Let her stay there for the bull to see. Maybe he'll follow her."

"Good idea, now let's chase the bull out."

Hammering on the rack to no avail, the truck driver finally handed out tools, hammers and lug wrenches to hammer on the rack with. A bedlam of sound and activity followed as they pounded the sides of the rack with them. The bull stood still, oblivious to the din. He looked like a statue looking out the open door from the middle of the truck box.

The stand-off continued for over an hour. New strategies were developed of getting the bull off the truck, but nothing seemed to work. Finally Tomlinson suggested, "Let's just leave him. He'll get off when he's ready."

The truck driver objected.

"I'm supposed to be up a Sandhill by 2 p.m."

Tomlinson insisted, "I think that's the only way we'll get him off."

Raised on a farm, Chizek felt his superior experience handling livestock put him head and shoulders above the rest. *I know darn well I could just jump up in the truck with him and shag him out of there. He looks dumber than a rock.*

"Hey guys you want me to show you how to get him out of there?"

Mills asked, "Do you think you can? How would you do it?"

"I'd just get in the truck, get up behind him and chase him out."

"I don't know Jim, they say buffalo are ornery as all hades."

"Kenny, I've been around livestock all my life and never found anything I couldn't handle. What do you think Frank?"

"I don't think you should get up there with him. He might hurt you."

His reasoning questioned, Chizek responded with action.

"Just watch me," he quipped and ran up the ramp. Stopping in the door he sized up the animal facing him. *Stupid looking shaggy beast,* he thought.

Advice was now being given freely from the watching crew. "Get out of there Jim. He may hurt you. Buffalo are supposed to be mean."

"But this is just a little guy. He'll be easy to handle."

Now how do I do this? Just walk past him and pat him on the hinder and out he pops. Putting his thoughts into action, he slowly eased his way along side the animal into the rear of the truck.

"I told you he wouldn't hurt me."

"Its not over yet. Get out of there."

With a wide grin on his face, Chizek approached the buffalo from behind and slapped him sharply on the rear. He expected him to bolt out of the truck, but he was wrong. Instead, the bull turned 180 degrees in one liquid movement, his feet never touching the deck. Staring at his still outstretched hand, now near the bull's head, he instinctively jerked it back. He stood befuddled, staring at the bulls head where his rear had once been.

Advice from the watchers was now muted as he concentrated on the improbable position he had put himself in. *Oh, oh maybe I made a mistake. No sweat I'll get out of here O.K.*

Head down, the bull began taking mincing steps toward him. Backing toward the rear of the truck his mind raced, desperately trying to come up with a way out of his predicament. *Got to do something, his muddled mind screamed.* Reaching out he firmly grasped the bull by the horns. The reaction was sudden, unexpected and violent as the bull began jumping up and down his knees frozen in a stiff legged jump, rocking the truck on its springs. *Whoops, wrong thing to do.*

Frightened to the point of desperation at the outcome of his foolhardy bravado, Chizek released the horns and stepped back several steps to study the beast who was belligerently staring back at him. The little bull had somehow grown to a gargantuan size.

Suddenly, the tales he had read of buffalo encounters flashed through his mind. He remembered tales of people being injured and killed by them. He also remembered them described as plodding, but their great lung capacity allowed them to run 40 miles and easily wear out three changes of horses. He was haunted by the thought of how buffalo fight. *Man, they throw you through the air with their horns and gore you on the ground. That could happen to me! How am I going to get out of here? I'm almost at the end of the rack. No more room to retreat.* Turning his glance to the sides of the covered enclosure for a means of escape, he spotted a small square hole in the corner of the rack. He contemplated dashing for it. *Better not try it. Looks like it's too small. I'd never squirm through it. He would get me before I could get out.*

Immobile, he consciously worked on his fear. *Take it easy Jim. Panic will not get you out of this. Help me Lord. If I get out of this I will never go near a buffalo again.* Calmness slowly returned and he analyzed his situation. *Buffalo respond to fast movement. Got to move very slow. Just slowly walk around him like I did on the way in.*

More composed, he slowly and deliberately stepped to his right in an exploratory move. The bull stood as though bolted to the truck. Slowly holding his fear in check, he walked, step-by-gentle-step, past the bull. Once in the clear, he made a desperate leap landing on the ramp. A second jump took him clear of it.

Wringing wet with sweat from head-to-toe Chizek was speechless. He spent about 10 minutes walking around before he was able to discuss the incident with the others.

"I have just one thing to say. I'll never go near a buffalo again," he said.

Though his pride took a fall that day, he took it in stride, thankful his prayer had been answered. He didn't even mind being called Buffalo Jim for a time by the game farm crew.

Not intimidated by his tormentors, the bull stayed on the truck. Finally, the crew decided to take Tomlinson's advice and leave. The bull stayed on the truck most of the day. For no apparent reason, he jumped off the truck as dusk darkened the evening sky.

Within a year after arriving at the farm, the bull gored and killed the cow buffalo.

BETTIN' ON THE BUCK

In 1944, at the age of 14, Jimmy Chizek was hunting deer south of his parent's dairy farm in Price County near Fifield. Without a sun to guide him, he got lost while hunting the wilderness area between highway 70 and Lugerville, a wild trackless area of approximately six-square-miles. He dug in his pocket for the old beat-up compass he always carried. *Good thing dad made me take my compass along.* Heeding the north-pointing-arrow he headed straight north reaching the long abandoned Wilson-Martin homestead. Recognizing where he was, he followed the dirt trail the quarter-mile to highway 70. Walking briskly to beat the darkness, he followed the highway east toward his home several miles away.

With darkness coming on, he hurried his steps through the spruce and cedar swamps growing along the highway to the intersection of county B–the home of Shorts Tavern. He slowed his steps to listen to the merriment of deer hunters within the tavern and saw a middle-aged man leave the bar. The man drove unsteadily north on county B. He recognized the man as John Lubbock. *Looks like John's had too much to drink, hope he makes it home.*

Watching the old car rumble slowly along the dirt road, Chizek saw a large buck walk in front of Lubbock's car. Braking to an abrupt stop, Lubbock's auto sat momentarily still. Suddenly, a rifle protruded from the driver's side of the vehicle. Flames shot from the barrel in the semi-darkness and rifle shot reverberated through the silent, wooded area. The buck dropped into the ditch and floundered. Tossing the rifle swiftly into the rear seat, Lubbock struggled out of the car and slid down the snow-covered slope on his rear. He grasped the buck by the antlers, and in a seated position, dragged him up the bank in a series of jerks to the ice-glazed road. Lubbock fell several times while struggling to drag the deer toward the car.

Chizek watched in awe. He was afraid to be near such a brazen violation, yet was inexplicably drawn to the drama.He was reluctant to leave. *Should get home. Someone is going to get in trouble here. Maybe I could just hang around a little while and see what happens. Should I tell someone?*

Not knowing what to do he entered the tavern and ordered a bottle of soda pop. The pop was barely set in front of him when Lubbock threw open the tavern door his voice booming, "You should schee what

I got."

"What do you have, John?"

"I jus sshot a big buck, a big, big 'un. Was drivin' up the road, he scteptted right in front of me."

"Come on. You just left here a few minutes ago."

"Yep, Sshot him about a hunnerd yards up B. Come on I'll show ya. Cum on, cum on, he's in ma trunk."

Lubbock ushered the dozen hunters clad in mackinaws speckled with red swatches out the door. He walked unsteadily to his parked sedan which he had unceremoniously braked to a halt in front of the tavern door.

He turned the trunk handle, jerked it open, and out jumped an enormous 10-point buck. It landed on the icy parking lot, skid on the ice, and slid into the gathered throng. Everyone scampered to get out of its path. Terror in it's eyes, the buck slipped and skidded, his hooves throwing ice until he righted himself and bolted into the woods behind the tavern.

Subdued silence was suddenly replaced by embarrassed laughter. It rose rapidly into a crescendo as the crowd realized what had happened. Having spent a considerable time imbibing in spirits, the mischievous nature of the troop now exploded into rowdy laughter and derisive comments, "Ha ha. Now what're you going to do John? The buck's gone and so is your deer tag."

"Bye-bye buck, ha ha, Bye-bye tag."

"Ma tags not gone...never tag ma deer till after the season ennaway. Get outta the way...gotta get my rifle. I'll get 'em."

Pushing through the crowd he repeated, "I'll get 'em, out of the way."

In spite of his inebriated condition, Lubbock moved swiftly toward his car. He reached in and grabbed the loaded rifle from the back seat and swung the muzzle dangerously toward the crowd. Stampeding en masse, the crowd scattered to avoid the eminent danger of this drunken mad man.

"Hey John your hammer's back."

"You'll shoot someone if you're not careful."

The group made a hurried second retreat when Lubbock once again swung the muzzle menacingly in their direction as he ran to the auto's open door and snatched a flashlight off the front seat. He spun in his tracks and followed the light beam toward the underbrush where the buck had disappeared. Reeling into the woods he swore at the buck who was causing him this deep embarrassment.

The assemblage watched as the flashlight beam darted hither-thither among the tightly-bunched spruce trees to ferret out the wounded deer. Their raucous cries were now openly for the buck.

"You'll be out there all night John," shouted one reveler with a wide grin.

"We're bettin on the buck!"

"John, now you're going to get pinched for shining deer, hee hee."

"Let's here it for the buck, hurrah, hurrah!"

Lubbock disappeared into the thick foliage now shrouded in darkness. Wagers were made on the outcome, with the odds heavily weighted toward the buck.

"One will get you five the buck gets away."

"He's too drunk to hit the deer if he does see it."

"That buck is pretty lively. Bet he gets away."

About 10 minutes lapsed before Lubbock's rifle barked as he put the buck out of his misery.

Deep in thought, Chizek returned home. By the light of the moon, he tripped along, letting his thoughts go over the episode he just saw and the hundreds of hunting, violating and game warden tales he had grown-up hearing. The events of the evening had made an indelible image in the young man's mind–an image to last a lifetime.

Still concerned about this knowledge and the consequences of being present when the buck was killed, he ducked into the woods each time headlights warned of an approaching car. His imagination was running wild thinking of the super game wardens his family often spoke of. *I just know the game warden is on his way out here. He must have heard about what happened. Hate to have to explain what I'm doing out here so late with a rifle. Wonder if I could be arrested for being at the tavern when John brought the untagged buck in? I wouldn't even want to be asked about it. What would I say to a warden? With all those people watching him one would think he would tag the buck. Guess he's just not afraid of the game warden. I'm thirsty. Never did get to drink my pop, didn't pay for it either.*

Author's notes: About 30 years later, while working as an undercover game warden, I often wondered if I might be in a tavern some day when a person would show off an untagged deer. It never happened.

PUGH-JA-LIST

In the 1940s, diminutive game manager George Kern was sent to Antigo as a special warden to assist in game enforcement prior to and during the deer season.

Carl Miersch, who worked Langlade County, was glad to have Kern working for him. His reputation as a good special warden was well-known throughout the state. His tenacious bulldog personality also preceded him. Kern constantly bragged that he had been a golden-glove boxer. Miersch found this curious.

"Good morning George," drawled Miersch, in his slow mischievous way. You ready to go out and have at 'em?"

"You bet," said Kern impatiently. He bobbed and weaved, throwing a few fainting punches at an invisible foe. "Lets go."

While working deer hunters, there are many hours of waiting for something to happen. During these boring moments Miersch and Kern, as hundreds of wardens before them, discussed happenings in their lives.

Miersch, a polished, suave interrogator slowly drew out of Kern the story of his prize fighting days. It was obvious he was very proud of his boxing ability. Their conversation left no doubt that he would relish having a violator resist arrest or try to assault him. He liked being known as a pugilist.

"You just give me the word Carl if you want someone's clock cleaned. I'll take care of him."

"Well now lad we don't go around lookn' for a fight, but if one shows up, I'll give you the nod."

He let his mind wander. *I wonder if George is really such a good fighter. No way to find out of course, but I wouldn't mind seeing him in action. He claims he's good and likes to be known as a pugh-ja-list.* Miersch always drawled the word pugilist making it sound like pugh-ja-list.

Little did Miersch know that he may have a chance to see Kern use his pugh-ja-listic prowess.

Approaching a fire lane with a locked gate in a huge wilderness area, he nonchalantly handed a key to Kern, "Unlock that gate and we'll take a look see. We sometimes have some impatient partridge hunters, prone to hunt deer before the season opens."

They raised a plume of dust as they drove down the lane. A sharp, northwest wind whipped about their car as they slowly proceeded, all the while looking for hunting activity. Rounding a turn in the road, they saw a tall well-built man, gun at port arms sneaking along the road and peering into the woods on both sides. The heavy wind blew the dust cloud to their rear and drowned out their approach. They drove up behind the hunter without being heard. Stopping the car Miersch said, "Go on check him George."

Carefully opening the door and pushing it quietly shut, Kern walked up behind the unsuspecting hulk of a man. He reached out and touched him on the shoulder, "I'm a game warden and would like to see your license."

Startled, the huge man swung around raising his fist, "What the hell is goin' on?"

"I want to see your hunting license."

In a Kentucky twang he growled, "What raght do ya have of sneeken' up on me like this?"

Pointing to his badge Kern replied, "This gives me the right."

"Why you little weasel, I've a notion to jam that piece of tin whar the sun don't shine."

"Oh you would, would you? Come on, see if you can. I'll put that light in your lantern jaw out."

Miersch saw the men's jaws working, arms swinging, and balled fists rising, and jumped into action. He scampered to the scene and pushed his way between them.

"Hold 'er boys, this thing is gettn' out of hand."

"You bet it's getting out of hand," announced Kern. This guy wants to fight."

"Ya bet aw wants ta fight. I could eat this pip-squeak fer breakfast."

"Let me at 'em Carl, He called me a little S.O.B. I'll trim him good."

"Well now lads if you want a friendly fight, guess it's alright with me." He pointed to Kern and said to the brute, "I should warn you though, this man is a pugh-ja-list.

"A pugh-ja-list ya say...and then ya laugh at the way us Kaintucks talk. But we all ain't here to talk, we're here to fight. I won't even work up a sweat whippin' this little jayhawk."

"O.K. lads you just go at it."

He took the man's gun and said, "A fair fight though. The first one to pick up a stone or stick will get it from me. Go to it!"

Now we'll see how good old George really is. Stepping back, he broke the single-barrel shotgun and palmed a six-chill shell. *Looks like he was hunting partridge alright.* "O.K. guys go to it!"

Smiling in elation, Kern never blinked as the man hit him with roundhouse swing right on the nose. Flying through the air he landed with a whooosh hard on his back.

Miersch thought. *Oh oh, what did I get little George into? He's going to be killed.*

Shaking his head, to clear the cobwebs, Kern slowly got to his feet and scuffled slowly toward the giant both hands high in a true boxers pose. Diving in, he jabbed the man several times in his face without the other man so much as taking a swing. Faking, diving and jabbing he slowly cut the man's face to ribbons. Beyond several wild roundhouse swings that never touched Kern, the man's only blow was his first. Slowly, the man began to sag and weaken. Suddenly he backed off, "Nuff, nuff," he panted. "Ya'll wins."

Miersch enjoyed the entertainment. The man went down several times and on one of the falls, he noticed a shotgun shell fall out of his pocket. After the fight, he picked it up and found it was double-zero buckshot, illegal at that time of the year in areas inhabited by deer.

While the man wheezed to catch his breath, Miersch wrote him a summons for the buckshot violation.

GOOSE POND WRANGLE

In early 1958, Poynette Game Manager, Thurman Deerwester, received a petition signed by 19 property owners in the townships of Arlington and Leeds, Columbia County. The petition asked that an area be closed to hunting on the Arlington Prairie. The proposal was to close approximately 2,800 acres to hunting around and including Goose Lake, an 80 acre lake commonly called Goose Pond. Goose Pond had traditionally attracted fair numbers of waterfowl and was heavily hunted for generations.

The landowner's contended that larger numbers of waterfowl would congregate if protection was provided around Goose Pond and that protection would provide better hunting and waterfowl viewing. The lake was divided roughly in half by a road. Culverts beneath the road allowed the free passage of water. This is where many people viewed waterfowl.

After many meetings between game managers, game wardens, legal staff, and other Wisconsin conservation department personnel, it was decided that too many problems were associated with the proposal. All agreed that closing the area, as the petitioner's proposed, would increase the number of waterfowl using the area. In fact, the consensus was that the petitioner's expectations would be far exceeded. Concern was for the east half of Goose Pond, where one person owned all the land surrounding it. This owner, Darrell Walter had not signed the petition. In order to make the closed area effective, his land must necessarily be closed. Legal services in the department ruled that closing his land to hunting without his permission, while legal, would create a public relations problem and perhaps a legal challenge. Darrell Walter, an outspoken opponent of the closure, would most likely contest the closing of his land to hunting without his permission.

The decision to not go forward with the closure, brought a horde of complaints from the petitioners. After meeting with them several times, the department decided it was worth opening the proposal to a public hearing.

The public hearing was held in May of 1958, with a final vote of 21 to 11 for the establishment of the closed area.

Reluctantly, the department closed the area to hunting on September 1, 1958. This decision would throw the Arlington Prairie into a prolonged squabble between neighbors, hunters, and the conservation department.

The closed area worked beautifully, just as the petitioners had predicted. Each spring and fall, the number of waterfowl using the Arlington Prairie increased. Between 1958 and 1961, geese using the Goose Pond increased from approximately 700 to 10,000, and duck usage increased from about 2,500 to 7,000. Other species also benefitted, including a few rare species like white-fronted geese and cinnamon teal. Shorebirds such as egrets and herons also increased in number. Waterfowl viewing and photography became legendary as cars were forced to stop for ducks and geese crossing between the two halves of the lake–all this during the open season for waterfowl.

Hunting on the prairie began to blossom, with large movements of waterfowl to Schoenbergs Pond and marsh en route to the Mud Lake Wildlife area 8 miles to the northeast along with flights to Lake Wisconsin 10 miles to the west. With waterfowl hunting increasing in an area posted to hunting, complaints of trespass were greatly increased. Illegal hunting became a concern as Chizek made arrests for hunting in the closed area. Some arrests were made of the petitioners friends and relatives.

During these years, Darrell Walter, a non-hunter, continued to protest the closure of his lands to hunting without his consent.

"You mean I can't even hunt on my own land?"

With his discourse growing ever louder and complaints continuing to grow, sentiment around the Arlington area began to swing in his favor. Another petition, with some of the original signers names on it, now came before the department requesting *removal* of the closed area. Appearing at the annual conservation congress public hearing in the spring of 1960, Walter and nine other landowners made a strong case for removal of the closed area. They complained that the waterfowl were doing damage to their crops. So strong was their plea that the sportsmen at the meeting voted to have Goose Pond closed area removed.

By this time, the department had spent considerable time and money implementing the closed area. Because of its success in protecting waterfowl, they would not consider its removal.

Finally, In October 1961, Warden Jim Chizek began to hear rumors. Walter was leaking the word that he was going to hunt on his land included in the closed area. The morning of the opening of the waterfowl season found Chizek patrolling the Goose Pond closed area in an effort to ascertain if the rumors were true. Upon approaching Darrell Walter's land, Chizek was surprised to see him posting no trespass signs.

What do I do? Should I approach him and ask him if he's going to hunt? Why not? Parking his auto nearby, Chizek stepped out, "Hi Darrell, I see you're posting your land."

"Yeah, I usually don't allow any hunting on my land. What are you doing? Patrolling for early hunters."

"Well, I did some patrolling, but I really came down here to see if the rumors I've been hearing are true."

"They probably are."

"You're going to hunt on the closed area?"

"Yep, glad you stopped. I need to ask some questions."

"I'd be glad to answer them, but if you're going to try the law, we may as well get together and plan this out so neither of us will waste any time. Now what are your questions?"

"As you know, I don't hunt so I don't know the game laws. I want to be arrested, but only for hunting on my own land that you've closed illegally."

Handing Walter a note pad and a pencil, Chizek said, "O.K., you better write this down so you don't forget. You must buy a small game license and a waterfowl stamp. The license you can get at the county clerk's office, the federal stamp at the post office. Make sure you have your gun unloaded and fully-encased in a carrying case while it's in your car."

"What kind of gun do you use for killing ducks?"

"A shotgun larger than a .410-gauge. By the way, the shogun must be plugged so it'll hold no more than three shells. The shells must contain shot no larger than number BB."

"BB? What does that mean?"

"When you buy your ammo, just tell the clerk you want shot smaller than BB and you'll be using it for hunting waterfowl. They'll help you get the right shells."

Busily scribbling in the notebook, Walter continued, "Will you take the gun when I shoot the duck?"

"Yes, the gun will be held for evidence."

"Guess I'll borrow my neighbors."

"Remember, should you be convicted the gun may be confiscated by the court."

"I don't think his gun is much good anyway."

"O.K., where and when do you want to meet?"

"How about on Goose Pond Road where it crosses the pond?"

"That'll be fine with me. What time?"

"When does the season open?"

"At noon. Why don't we meet there at 12:15?"

"That's fine with me. See you at 12:15."

"After leaving Walter, Chizek immediately radioed for assistance from Leonard "Len" Tomczyk at Columbus and his supervisor Louis

“Pat” Oshesky. He asked them to meet him as soon as possible. Upon their arrival he quickly briefed them as to what was to take place.

As noon approached, they drove to the prearranged meeting place and parked. At exactly 12:15 p.m., a car approached from the rear and parked behind them.

Chizek greeted Walter as he uncased a shotgun.

“Did you get everything straightened out?” Gesturing toward several teal sitting on a muskrat house he said, “I think so. Would it be O.K. if I just walk out in my field and shoot a duck?”

“It’s up to you. I must warn you that if you do you will be arrested for hunting within an area posted as closed to hunting.”

“That’s what I came here for.” He swung the muzzle dangerously toward Chizek’s middle as he shoved shells into it.

“Careful with that muzzle. Do you know how to use that gun?”

“My neighbor showed me how.”

Pushing the barrel aside, Chizek instructed, “You never point the muzzle toward anything you don’t want to kill.”

“O.K., I’m not used to handling firearms.”

The gun loaded, Walter walked gingerly in his street shoes down the bank into his field off the road right-of-way. He aimed and shot a teal sitting on top of the muskrat house.

The blast reverberated across the open prairie causing thousands of ducks and geese sitting on the pond to rise in a maelstrom of sound and motion.

While Supervisor Oshesky watched from the road, Chizek motioned to Tomczyk who then directed his labrador to retrieve the duck. Chizek focused on Walter.

“I’ll need your gun and hunting license.” Little conversation was carried on as Chizek wrote the citation.

“Do you have an attorney?”

“I hired T.J. Sanderson of Portage.”

“He’ll do a good job for you. We’ll see you in court next Thursday.”

Leaving the scene, Oshesky chuckled, “Pretty easy case. He surrendered. Seriously though, I believe I should sign the complaint on this one. It’ll demonstrate that the state is backing the arrest. I believe this will be a hot one. It sure is different. I know Sanderson will give us a fight.”

Putting on his best smile, Chizek commented, “I’m not worried. From now on I’m going to have them call the house when they want to be arrested.”

Shaking his head Tomcsyk joined the conversation, “You sure come up with some interesting situations Jim. It’ll be interesting to see how this turns out. Personally, I think we’ll lose. Let Pat lose the case!”

“To be sure, I’ve had a bad felling about stopping hunting on a man’s land without his permission from the beginning. Guess I’ll let you lose this one boss.”

Appearing in county court for Walter, T.J. Sanderson entered a not guilty plea and asked for a trial before Judge Daniel C. O'Connor. An agreement was reached to file briefs.

No witnesses were called on July 27, 1961. In place of testimony a 12-page stipulation agreed to by the attorneys was presented. The court ordered the defense to file another brief within 30 days, answering the charge of hunting on a closed area, with District Attorney David Bennett to file a reply brief within 21 days, so the court case could be disposed of on October 2, 1961, just days prior to the opening of the waterfowl season.

The court ruled, as Walter had claimed, that the state can not close land to hunting without the owner's consent.

After losing in court, Chizek, Oshesky and Tomczyk stopped at the Walgreen Drugstore for coffee and to commiserate their loss.

In an effort to lighten the occasion, Chizek cuffed Oshesky's shoulder, "Sure glad that wasn't my case Pat, only a supervisor could lose a case handed to him on a silver platter."

"Ha," snorted Tomczyk, "Maybe next year Jim and I can share that pay raise you were going to get."

As a result of the loss, the closed area signs were immediately removed, and hunters had a heyday on the prairie that fall. The waterfowl accustomed to protection in the area were soon shot out and the prairie didn't draw and hold waterfowl to any great extent for the next 10 years.

Several years later, in the spring of 1964, whistler swans using the lake suffered a huge die-off. Warden Jim Chizek and his black labrador Peggy retrieved about 50 dead or dying swans. The birds were frozen and held at the Poynette Game Farm and turned over to Daniel Trainer and R. A. Hunt of the department of veterinary science at the University of Wisconsin. Their investigation determined that the swans had been poisoned by lead shot. Over 200 swans were recovered and tested that spring in Wisconsin. The number of pellets recovered from the birds gizzards ranged from zero to 201, with an average of 50 pellets per bird.

Goose Pond was heavily hunted for many generations, and was ideally suited to kill the long-necked swans. In spring when water levels were low, they dipped for food in shallow water and consumed more than just insects and algae.

In 1967, the Madison Chapter of the National Audubon Society, consisting of 3,500 members from Dane, Columbia and Sauk counties, began buying land on the Arlington Prairie with the goal of protecting migrating waterfowl. Around 1979, the area was posted as a sanctuary. Today, no hunting is allowed on 272 acres including the lake, which is owned by Madison's Audubon Society. Their goal is to acquire 1,000 acres.

With complete protection, resident managers Mark and Susan

Martin say waterfowl numbers are again rising. Recent estimates include 10,000 ducks, 25,000 geese and 1,000 swans frequent the area. Rare birds can also be seen at Goose Pond such as cinnamon teal and white-fronted geese. These sitings have been confirmed by the Martins.

CROW INVASION

Beginning the late 1950s, some special trees at the Poynette Game Farm became threatened by an unlikely culprit–crows. The trees were diligently planted and nurtured under the direction of Harley W. "Mac" MacKenzie as Director of the State Conservation Department many years earlier. As the former chief warden and director of the department, Mac had the respect and admiration of thousands of Wisconsin sportsmen long after his retirement in 1942. To many conservation department employees of the day, when Mac spoke, they responded.

Thousands of crows gathered in the Poynette area during the early winter months of these years and roosted in the pine and spruce windbreaks and plantations at the Poynette Game Farm. Crow numbers increased in direct proportion to the severity of the winter. The roosting hordes began to break and destroy the trees it had taken years to grow. Each year the number of crows increased, causing ever more damage to the trees.

Bill Ozburn, director of the farm gave hunters permission to enter parts of the game farm posted as a refuge to harass and kill the crows. Soon game warden Jim Chizek was summoned to Poynette by Ozburn.

"Jim we've got problems on the game farm. Guess I'm part of the problem as I've allowed hunters to enter the refuge. Our workers have found where a number of pheasants have been killed."

"Did they kill them right in the pens?"

"They not only killed them in the pens but they cut the pens to get them out."

"You gave them permission to enter and hunt in the refuge?"

"I know I shouldn't have done that, but I was desperate and Mac was on me to do something to protect the trees."

"I knew there were a lot of crows roosting here, I've shot them myself on the plantations outside the refuge. Do you have a list of the hunters you let enter? Maybe we could contact them and in that way stop it."

"No, I never kept a list, but remember some of them."

"How many have you given permission?"

"I don't know, quite a number."

"Well Bill I think we must put a stop to it. Will you call all you can remember and inform them it will no longer be allowed."

"I will do that, however, I'm afraid there'll be quite a number that I just can't remember."

"Do the best you can, and I'll run articles in the Portage Daily Register and the Poynette Press warning people that they'll be arrested and prosecuted if they hunt in the refuge. Both papers have always been very helpful to our causes and I'm sure they'll help us on this. I'll begin patrolling on a regular basis and warn hunters entering at first that we'll no longer allow them to enter. You have a number of employees carrying warden credentials, so I suggest you encourage them to patrol and do the same."

"O.K., I agree. Will you make any arrests?"

"Not right away. We'll see how it goes."

"What about Mac's concern for the trees?"

"Leave that to me. I'll talk to Mac. He's an old game warden and a friend. He'll understand."

With Christmas drawing near, the days grew shorter and colder. Flocks of crows continued to obey their natural instinct to roost in a area protected from the wind. Each day, the flocks grew larger as temperatures plummeted. Chizek responded along with Warden Leonard Tomczyk of Columbus. Many nights as the sun set, the two were to be found walking the windbreaks in the bitter cold shooing hunters off the grounds. On several occasions arrests were made when hunters were found in possession of pheasants. After warning people for weeks on end, not able to stem the flow of hunters entering the farm, the two wardens called a meeting with Warden Supervisor Louis "Pat" Oshesky and Ozburn. Media publicity was discussed along with the warnings handed out. It was clear to all that the effort had not succeeded in alleviating the problem. They agreed to make one more news release–a final warning stating emphatically that arrests would be made from this day forward.

Several days later, the wardens found a half-dozen men, blasting away with shotguns to flush crows from the windbreaks within the refuge. Summons were summarily handed out to loud protests.

"We've been hunting the Poynette Game Farm for several winters now. How come we all of a sudden get tickets. We're just helping the department protect their trees."

Tomczyk interceded, "I remember you. We contacted you a few weeks ago and you were told to stay out of here or you would be arrested."

"Yeah, but a lot of people have been told that and they weren't arrested."

Chizek jumped in, "We've decided warnings do not work and everyone hunting in here will be arrested from now on. I have discussed this with District Attorney Howard Latton and his orders are to arrest anyone found hunting within the refuge."

The following week, the *Wisconsin State Journal* carried a stinging story criticizing the department, Chizek and Tomczyk for arresting people assisting the department in the control of crows doing damage to state trees. The fact that people had been allowed to enter the refuge and hunt was also a part of the criticism

A hurried meeting between Oshesky, Ozburn, Tomczyk, Chizek and Area Game Manager, Deerwester was held at the game farm office.

All felt the department had egg on its face. They discussed tactics to recover its credibility. To quiet both the critics and protect the trees and pheasants, the group decided to allow crow hunting to continue both inside the refuge and in the game farm plantations bordering the refuge.

Chizek and Tomczyk were in a good position to make a recommendation having spent so much time patrolling the area. They knew the crows' roosting habits and exactly how they reacted to the shooting. At dusk, the staging began along the perimeter of the farm. The oak hills on the perimeter became a bedlam of raucous cries, making it difficult to hear. There they remained until darkness began to fall. Suddenly, as if by signal, the crows were aloft and vying for shelter in the pine and spruce windbreaks. The roar of wings flapping and birds cawing created a discordant canopy almost unbearable to the human ear. As the shadows lengthened, the madness increased as they started to roost. Their silhouettes darted every which way creating an unbelievable scene of chaos no amount of shooting could stop.

The shooting was fast and furious with hunters desperately attempting to silhouette the darting shadows against the night sky. *Which one should I shoot at? Oops got by me. Here comes some more. Missed again. How could I miss at 15-feet? Man I think I've shot a whole box of shells. Didn't hit one yet. Hope I don't run out of ammo.*

Often they seemed to disappear in the darkness as they turned their thin side toward the hunters in a mad dive rivaling the stoop of a peregrine. Hunters often shrugged their shoulders in disgust at their poor shooting ability. The birds would often zip within 10-feet of hunters en route to the trees. This angered hunters so much that they often began shooting at them as they rustled about in the trees. Yet, they couldn't hit them because they couldn't see them. Most hunters were awed at the flying ability and agility the crows demonstrated. They often questioned their shooting proficiency. Some blamed it on the hot barrels of their shotguns. Once roosted within the refuge area, they would rest for the night. Hunting within the refuge flushed the crows and forcing them to fly to the ambush waiting for them as they attempted to roost outside the refuge.

Thurman Deerwester estimated 100,000 crows roosting in the game farm trees. The group decided to get approval from the department director to issue permits to department employees allowing them to hunt within the refuge in an attempt to disrupt the crows roosting pattern forcing them to fly to waiting hunters in the open hunting areas on the perimeter.

As soon as the plan was accepted and signed by the director, publicity of the plan was greeted enthusiastically by the public. Mac MacKenzie was highly pleased that the crows were being shooed from his beloved trees.

While arrests continued of people who would not comply with the refuge boundaries, most enjoyed some of the best crow shooting action in the Midwest. Most nights there were a few department employees walking and shooting the windbreaks, which provided terrific shooting to sportsmen outside the refuge. While shooting is very difficult in the dark, many people chose to hunt very late. As long as crows were flying, shooters would stand along the plantation edge in the bitter cold to shoot at the flitting shadows. The colder the night, the more anxious the crows were to land. Many hunters stayed well into the morning hours when the moon was full and the night bitterly cold.

Shooters often left disgusted with their shooting skills. However, many crows were fatally hit and dropped out of view of the hunters. Each morning, game farm crews finished off crippled birds and picked up dead crows while making their rounds. Pickup truck loads of birds were buried in a pit provided for the burial of car-killed deer.

During these years, wardens held their area meetings and training sessions in the mess hall or at an old barn at the game farm. In the evenings, they went to the Owl's Nest night club in Poynette for dinner. Now, wardens also could hunt crows in the evenings for recreation. Most of the approximately 20 wardens in the old southern district were hunters. After dining at the Owl's Nest, most unlimbered their shotguns to try a little crow shooting. Jim Chizek, Len Tomczyk and Owen Anderson guided the group. Wardens with permits entered the refuge while others stationed themselves along the perimeter near the plantations. A number of very memorable combination area meetings and crow hunts resulted.

Now retired, Bill Ozburn recommended to Rudy Teschan, the new game farm manager, to continue the hunt as it seemed to be slowly stemming the large flocks. Soon complaints began coming in from the surrounding area as crows began roosting in other area plantations. Wardens gave hunters the names of landowners which gave them access to even better hunting on plantations not previously shot over.

A memorable warden crow shoot was held after an area meeting in the bitter cold of February. Riding with Jim Chizek was Warden Norm Wood of Milwaukee and others. Wood and the other wardens were directed to walk a windbreak about 9.30 p.m., so Chizek dropped them off and agreed to pick them up around 11 p.m. at which time they were to proceed to the Owl's Nest to imbibe in refreshments. Chizek joked with the other wardens he picked up at 11 p.m. and drove to the Owl's Nest. After about an hour of commiserating with friends, a half frozen, stormy faced Norm Wood stumbled into the welcome warmth of the tavern. Chizek was startled as the door flew open.

Chizek tried his best to be inconspicuous. Norm removed his steamed up glasses and gazed angrily up and down the crowded bar for the one who had forgotten and left him to walk several miles in the bitter cold. Desperately looking for a way out of the lashing he knew he deserved, Chizek chose to go on the offense. Having imbibed in just enough joy juice to give him courage, he blurted, "Where were you Norm? I looked for you. Were you lost?"

"Lost? Me lost? Where were you? I waited until I almost froze and then walked here."

"Aw, you were lost."

"Not lost. You're buying a drink for the house."

"Bartender give Norm a drink. He needs something to warm him up."

"I said a drink for the house. Neil give everyone a round. Jim is buying."

Reluctantly Chizek produced his wallet, "Hope I have enough to pay for this."

"If you don't Neil will trust you. He can pay later. Right Neil?"

"You see me pouring, I trust Jim."

Slowly the shooting on the farm had an impact. The flocks of crows diminished with each passing winter until only normal numbers roosted in the game farm trees. Although there was significant damage, the trees eventually recovered.

Mac was happy his trees were saved.

SUFFERIN' SUPERVISION!

In the early years, funds were always very short for the purchase and maintenance of warden equipment. Wardens were expected to do their own maintenance, including wiring boat trailers, painting boats and reriveting their leaky boats. When boat lights and life preservers became mandatory, the cheapest products were the norm and included disposable boat lights. Supervisor Pat Oshesky was a stickler on the care and maintenance of state equipment and southern area wardens thought his concern ran to the extreme. Under their breath a few called him cheap. It appeared that Supervisor Vince Skilling of the northeast area always outdid him when annual equipment budgets were established.

During the warden conference held in Stevens Point in the winter of 1959, a number of warden cars were either broken into or opened because they weren't locked. A substantial number of state issued handguns were stolen. Several weeks after the conference Supervisor Oshesky sent a memo to all wardens in the southern area advising them of the theft. He asked everyone to check their handgun, so an accounting could be made of the losses. About six months later, the Stevens Point Police Department arrested the thieves and recovered the stolen handguns.

Oshesky called Warden Jim Chizek who lived a few miles south of his Portage station one evening. Chizek was eating supper.

"Come on down. I've got a good one to tell you."

Arriving at Pat's country home he was greeted by a smiling Oshesky, "You'll never guess what happened. Remember when all our guns were stolen? Well they were recovered and we have an extra gun."

"An extra gun? How can that be? You mean someone doesn't know his gun has been stolen?"

"You got it. Guess who."

Without waiting for an answer he burst out laughing, "Clarence Wilger. He never reported his missing. I don't think he ever checked and he doesn't know it's missing."

"My God. How can a warden not know their sidearm is gone?"

"Goes to show you how much Clarence carries his gun. Do you remember the memo I sent out asking about the stolen guns?"

"Yeah, but that may be one of those empty envelopes Clarence keeps getting."

"I've got a notion to burn his tail on this, especially after sending out a memo with specific instructions to check his gun. Maybe a little humor and embarrassment will do just as well. I'll send out a memo scheduling an area meeting and order all handguns be brought in for a safety inspection. We'll see what Clarence has to say. Don't say anything about this. We'll have a little fun with Clarence."

Several weeks later, Oshesky called the meeting in the mess hall at the Poynette Game Farm. "The first order of business will be the safety inspection of our handguns." he announced. Oliver Valley evidently in on the secret, marched to the front of the room and told the assemblage to file past and he would look each gun over.

In the back of the room Wilger shifted uncomfortably and stuttered, "Ah...Er...Ollie, er...Pat I...I have a problem. I can't seem to find my gun."

"You lost your gun?" Oshesky seemed surprised.

"Well no. I...I don't think so. I must have misplaced it. I've looked everywhere."

Looking around the room, Chizek noticed a number of smiling countenances. Evidently he wasn't the only one in on the secret.

"Oshesky now rumbled, "Where do you keep your gun?"

"Well...I always keep it in the glove compartment of my car. But...Er...it's just not there."

"Unable to contain the smirk on his face Oshesky continued, Did you have it after the conference?"

"Well...I don't know, Pat."

"I sent you a memo instructing you to check on your gun. Did you check?"

"Ah, guess not. I knew where it was. I must have laid it aside when I was cleaning it, or something. I'll keep looking."

"No need. I have it right here. Oshesky's voice now carried the tenor of an enraged polar bear, "It was stolen at Point along with the others and you didn't even know it was missing. The rust on it belies your claim of cleaning it. It looks like it hasn't been cleaned in years."

The room full of wardens broke into a roar of laughter at Wilger's embarrassment.

The smiles slowly turned to frowns as Oshesky began to reprimand them all for their careless use of equipment.

"You all know we have a hard enough time to get equipment. It's time we start taking care of it. We've had equipment broken, stolen and not properly maintained. Just because you're driving your own cars, doesn't mean you can leave it unlocked with state equipment in it. I see binoculars and other valuable state equipment in plain view.

The least you could do is cover it up. These careless practices will stop!"

His harangue continued well into the meeting as he continued to come down on his charges. It had been fun when the barbs were aimed at Wilger, but not so much fun now that all were receiving a dressing down.

As the meeting ended, all was quiet as the subdued group filed out of the meeting room.

Several days later, Chizek received another call from Oshesky. His usually low gravelly voice was even lower and more gravelly, He droned, "Come on down."

"What's up Pat?"

"Never mind, I don't want to talk about it over the phone." He droned on, "This neighborhood has ears."

"O.K. Pat. I'll be down in a little while."

Upon arrival at Oshesky home, he was greeted by a somber, beaten man. His husky voice droned, "You'll never believe what happened to me. I lost my binoculars."

"How did...?"

Impatiently Pat interrupted, "Listen to me. I pulled the dumbest stunt I've ever heard of. Oh I know how I lost them. On the way to work at the Nevin Hatchery, I often stop at the Goose Pond Closed Area and check a few hunters. Yesterday I checked three fellows hunting near the closed area. When I left my car, I took my binocs with me. While checking their guns, I reached into the back seat of their car still holding the binocs in my hand. I laid them on the seat when I picked up the first gun. As I put the guns back in their car, I noticed a pair of binoculars laying there. I even commented, nice pair of binoculars you have there. I closed the door and left. They said nothing. I can't believe I did that. You check the area all the time. Watch for these guys and see if you can get my binocs back."

Chizek immediately recognized the description of the car and drivers.

"I remember those guys and their car. They've been hunting that area regularly. I may run into them."

"For Gods sake, don't mention this to any of the boys."

"Your conscience bothering you boss?"

Chuckling for the first time, he conceded, "This would have to happen right after I dress everybody down about being careless with their equipment."

Several weeks later, Chizek entered the closed area and came upon the car Oshesky had left his binoculars in. Pulling alongside, he waved them over.

The driver got out as Chizek approached.

"Do you fellows have a pair of binoculars that don't belong to you?"

"Nope. We have binoculars, but they belong to us."

"Then you won't mind if I look at them?"

"Go ahead," gestured the driver toward the man in the back seat. "Give him the binocs."

Checking the serial number of the binocs with the one in his book, Chizek asked, "Where did you get these?"

"We've had them for some time. Why?"

"These glasses belong to Pat Oshesky, my boss. He left them in your car when he checked you fellows a few weeks ago."

"Well, guess they belong to him then. We sort of found them in our car."

"I believe you knew he left them in your car and you neglected to tell him as he was leaving them. But it makes no difference, because I'm taking them. I'll give you a receipt for them. If you have a problem with that you can contact Oshesky. I'll give you his address and phone number. O.K.? He may want to prosecute you for the theft of the glasses."

"O.K., what ever you say. We didn't steal the binoculars. We just found them in our car. You tell Mr. Oshesky that."

Without further conversation Chizek turned on his heel, returned to his car and left.

Upon receiving the binoculars Pat was relieved, "Thanks a lot Jim. Guess I'm lucky to get them back. Now remember...your lips are sealed."

Well, a secret like this is a heavy burden to bear and alas the story leaked. The story became widely known and gave Oshesky catfits when wardens subtly mentioned the lost binoculars.

WHO SHOT MATT DILLON?

The sun shone bright on a pleasant, warm, October afternoon as Game Warden Jim Chizek and Special Warden Jack Allen patrolled the Pine Island Goose Refuge near Portage. Answering a radio call, they immediately responded to a request to stop at the Portage Police Station.

Police Chief Francis Riley met them at the door, "Jim our dispatcher received a strange telephone call. I believe there's been a hunting accident on the outskirts of the city. The dispatcher said an Ed Connors wanted to see you because he shot someone. Do you know this Connors?"

"Yeah I know him. Was he drunk?"

"Maybe. The dispatcher said he couldn't understand the fellow very well and was unable to find out exactly what the problem is. He said he wanted to see you. He's out at the old Taylor farm."

"The guy's a lush. He contacts me all the time. He is an ardent hunter and trapper, so what he's saying may be on the up and up. I'll run out there and see what's going on."

The sun was fast fading, as the two wardens drove into the ramshackle Taylor farmyard. Their car headlights flashing across the yard, picking up an odd looking object hanging from a standard jutting out from an old shed. Approaching the object, a freshly butchered cow loomed in their headlights.

Without further examination they drove to the old farm house. Braking, Chizek glanced at the door as a lanky old man stepped unsteadily forth. "Is he drunk Jack?"

"Looks like it, but I've never seen Ed sober so its hard to tell."

"Well, we'll find out."

Stepping quickly from their vehicle, they noticed the tall man sway as he walked toward them. "Jim, I'm shure glad to shee you. Think I sh...hot shomeone."

"Where's the man you shot Ed?"

"In the shhed, I think."

"In the shed? Aren't you sure? Lets look."

Opening the shed door, Ed directed them inside with a flourish of his arms. "R-Right here shomewhere."

A quick search revealed no body. A little disgusted, Chizek scowled, "Lets get to the bottom of this Ed. Did you shoot someone or not?"

"Well...ll..., I thought so. One of...f...the bullets came right through here."

Looking among the scattered junk stored in the shed Allen exclaimed, "Look here Jim he shot a hole through the picture tube of this old television set."

"My god Ed what were you shooting at?"

"The cow."

"You were shooting at a cow?"

"Yep, butcheerin,"

"You butchered that cow hanging outside?"

"Damn thing wouldn't sshtand still."

"Let's take a look," Chizek led the three out to the stark carcass hanging by its gambrels and the gaping bullet holes through the ribs and front and rear quarters.

"Ed, this is the damnedest thing I've ever seen. How many times did you shoot this cow?"

"Don't 'member, she wouldn't schtop, shhe kept runnin."

"You were shooting at her on the run?"

"Told ya...wouldn't shtop."

"I count four large bullet holes through her. What kind of a gun were you using?"

"Thutty, thutty...wouldn't sthop."

"Where was she running when you were banging away at her?"

A swing of his arms indicated a path past the shed.

"Jack, take a light and see if he hit anything else." Smiling a little now he murmured, "Keep an eye out for a body."

Flashing the light along the front of the shed, Allen carefully searched the shed and yelled, "A bullet hole here through the wall...another bullet hole here," He found where five bullets had past through the shed.

"O.K., Ed," Chizek demanded. His voice now low, leaving no doubt that the games were over. "Did you shoot someone? If you did you better hurry up and show us a body."

"Ghuss not, don't see nobody."

"O.K., what made you think you shot someone?"

"Could've been shomebody in the shed...th-thought I heard shomeone."

"You probably heard the bullet hit the picture tube of the TV."

Despite the potential seriousness of the situation, the improbable nature of this thought brought an involuntary smile to Chizek's face, "Maybe Mat Dillon was on." A twinkle in his eye Chizek questioned, "Ed ! Did you shoot Matt Dillon? Whose cow is this?"

"Taylor's, I was butcherin' it fer 'em."

"Don't look like he has much left to eat. Pretty shot up."
"Wouldn't sthand sthill...dumb cow."
"Not so dumb, Ed. She was running for her life."
After questioning John Taylor, it was determined that Connor was falling down drunk when he attempted to butcher the cow. He had first tried shooting the standing cow in the head and missed.
"John, you say he missed a standing cow?"
"Yep, as the cow ran past the shed he blazed away, shooting through the cow and the shed several times. He was so drunk he imagined he had killed someone. He said he had to report the shooting to the game warden."
Shaking his head in disgust Taylor murmured, "I'm not going to pay him for butchering. Hell, he ruined the cow."
Turning back to Connors Chizek retorted, "Ed, you go to bed here and sleep off your drunk before you drive. And leave that rifle in the house. Come on Jack, lets get out of here."
As they wheeled out of the driveway Allen chuckled, "Who shot Matt Dillon?"

TIP A SKIFF FOR A PINCH

It was a beautiful balmy July day in the late 1930s, when wardens Louie Giesen of Fountain City and Elmer Lange of La Crosse developed a new strategy to fool some very alert, tough fisherman.

The wardens knew these fishermen were taking and keeping game fish caught in their hoop, frame, gillnets and seines, and had tried unsuccessfully to catch them many times. Always on the lookout for wardens, the fishermen would transfer the fish from their nets into a holding tank aboard their boat and then take them into their pier and make a second transfer into other holding tanks. Using the pier in this manner was a clever way to elude the wardens–they could keep the fish alive and return them to the water when they spotted the warden's skiff approaching. The wardens couldn't close in fast enough to catch them before the fish were thrown into the river. Without the actual fish to present as evidence, the district attorney and courts would not prosecute. Many times the live fish were dip-netted back into the water as the two wardens paddled their skiff mightily in an effort to preserve evidence.

The two wardens decided on a mission to entrap the wary duo.

They arrived well before the fisherman normally ran their nets to set up an ambush. Anchoring their boat about 100 yards from the fishermen's pier, they baited their trap. Giesen, a large rawboned man, unpacked and donned women's clothing. Lange donned a pair of bib overalls often worn by farmers in the area.

"Louie, how come you brought women's clothes for yourself?"chortled Elmer as he pulled on the bib overalls.

"I'm much smaller and cuter and would make a better looking woman than you. Got 'em from Mrs. Green, my neighbor. It's her size. No one argues with her."

Putting out cane poles, their bobbers lazily drifting in the slow current, they gave the appearance of a man and wife peacefully fishing in front of the suspected pier. They had essentially gained the 100 yards they were normally short, as the illegal fish were being dumped back into the river.

Arriving at the time they usually did, the two fisherman ran their nets. The lazy appearing fishermen watched. Rowing into the pier they began unloading and sorting the fish. Game fish, bass, pike and panfish were thrown into one tank, and the carp, buffalo and catfish into another.

Appearing not to notice, the couple continued to fish, until they were sure there were a number of game fish in the tank. Giesen gave the command that would put them within arms reach of the illegal fish.

"Now," he whispered.

With that, they both grasped the gunwales of the boat and in one giant heave overturned the skiff in the still waters of the slough. With a loud splash both of them landed in the river, shouting for help. "Help, I can't swim. Quick Marge grab the boat and hang on."

I have it," squeaked Giesen in his best rendition of what Marge would sound like. "But I can't swim. I'm scared. Help me. My dress is tangled up in something on the boat. It's dragging me under. My God we're going to drown. On the dock, help us!"

"This water is cold, I don't know if I can hold on much longer."

On the dock, the two men heard and saw the disaster unfolding before their eyes. Reacting as any good Samaritan would, one yelled, "God those people tipped over. They could drown. We've got to help them. Come let's push the boat out and pick them up."

Swiftly they boarded the flat-bottomed scow tied to their pier and pushed it into the slow river current. They rowed furiously toward what appeared to be a tragedy in the making. In a matter of minutes, they were alongside the floundering people.

"Here take my hand mam," the bow man grunted, surprised at how heavy the woman was as he struggled to pull her into the boat. The other man pulled the smaller person in on the other end.

"What happened?"

"I stood up to move and tipped the boat over." squeaked Giesen, in his best soprano voice.

"Well your O.K. now, We'll take you to our pier."

Playing the part to its end, the couple lay gasping on the bottom of the boat until they reached the pier.

Tying the boat up, the man in the bow nimbly jumped onto the pier, reached out in a grandiose manner and assisted the helpless damsel out of the boat.

"Are you all right mam?"

"All right? I'm great," chortled Giesen, flashing his badge. "And you my friend are under arrest."

"Under arrest? You're wardens? Wait a minute, is that you Louie? I don't believe this."

The other man sputtered, "You can't be Giesen, You're a woman. Women can't be wardens."

"Why can't women be wardens?"

"Don't know, just never seen one before. Are you really wardens?"

Both displaying badges, Lange snorted, "We're wardens all right and this time you don't get a chance to put those illegal fish back. You're both under arrest for taking game fish with gear legal for taking rough fish only."

Both wardens gloated over the tank. They finally had caught the two clever operators. They marveled at the game fish swimming about –the fish they had worked so hard for so many years to see.

FEAR IN THE NORTHWOODS

It was with a sigh of relief on March 23, 1973, that special investigator wardens and local conservation wardens heard a Forest County jury proclaim Larry Jones guilty of illegally selling deer and possessing untagged deer. The case culminated from investigations going back to the deer gun season of 1971. The scene for this trial had been set a year earlier when Norman Kolman, another notorious commercial hunter, had been convicted of selling deer. Kolman had several years earlier been freed of the same charge by a hung jury. George Patak, among others, had also hung a jury about the same time on deer selling charges brought as a result of deer bought by Joseph "Joe" Rubesch, chief of special investigations.

The Crandon area located in Forest County had a notorious reputation of moonshining during the prohibition era. It was also a hotbed of illegal activity concerning the illegal taking and sale of fish and game. The old conservation department and the newly organized department of natural resources had battled for years to curtail this activity.

During the 1960s, there were several successful prosecutions of a cartel of people who hunted and fished together as a result of efforts of warden special investigators purchasing illegal game. Penalties handed down by justice court ran from $50 to $100 plus costs which the violators paid and wrote the experiences off with a laugh. Pride reared its ugly head as the violators began to be ridiculed by the local citizenry. This brought about a number of not guilty pleas. On the premise that a local jury would not find them guilty, especially if the jury could be frightened, proved to be true. Juries intimidated by local hoodlums soon began to say, "not guilty" or would become hung because a large enough number of jurors were afraid to find violators guilty of charges of selling game or fish. Another factor entering their decisions, in spite of ironclad evidence, was an attitude of protecting their own handed down from prohibition days and the Great Depression. It was O.K. to take game to feed ones family. It was only another small step to saying, "O.K., he only sold one or two deer or fish. What's the big deal? The money from the sale will help to feed his family." However, attitudes were slowly changing. People began to realize, even in Forest County, that to let violators off the hook wasn't fair to the resource or other users.

In the 1960s, the greater reason for letting violators off the hook was out and out fear. People chosen as jurors had to live with the people they were convicting. The band of pirates they were dealing with and their reputations of taking revenge were well known by all in the tightly knit community. The cartel was also involved in many other illicit activities such as burglary and timber theft being among the most prevalent.

They not only threatened revenge to any juror voting for conviction, but ruthlessly followed through with their threats. A stark reminder as to what could happen occurred several years earlier when conservation warden Clyde Sundberg brought charges of selling deer against Jerry Busher, a self-proclaimed attorney who was coyote smart and had considerable knowledge of law in spite of having no parchment to back up his claim. Even though he was found not guilty of the charge, it became public knowledge that the owner of the Cedar's nightclub had voted for conviction. Shortly after the trial, bullet holes mysteriously appeared in his establishment. All knew of the threats and knew who shot through the Cedars. Therefore, Forest County juries were not apt to find any of the bad bunch guilty of any crime. Regardless of the evidence, this knowledge was always something a criminal investigator had to face.

At this juncture, Ed Hill, supervising warden at Antigo, requested the aid of the special investigation section of the bureau of law enforcement at Madison. Prominent among a long list of known commercial violators in the Crandon area was Larry Jones and Norman Kolman.

With this history in mind, Warden Chief Special Investigator Joe Rubesch directed Warden Special Investigators Jim Chizek and Jack Y. Miller into the Crandon area shortly after the November 20, 1971 opening of the deer gun season in Wisconsin. They were determined to make buys of illegal deer of these cagey operatives in such a manner that entrapment could not be a defense issue. They wanted to end the era of not being able to get a conviction before a Forest County jury. Rubesch stayed in the shadows as he was known in the area, having made buys there several years earlier. He would enter suspect establishments only to affirm and measure the investigators progress.

Chizek walked with a cane and limp from a recent total hip replacement. Miller was a slightly overweight, balding middle-aged man who feigned a Chicago accent and overbearing attitude. They gave the impression of two wanna be hunters who drank too much, talked too much of their hunting exploits, but scarcely entered the woods. Special Warden Miller drove his wife's fancy, black, four-door Thunderbird car, bearing Illinois plates to complete the illusion they intended to project. Frequenting local saloons, their conversations with local hunters was readily noticed in the small communities of Hiles, Wabeno, Laona, Armstrong Creek and especially at Ducks Bar in Crandon. It was here that Larry Jones was known to hang out.

Larry Jones was a slight, trim short man in his mid-thirties with a mane of flaming red hair. He was known for his unusual behavior and his tendencies to break almost every law. He was a repeat game violator who constantly challenged the local wardens. He had woods and street savvy and was difficult to fool.

While getting acquainted with Jones they also frequently dropped into Bocek's, another small country bar several miles west of Crandon on highway 8 where they hoped to encounter Norman Kolman who was known to hang out there. Dropping bait each time by loudly complaining of their bad luck in hunting, they left them with the impression they would do almost anything for a deer. After many stops, they became known by most of the customers. In an attempt to break into local groups, Miller would go into what he called his 'act.' Knowing the small town bars would not have it, he would feign a tantrum when refused Chevis Regal whiskey.

"Ah ah," he would grunt, "Look on the top shelf you may find a bottle of real whiskey. Nothing is too good." He constantly complained about the bar's service. "Drinking in this joint ah hah, out here in the sticks is really beneath my dignity. But, ah ah, I'm no camel. Give me a shot of the best stuff you have on the top shelf."

It became clear the bartender hated to see them arrive, but everyone identified and remembered the two they dubbed the cane man and the fat man, as a pair who would undoubtedly buy a deer if offered. After many stops with no luck, they began to think they were not to be lucky enough to contact Kolman. On the sixth day of the season they left Bocek's discouraged because they had not been able to make the planned contact. As they entered their auto a slim young man wildly waving his hand came running across the parking lot shouting, "Hey wait".

"Oh oh, ah hah, looks like we're in business winked Miller."

"Rolling down his window he said, "Ah hah, What do you want?"

"You lookin' to buy a deer?"

"Ah hah, don't know. You got one?"

"Ah don' have but my uncle's got three bucks fer sale."

"Your uncle, who?"

"My uncle Norm Kolman."

"Oh well, ah hah, guess we're interested. Where are these deer?"

"Falla me."

Following the beat up red pickup along highway 8 for several miles they turned north on county S and stopped at a modest farm residence where on a meat pole near the road hung three nice bucks.

Approaching their car the young man said, "Take a look at these beauties. I'll go get Norm."

Gazing at the deer Jim commented.

"Hanging close to the road. Looks like he's advertising. I remember Pat Oshesky saying, "When bucks are displayed near a road, I would bet I could buy them."

Soon George returned, "Unca Norm ain't here. The price of the deer is $85 for the big buck, $65 for the middle-sized one and $55 for the smaller one. He'll be here later. Can you come back about six this evening? He'll be here then."

Traveling south on county S, they came upon a car that had slid off the icy road and was deeply buried in the snow plow ridge in the ditch. Stopping to assist the elderly gentleman they were along with other hunters pushing on the car to extract it from the ditch when the red pickup came speeding from the north. Sliding to a halt George approached the two investigators, "It's O.K., Norm is home," he whispered. "He wants to sell you the deer."

Following George back to Kolman's place the two discussed their approach to Norman. Jim said, "We must make sure we can establish who we're buying the deer from."

"Yeah, ah hah, Guess we don't really care. Perhaps we ah hah can implicate both of them."

After exiting their autos, George went to the house and brought Norm outside. "You guys want to buy these deer?"

Miller replied, "Ah hah, We only want one."

"How much will you give me for one?"

"It's your deer. What are you, ah hah asking?"

"As George told you before $85 for the big one, $65 for the middle-sized one or $55 for the smaller one. They're all nice bucks. You pick the one you want."

"Ah Hah, We didn't want to pay that much."

George interrupted, "I've got to leave. Meeting my hunting partners. Bye unc."

At that juncture Jim commented, "Maybe we could take one of the smaller ones?"

"I would prefer to keep the smaller ones." Pointing to the huge 10-point buck with antlers that would place well up in Boone and Crocket, Kolman continued, "Tell you what, you're pretty good guys. Why don't you take the big one for $55. Who wants him?"

"I'll, ah hah, take him," said Miller. "Nice Antlers. My buddies will never believe I shot him. Ah Hah, you won't tell will you Norm?"

"For $55 I won't. You have huntin' podners in the area?"

"Yeah answered Jim, "They are hunting in the Hemlock Lake area."

"Would they be interested in buying one of these deer?"

"Ah hah, they may be, "We'll ask them. You may hear from us.

"Norman assisted Jim in cutting the buck down and tying it on the trunk of the Thunderbird as Miller struggled to get his wallet from under his hunting trousers. Handing his tag to Chizek he said, "Tag, ah hah the deer for me."

Kolman took the tag from Jim, "Here I'll take care of that." Reaching into his pocket he pulled out a jack knife, cut the tag from the buck and snapped Miller's tag onto the gambrel of the hind leg.

"$55 please," said Holman as he reached out and accepted the proffered money from Miller.

Returning to the house, he entered and came back with a middle-aged woman. Pointing to the investigators he confided in her, "Take a good look at these fellows, if I'm not here when they return, sell them the deer."

After buying the deer from Norman Kolman and tagging it with a metal evidence seal, the three investigators met with local Ranger Loyal Abney and hung the deer at his farm. As a group they made a decision not make an immediate arrest or seize the other two bucks offered for sale as they were short of time and wanted to proceed with their investigation of Larry Jones and other suspects in the area.

Since it was earlier than Jones usually appeared at Ducks Bar they agreed to eat supper at the Cedars where they could relax a little after a grueling week of investigation and revel in their success at making the buy from Kolman.

Looking forward to a leisurely supper, they made one last check of Ducks on the way to the Cedars. Suddenly the investigators came to life as Jones' car was spotted.

"He's here now," exhorted Rubesch as Jack wheeled his Thunderbird around the block.

Always serious Rubesch put the damper on their enthusiasm, "I hope Kolman doesn't realize he's been had and spread the word. These guys all know each other and keep each other posted."

"I don't think he's had time to tell many people," interjected Chizek.

"We'll give old Larry, ah hah, a try right now," breathed Miller, "Time to go into my act."

"But what about deer tags?" wondered Chizek. "We've just used your buck tag Jack. What do you think Joe?"

"We don't have time to go back to Hiles and pick up more tags. We'll just have to wing it. He probably won't know the difference anyway. Drop me off at my car and try Jones."

Entering the bar the investigators immediately seated themselves alongside Jones in the middle of the bar.

"How ya doin' Larry,?" asked Miller.

"Real good. Did you guys do any good today?"

"We haven't shot a deer yet."

Hesitating in his reply Jones breathed, "Well maybe I can help you out."

"We may take you up on that," replied Jack.

"You guys look thirsty. I'll buy a round. What kind of deer do you want. A big one or a little one?"

"Ah hah," grunted Miller, "Guess."

Jones turned to Chizek, who said, "A deer is a deer."

As the drinks were served Jones gestured toward the booths at the rear, "Let's go back there and discuss a transaction. As they sat down he asked, "Now where are you guys from?"

Chizek replied, "I'm from Portage and Jack is from Antioch."

"How do I know that? Are you guys willing to prove where you are from. I know game wardens sometimes buy deer in taverns. Happened to a friend of mine. Right here in this bar. That warden better never set foot in here again. You guys are not game wardens,? Are you?"

"Are you kidding jibed Chizek. The last person we want to see is a warden."

"O.K. get out your drivers licenses."

"Hmm, let's see, Jim Sievert from Portage. O.K. and your Jack Millston from Antioch. It just happens I have a friend here who now lives in Antioch. Hey George," gestured Jones, "Come over here."

As the tall hefty man shoved into the booth he said, "George this man is from Antioch. I want to sell him a deer. Check him out."

"O.K., Where do the main highways run in Antioch?"

Sure glad I went to Antioch to check it out. He answered, "Highway 83, ah hah, runs north and south and highway 173 runs east and west.."

"Anyone could know that by just looking at a map. Where is the firehouse in Antioch?"

"It's located near the old hotel directly across the street from the John Teresi auto dealership and furthermore the mayors name is, ah hah, John Tobeson."

Turning to Jones, George said, "Sell them the deer."

Pointing to Chizek, Jones asked, "You want a deer too."

"Yeah, I don't have a deer yet."

"I have two bucks for sale. The price is $75."

"Seventy five dollars," That's a little high."

"Take it or leave it," he angrily blurted. "I'm taking a big chance selling you the deer. Well what's your answer?"

Chizek reigning reluctance, replied "Think its a little high but I'll take it."

Face lighting up, Jones retorted, "You won't be sorry. I have two nice bucks for you."

"O.K. ah hah, "Let's go out and load them on my car."

"Not now, I don't have them here."

"Well then, ah hah, how about delivering them to the motel at Hiles. That's where we're staying."

"Are you going there now."

"We're going to eat," said Chizek. "I'm mighty hungry. We'll be eating at the Cedars."

"O.K., Don't worry about it. I'll contact you. Go on and enjoy your supper. What room are you in the motel."

"Number one."

Partially through their meal at the very quiet, half-empty Cedars nightclub, Jones walked toward their table, his disheveled flaming red hair giving one the impression he was excited and scared. He shouted, "I'm ready to deliver your deer."

"Can we finish eating first Larry?" asked Jim.

"I want to see your deer tags first."

"Deer tags, Why?"

"Voice increasing he responded. Get 'em out. I want to see 'em."

"O.K.," said Chizek unwinding the tag from his hunting hat.

Handing it back he continued, "Where's your tag Jack?"

Miller thought, *man what a situation. Many tags for every unit in a box and I don't have the right one.*

"I've got to tell you the truth, my tag is on a buck."

"On a buck he shouted. And you want to buy a deer?"

Suddenly embarrassed, the investigators glanced around the room at the diners. They were stunned by the wild scene and sat silent staring at them, some with forks or spoons suspended motionless in mid air.

"Well Larry I do have a ah hah, party permit tag."

"Party permit," he blurted, his red hair now flying about as in a high wind. What do you take me for? There's no party permit in this area."

"My party permit is from the, ah hah, Prentice area."

After a string of profanities he shouted, "I'm not selling you a deer on a party permit. I've got a buck and it takes a buck tag."

Chizek interrupted to see if he could salvage the deal. "Look Larry, what difference does it make what kind of a tag Jack puts on the deer. Selling it is illegal anyway and so is buying."

"But Jack may get caught with the wrong tag on the deer."

"So what. How will that effect you?"

"You may tell where you got it."

"We won't tell. Let us worry about it. If we get caught we'll just have to pay up."

"Well maybe. O.K.. You guys just lay $150 on the table and leave. The deer will be on your car."

"On my, ah hah, car? Do you know which car is mine."

"I know. The Thunderbird with Illinois plates on it."

With a fearful glance about the room, he realized that everyone had heard and turned to leave. Stopping just short of the door he turned and yelled, "Leave the money, the deer will be on your car in five minutes."

Gazing at the perplexed faces of the other diners, the two deliberated as to how they should proceed. Chizek broke the silence. "Get out your money Jack," he said with a wink and a smile.

"The guy must think we're crazy if he, ah hah, believes we're about to leave a pile of money on the table."

"The waitress will think, what a tip. Let's just wait around a little and see what happens." After a half-hour the two paid their bill and retreated to their auto where they waited another 15 minutes.

"What do you, ah ah, think Jim?"

"I think the guy is crazy dangerous. Perhaps the deal is off. I just don't know. I certainly can now understand why the people around here are afraid of him."

"He may still come through at the, ah hah, motel."

Meeting Rubesch at the motel, the three discussed the unusual way things had played out while unpacking their bags. Their conversation was interrupted by a loud knocking on the door. The motel owner delivered a message that their was a phone call for the man with the Thunderbird.

Upon answering the call Miller found it was Larry Jones. "Why didn't you guys wait? I brought the deer to the Cedars and you were gone."

"You said you would deliver the deer in five minutes. We waited over a half hour."

"O.K.. I'll be at your motel within a half-hour with the deer."

"We'll be waiting."

At the knock on the door Rubesch hustled into the bathroom where he could hide and listen to the conversation.

Opening the door Chizek was greeted by Larry Jones and a young man he had never seen before.

Jones said, "The deer are here."

"O.K.. we'll take a look at them."

Stepping into the cold, starlit, snowy night the investigators saw a black sedan they had never seen before parked alongside Jack's Thunderbird with two buck heads covered with powdery snow protruding from under the trunk lid.

"Gesturing broadly Jones said, "Just as I said two nice bucks."

"Are they shot up?" asked Chizek.

"Shot up. Of course they're shot. Do you want them or not?"

"Well I think we should take a look at them."

"Look you'll take them as they are or we're leaving. I don't want this deal to take any longer then necessary. Do you want them?"

"O.K., ah hah," said Miller, money in hand, "We'll take them."

The men cut the rope with a large hunting knife and jerked the two deer from the trunk as Chizek, heart in throat, tried to make himself invisible. He made several swipes at the snow-covered license plate in an effort to get the number in the pale light. The two men swiftly dragged them around their auto and loaded them into Miller's trunk.

Extending his hand, Jones whispered, "Quick give me your tags.

Let's get these deer tagged and get out of here before someone suspects what we're up too." Fumbling at his hip, he again produced the large hunting knife. He leaned over and deftly slit the gambrel of each deer's legs and snapped on the tags. Turning to Miller he remarked, "There now it's up to you to explain why you have the wrong tag on your deer." Turning he again extended his hand, "That will be $150."

"O.K.," murmured Miller handing his pre-recorded bills toward the unknown man.

"Wait just a minute," shouted Jones, holding out his hand, "Pay the boss."

"Oh you're the boss," Gesturing toward the tall thin man he asked, "Ah hah, Who is this?"

"Never mind, just give me the money." Thumbing through the bills, he extended his palm toward Chizek and said "$75." He again was paid with pre-recorded bills.

As the car headlights disappeared Miller asked, "Did you, ah ah, get their license number?"

"I only got the first three digits. The snow was packed on that plate so hard I couldn't knock it off. I was afraid they would see me do it. I tried about half a dozen times. No soap."

After the two had left Rubesch said, "I'm going to Ducks to see if Larry comes back to brag about his sale and see if I can identify the other guy."

"You be careful Joe," warned Chizek, "Jones threatened you."

"It's been a few years. I'll make myself as inconspicuous as possible."

After tagging the deer as evidence, the two began writing their incident reports, waiting anxiously for Rubesch's return.

Entering Ducks Bar about 8:45 p.m. that evening Rubesch luckily found the establishment crowded. He melded into the red and orange clad mass. Looking the crowd over, he was relieved that George Patak was not among them. He recognized Larry Jones as he entered the bar with Jerry Busher the self-proclaimed lawyer that the courts sometimes allowed to represent defendants in spite of the fact that he had never gone to law school. From the investigator's description, it was obvious that Busher was not the unidentified man who had delivered the deer. Sitting several bar stools from them he ordered a hot beef sandwich and listened to Jones brag to a group of about seven or eight men and several women.

He told of how he had sold the deer and how he had hurried the transaction so the hunters would not look the deer over as one of the bucks was a car killed deer with several broken legs. He related the best buck was the one with the small rack. One of the ladies asked him if he thought the purchasers were the law. He replied, "I was scared, but I'm sure they weren't wardens."

His jovial mood was shattered when from the rear of the room another lady came forward, "You sold deer to those guys?"

"Well yeah, Why?"

"I recognized one of them. I can't tell you his name but I know he is a warden from south of here."

Suddenly the bar became silent as Jone's face paled and his jaw fell slack in despair.

Rubesch gaining as much information as he needed left the bar to return to Hiles and report what he had heard.

Since Jones and his friends knew where they were staying, they discussed whether they might exact revenge. Knowing the reputation of him and his cronies, they concluded the best part of valor is cowardice and decided the state would have to pay for two rooms that night as they retreated to the Cutless Motel in Antigo.

Milling about, happy about their recent success, the trio began jesting and telling stories of past experiences. Chizek asked Miller, "Is this where you stayed with Ernie and Joe when you bought the deer they couldn't?"

Miller told the story of how he tested the temper of Warden Ernie Meress at Marshfield.

"Yeah, ah hah. It took skill and talent."

Even though he had heard the story before, Chizek said, "Tell me about it."

"Ah hah, they needed the A-Team up near Pickerel so Joe sent me up there to, ah hah, buy a deer. Not much of a task for the old master. I bought the deer and met Joe, Ernie and Ed Hill here. They told me how they, ah hah, had screwed up and scared the guy off when he was offering his deer for sale. The guy told them, ah hah, they were wardens and to get the hell out of his bar. He said he could spot them as wardens a mile off. Didn't surprise me. Ah hah, I started to rib Ernie. Well you know how damn mad he, ah hah, gets. Temper like a firecracker. He just can't take a ribbing so I, ah hah, poured it on."

Finally Ed said, "We're not far from that bar. Why don't you go over there and show us how the A-Team works. I said O.K.. It'll, ah hah, be like taking candy from a baby. I said I'll be right back. So, ah hah, I went over to the bar, went into my act and bought the deer and returned. Ernie, ah hah, really got steamed when I told them what the bartender told me."

"What did he tell you?" Chizek asked with bated breath.

"You know how Joe always wears those moccasins thinking hunters will be convinced ah hah, that he has just come in from hunting and changed out of his field boots? Well this guy said, ah hah, Two guys were just in here trying to buy my deer. But I knew they were game wardens. Ah hah, because the tall one was wearing bedroom slippers and the little one was just plain stupid. Ah hah, Ernie began to swear at the guy. Ah hah, ha ha I couldn't pass up the opportunity to give it to Ernie. I ah hah, told him 'stupid' was not my word, the guy just picked him out. I had him so mad, I Ah hah thought for health reasons I'd better clam up."

"Later, as I was writing my incident report I couldn't ah hah, resist one more jab, So ah hah, I asked him how do you spell stupid, with one or two 'Ts?' Jim, I actually thought he was going to kill me."

"Does that mean I'm on the A-Team?"

"Ah hah, you bet. Anyone working with me is on the A-Team."

On November 30, the day after the deer season, Chizek journeyed from Park Falls to Crandon to discuss the deer selling cases with District Attorney Robert Kennedy.

Upon entering the courthouse, Chizek met local Warden Max Harter, who asked, "Jim would you like to say hello to an old buddy?"

"Old buddy? Who?"

"Norm Kolman."

"Is he around?"

"Yeah, just saw him downstairs. It would be fun to see his expression when he sees you in uniform."

"It sure would. Lead on."

Following Harter's direction Chizek spotted Kolman in the corridor. Approaching from the rear he was along side of him before he spoke, "Hi Norm."

A combination of recognition, fear and confusion crossed Kolman's face, his mind attempting to comprehend and deal with who he was seeing. "Ah ah."

"Remember me Norman?"

He visibly tried to control his concern and voice, "Ah, ah, ah, No sir. Ah, I've never seen you before in my life."

"Come on Norman, the fat is in the fire, You've seen me before."

With the guilty look of a dog caught stealing eggs, Kolman turned on his heel and beat a hasty retreat down the hall.

Watching at a discreet distance down the hall Harter, chuckled with a wink, "He didn't remember you."

Chizek updated District Attorney Kennedy on the two individuals involved in the Kolman case. It was decided to charge Kolman with selling a deer. George Check, the middle man, would be called as a prosecution witness. It was further decided to charge Larry Jones with two counts of selling deer and two counts of possessing untagged deer.

Complaints were signed by Chizek before leaving Crandon.

In spite of the fact that key witness, George Check, who lived in Skokie, Illinois did not respond to a subpoena as a prosecution witness, the Kolman trial began at 10 a.m. on June 23, 1972 at the Forest County Court House in Crandon. A plea of not guilty was entered by his attorney Carl Jason of Milwaukee. The trial was long and bitterly fought out, Judge Fowle often interceding between the two attorneys.

Chizek was the first state witness. His testimony although very straight forward was pounded by Jason. Over the objections of the district attorney and admonishment by the judge, he constantly preached the theory of entrapment to the jury. His defense was based on the fact that the wardens had dressed as hunters, rode around in a fancy Thunderbird car displaying Illinois plates, and had entrapped him. He pointed out that Chizek was attempting to gather sympathy from the jury by walking with a cane. After five hours on the witness stand, Chizek breathed a sigh of relief as Miller took the stand.

At one time, he testified that the investigators had gone to the Kolman home to buy a deer. Jason hammered him on the statement. Kennedy brought out the fact the that the investigators had been directed to the Kolman residence by Check and that the wardens charge was to buy deer illegally held for sale.

Jerry Kryka and Dick Abney testified that along with Max Harter they had tagged the deer with an evidence seal and transported the deer to the Crystal Lake Fish Hatchery where it was held for evidence. He questioned Abney as to whether the seal placed on the deer could or had been tampered with or removed during the long storage period.

Throughout the case, Attorney Jason attempted to persuade the jury that the wardens had entrapped Kolman. He often tried to get their testimony thrown out when they testified to conversations held between them and Gerald Check because Check wasn't present for cross-examination. Judge Fowle stepped in several times to stop the wrangling over the subject. He firmly ruled the testimony could be taken as in every case because the wardens were testifying to something within their own knowledge. He further ruled the wardens were testifying as a result of a one party conversation which the hearsay rule didn't apply to.

Kolman in denying he had sold the deer to the wardens admitted he had taken the money and helped cut the deer down and tie it on their car. When Kennedy asked who he gave the money to he answered, "I kept it."

"Did you spend it?"

"You betcha."

After the prosecution had all its evidence in, Attorney Jason asked to make several legal motions in chambers. He began, "If it pleases the court, at this time the defense would move for dismissal based upon the testimony of Warden Miller which in effect proves entrapment in the matter of law and accordingly we would move that the matter be dismissed based on the testimony of the state agent, Mr. Miller, that they went out to the Kolman residence for an express avowed purpose of buying deer which indicates that it was the state agents that were the moving party who had intended to buy the deer...even assuming that all the rest of their testimony is correct."

District Attorney Kennedy responded, "They went there to buy the deer. They didn't go there to trap anybody. The thrust of the testimony is such that we didn't entrap anybody. It was obviously the testimony of Mr. Kolman that he spontaneously and readily sold the deer. He needed no persuasion and no persuasion was given. There is no evidence of entrapment, so I oppose your motion."

Judge Fowle ruled, "In denying your motion, I wish to cite Wisconsin law. It recognizes that, in the enforcement of the law, it is often necessary for law enforcement officers to set traps to catch criminals by offering them the freest opportunity to commit offenses which they are disposed to commit. Some inducement, encouragement, or solicitation by law enforcement officers is therefor permissible. But it is not proper for them to use excessive incitement, urging, persuasion, or temptation which is likely to induce the commission of an offense by a person not already disposed to commit an offense of that kind."

The jury retired to deliberate at 6 p.m. Eighteen minutes later they returned with a guilty verdict.

Judge Fowle imposed a penalty of $200 or 30 days in jail, plus a mandatory 10 days in jail.

Scanning the crowd Chizek noticed Kolman holding hands with two women who were crying, "Max, who are those women with Kolman?"

"They are his wife and his girlfriend. Guess they have an understanding relationship between them."

It was brought to the attention of the wardens in court that the witnesses after finding Kolman guilty, were afraid of retribution and requested an armed escort to there homes. It took several hours to round up enough law enforcement officers to do this. Between the wardens available and the Forest County Sheriff's Office each and every juror was escorted safely to their homes.

Because of delays in scheduling, the Larry Jones case dragged on for nearly two years. Finally scheduled for March 23, 1973, a last minute glitch threatened the existence of the case. The day before the trial it became known that the Forest County District attorney could not be available on the scheduled court day. Judge Fred Fowle declared because the case had languished so long he was not going to delay it further. He stated if the case was not tried as scheduled he would dismiss it.

In a quandary as to how to proceed Deputy Chief Warden Harold Hettrick contacted the attorney general's office and asked that one of their attorneys represent the state. He emphasized the importance of the case in that if dismissed the uncontrolled game violations and intimidation of the citizenry of Forest County would continue.

Assistant Attorney General Paul J. Gossens received a telephone call about 1 p.m. asking that he represent the state in the case on the following day.

Gossens a young passionate attorney called his wife and asked her to pack a bag for him and meet him at Truax Airfield. Little did he realize he was setting off to his greatest adventure as an attorney general. Without knowing what the case was about he packed a set of Wisconsin Criminal Statutes and hurried to Truax. He was met there by a department of natural resources plane who was transporting John Potter, chairman of the Natural Resources Board, to Wisconsin Rapids. After dropping Potter off, the plane landed at Clintonville where another board member, Larry Dahl disembarked on his way to Tigerton where he lived.

When the plane was back in the air the pilot, Kenny Beghin, asked, "Where too?"

Paul responded, "I have no idea. I thought you knew."

Beghin turned the plane and landed again at Clintonville where he used the pay phone. After many calls he finally made contact with Hettrick, who told him to deliver Gossen's to Rhinelander.

After landing at Rhinelander, Gossens was met by Joe Rubesch and Ed Hill in plain cloths who escorted him to the Cutless Motel in Antigo. There, they booked him under an assumed name. Wondering why all the cloak and dagger antics, he inquired as to what was going on and what was the case all about. He was told to go to his room. The case would be explained at dinner.

That evening, the two investigators accompanied by Ed Hill and Joe Rubesch met him. As they dined, Miller and Chizek told their story along with some of the history of the area and the terrible intimidation foisted on the people of the area and how important it was to not only get the case tried but to convict Jones in Forest County. They told him that as far as they knew, there had never been a conviction by a jury for selling deer in the county except for the recent trial of Norman Kolman. Rubesch related how he had bought a deer several years earlier from George Patak who was Larry Jones' buddy. He explained further that although Patak now lived in Antioch, Illinois, he often returned to Crandon where he was one of the bad bunch that intimidated the local people. He continued, "While we got him tried he got off on a hung jury." Gossens took it all in as the wardens told horror story after horror story of how the gang was decimating fish and game and stealing timber in the area.

Spending a good share of the night preparing the prosecutions case, Gossens was roused sleepily from his bed early the next day by Ed Hill, who along with Joe Rubesch proceeded to the Crystal Lake Fish Hatchery where the two evidence deer had been stored. Placing them on top of their vehicle they drove to Crandon.

Eating their breakfast in a restaurant, John Beggar, the defense attorney was pointed out to Gossens as he sat eating and priming his witnesses. He told the wardens he had previously met Begger while representing DNR on some environmental issues.

Chizek gulped in dismay as the two stiffly frozen evidence deer were carried into the courtroom and laid in front of the judges bench.

I can't believe this. Someone cut the tails off the deer. We may lose this case. The defense may get it thrown out if they can establish the evidence was available to a number of people and could have been tampered with. Cutting the tails off is obviously tampering. Hope Beggar doesn't come up with that kind of defense. We would be hard pressed showing they weren't tampered with.

The old elegant courthouse was spacious with perhaps room for 300 people, an eagle and a flag impressively displayed above the bench. At 8:00 a.m. the bailiff called out, "All rise." As the caped judge entered the room he called out, "Court is now in session. The honorable Judge Fred Fowle presiding."

Seated near the juror's box the defendant Larry Jones sat with his attorney. Jone's subdued demeanor and well-groomed red hair and clothing belayed the wild night at the Cedars.

Judge Fowle began by introducing himself, the defense and the prosecution to the jury. He continued, "First of all, I would like to tell you that this is a very important case that you are about to hear. It's of importance because it has to do with the preservation of one of the great natural resources of the state of Wisconsin. The case itself involves the alleged violation of game laws. The legislature has seen fit to develop comprehensive legislation, not only for the purpose of giving those people of the citizenry an equal right in perpetuating the herd, the herd of deer, particularly concerned in this matter because of its beneficial nature and connection with our recreation business. This is the fourth largest business in the state of Wisconsin and particularly in this area, we are well aware of the value it has for our economic welfare. Now this matter, you will hear is set forth in the form of a complaint, initially, and in this complaint, the defendant is charged with an alleged crime."

He then explained the specific charges, two counts of selling deer illegally and two counts of possessing untagged deer.

A six-person jury was solemnly seated by the bailiff and the trial began with Gossens laying out the prosecutions case.

"Members of the jury the state will demonstrate that Larry Jones sold two deer to Special Investigator Wardens James Chizek and Jack Miller. While perhaps the wardens provided Jones the opportunity, they in no way entrapped him into this illegal act. In fact they may have provided an inducement to sell them the deer. This is not an act of entrapment on their part. Mr. Jones had poached these deer with a purpose. He had them for sale. Further we will show that these deer were not legally tagged by the defendant."

Defense Attorney John Beggar made his opening remarks for the defense, "Members of the jury the defense will show to your satisfaction that these two gentlemen sitting over there, Mr. Chizek and Mr. Miller came to Forest County as strangers for the avowed and express purpose of hanging one on Larry Jones. Hanging the crime of selling a deer on Mr. Jones when it was their idea in the first place. We expect to show these gentlemen made the rounds of the local bars in the city of Crandon and enticed my client Mr. Jones with strong drinks. Enough drinks to induce Mr. Jones into selling them a deer. They weren't here in the first place, that is they weren't local residents and they were snooping around to try to entrap somebody into selling a deer which is prohibited, of course, by statutes of the state of Wisconsin, as his honor Judge Fowle read you earlier. Mr. Jones never saw these gentlemen before and I'm sure they never saw him before. We expect the evidence will show that they were setting Mr. Jones up into selling a deer. If you so find and you are satisfied that they were the moving party as agents of the state of Wisconsin and it was their intent, if they induced Mr. Jones to do this, then that is what the law calls legal entrapment."

"I object your honor," intoned Gossens. Entrapment is not an issue at this point."

"I have a right to tell them what we—"

Judge Fowle interrupted, "The objection of the prosecutor is sustained and for the record counsel I wish to point out that entrapment is evidentiary in nature and you are entitled to every affirmative defense for the welfare of your client, but this court believes that in your opening address to the jury, you are dealing in a conclusion when you talk about entrapment. I sustain the motion."

"But your honor I would like to just tell the jury what we expect to show and entrapment—-"

"Enough Mr. Defense Counsel. You will be given adequate opportunity to discuss entrapment at the time you and the Mr. Gossens make requests for the instructions to the jury when they are about to develop their verdict."

There were only two or three people in the front row of the court house as Gossens called his first witness. With local Conservation Warden Max Harter at the prosecution table, Gossens presented the states case. The two investigators were called to the stand where they related how they had spent several days in the Crandon area, habituating the local taverns in order to get noticed and give the impression they were slob hunters. Jack's rotund figure, balding head and his fancy Thunderbird car bearing Illinois plates fitted the bill to a tee. They admitted putting on an act to portray that they were not anxious to get into the woods. The fact Chizek could not walk very far and walked with a cane enhanced their portrayal. Gossens pointed out his use of a cane was not a visual aid as he had recently had a total hip replacement, the result of a car accident while working deer shiners.

He questioned the two wardens extensively as their story was listened to intently by the jury. They told how they had met Larry Jones in Ducks Bar and became acquainted with him as he was suspected of selling deer in the area. They testified that they had bought him several drinks during this period with him reciprocating in kind.

Chizek testified first. Gossens realizing that entrapment and inducement would be Jones' defense, concentrated on the number of drinks that were purchased by the investigators and the language used during the transaction.

"Mr. Chizek what was your purpose in being in the Crandon area during the deer season of 1971."

"Jack Miller and I were assigned to investigate the illegal selling of deer in the Crandon area."

"Now Mr. Chizek, how many nights were you in Duck's Bar in Crandon?"

"Four nights during the deer season, the 23, 24, 25, and 26 of November."

"And what night did you meet Larry Jones."

"The first night we were in Ducks Bar."

"Did you know who you were talking too?"

"Yes sir, we had a description of Jones. He was easy to spot because of his vivid red hair."

"And what was your conversation about?"

"Deer hunting. Everyone was talking about hunting deer."

"And did you buy him drinks?"

"Yes sir."

"How many?"

"Several each night."

"And was Larry Jones in the bar every night?"

"Yes he was."

"Do you know how many drinks you actually purchased for Mr. Jones?"

"Yes sir, I have them noted in my field notes. Can I refer to them?"

"Yes you may."

"Now wait a minute interjected defense counsel John Beggar. The defense hasn't been privy to those notes. I would like to see them."

Judge Fowle agreed that if the notes were to be used, the defense must be able to examine them. He called a short recess during which Beggar reviewed the notes. "Now Mr. Gossens you may continue."

"Mr. Chizek would you tell the court how many drinks you and investigator Miller actually purchased for Mr. Jones.

Notes in hand he read, "On November 23 we bought two, on November 24 we bought one, on November 25 we bought two and on November 26 we bought none as we were in the bar only about 15 minutes. Larry bought us one drink during the time the transaction for the deer was being made."

"And did Jones buy you drinks prior to the 26 when you bought the deer from him?"

"Yes he did, I didn't record them but it was one or two each night."

"Did Jones take any precautions before he sold you the deer?"

"Yes, he checked my drivers license which gave my name as James Sievert of Portage. He then had an acquaintance who we did not know question Jack about Antioch, Illinois where Jack claimed to reside. The man asked a number of questions to determine if Jack in fact lived in Antioch. Later we determined the man was George Patak who lived in Antioch. He finally stated, Sell them the deer."

"And did he tell you why he was questioning you thusly?"

"He said he had to be careful as he had been arrested for several game violations. He also said a friend of his had been arrested for selling a deer in Ducks Bar. He also kidded George Patak about being arrested there. George commented that he had the last laugh as the jury had hung and he had got off scott free."

"Did you ever ask to buy a deer?"

"No we did not."

"Did you give the impression you were open to buying a deer?

"Yes, our assignment was to investigate the illegal sale of deer in the Crandon area. We complained about our luck in hunting"

"Why were you in Duck's Bar?"

"Larry Jones was one of the suspects we were working on. We knew Ducks was his favorite hangout"

"Did you place a dollar figure on what you were willing to pay for a deer?"

"No, Larry offered the deer for $75 each. I complained it was too high, but agreed to pay the price."

"Was $75 more than the deer was worth?"

"No, we've paid much more for deer under the same circumstances. It's hard to place a fair price on something that's illegal to sell."

And what if anything then happened?"

"Jack and I went to the Cedars to eat. Jones followed us to the Cedars Night Club in an effort to sell us the deer."

"Yes he told us he would deliver the deer to the Cedars and we should leave the money, $150, on the table and leave. He said the deer would be on our car in the parking lot. He actually caused quite a ruckus in the nightclub,"

Begger objected, "Your honor this witness is trying to besmirch my client. This case is about selling deer. Let's stick to the subject."

"Objection sustained, carry on Mr. Prosecutor."

"And did you leave the money and leave?"

"No sir."

"You were not that foolish."

"Right."

"And then what did you do?"

"We went out to our car. There were no deer there so we went to our motel in Hiles."

"And did Jones know where you were staying?"

"Yes, we told him we were staying in the Hiles Motel in room number one while we were in Ducks Bar."

"Continue, Mr. Chizek what if anything happened then?"

"We were only in our room a short time when Jones called the manager asking for the man who owned the Thunderbird. Jack went to the phone. Larry was mad because we hadn't waited for him at the Cedars. He said he would deliver the deer in a half hour."

"Then what happened?"

"In a short time someone knocked at the door. It was Jones along with another man that we did not know?"

"At that time did you buy the deer?"

"Yes the two men had two buck deer in their trunk. They unloaded the deer and loaded them into Jack's car."

"Who accepted payment for the deer?"

"Jack tried to have the unknown man identify himself by paying him. Larry interceded by saying, Pay the boss and took the money."

"Did you stay in the motel in Hiles that night?"

"No, we went to Antigo to stay, because of Jones' actions in the Cedars and his reputation. We were afraid of being retaliated against."

Begger objected, "Your honor the prosecution is demeaning my client. This trial is not about his reputation. It's about selling deer."

"Objection sustained," intoned the judge."

"I have nothing further your honor."

Begger began cross examination with, "Mr. Chizek, That is your name isn't it?"

"Yes sir."

"It's not Sievert as you were known to Mr. Jones."

"No sir, Sievert was a made up name I used while doing undercover work."

"You used an alias as a means to entrap Mr. Jones."

"No sir, we did not entrap Jones."

"You and Mr. Miller came to Crandon in an automobile with Illinois plates on it using aliases and you say you did not entrap Mr. Jones. How were you dressed?"

"In hunting clothing, red jackets displaying deer hunting backtags."

"And were you hunting in the "Crandon area?"

"No, we were not."

"Your purpose and intent in coming to Crandon dressed like hunters, using aliases in an automobile with Illinois plates was an attempt to see if you could get my client to commit a crime."

"That's argumentative," objected Gossens."

"For selling deer."

"It is argumentative." repeated Gossens.

"Sustained, The officer testified that his purpose for being in the Crandon area was to investigate the illegal selling of deer. Next question Mr. Defense Attorney."

"I have nothing further."

Gossens then called Jack Miller to the stand. After identifying him as a special investigator he asked, "Mr. Miller have you been in court during this trial up to this point?"

"Yes."

"You heard the testimony of Mr. Chizek where he referred to you as Jack Miller. Are you that Jack Miller?"

"I am, ah ah, sir."

"And were you with Mr. Chizek at Ducks Bar on November 26, 1971 and left the bar together?"

"We did."

"What time did you enter Duck's bar?"

"About 5 p.m."

"And did Larry Jones offer to sell you a deer at Duck's Bar?"

"He offered to sell both, ah hah, Mr. Chizek and I a deer."

"Would you tell me how this transaction came about?"

"Yes, ah hah, Jones who we had met several days earlier and got to know asked me if we had gotten a deer yet. I told him no. He said maybe I can help you out. He then bought us a round."

"Did you or Mr. Chizek buy Jones any drinks that night?"

"We did not."

"Did you ever buy him any drinks?"

"We bought him several drinks in the days before the 26."

"O.K., Continue with what happened."

"Jones asked me, ah hah, what kind of deer do you want, a big one or a little one. I answered, him, ah hah, guess. He also asked Jim what kind of deer he wanted. Jim told him, ah hah, a deer is a deer. He then asked us, ah hah, to join him in a booth in the rear to make a deal. In the booth he checked our, ah ah, identification, because he said he was afraid we were game wardens. He knew I was driving a car with Illinois plates on it. When he, ah hah, found I was claiming to live in Antioch, Illinois he called over a friend who, ah hah, lived there. A man named George joined us and, ah ah, quizzed me on areas in Antioch. Having visited Antioch to back up my assumed name I, ah hah, answered his questions correctly. George then said, ah ah, 'Sell him the deer.' He then said he had, ah hah, two bucks for sale and he wanted $75 for each. Larry got mad when Jim ah hah told him $75 was too much. But we agreed to buy the two deer at his, ah hah, price.

"And was $75 too much to pay for a deer?"

A ripple of laughter echoed across the crowded courthouse at his answer.

"Now sir that was a very fairly priced deer. I have paid a lot more."

"Oh you have bought deer before?"

"I have sir, live and dead."

"What if anything happened then Mr. Miller?"

Because he didn't have the deer with him he said he would, ah hah, deliver them to our motel in Hiles. Telling him we were going to the Cedars to, ah hah, eat we left."

"Then if anything, happened?"

"We had just been served our meal when Jones, ah hah, entered the Cedars and wanted to deliver the deer right away. He checked my, ah hah, party permit and argued that he could not sell us a deer because, ah hah, my party permit was issued for the Prentice area. We finally convinced him, ah hah, it did not make any difference where the permit was, ah hah, valid because sale of a deer was illegal anyway. He told us to leave, ah hah, $150 on the table and leave and the deer would be on my, ah hah, car."

"Did you do this?"

"No, we finished eating and left for Hiles."

"Go on Mr. Miller."

I received a phone call at the, ah hah, motel from Jones who was, ah hah, mad because we didn't wait for him at the Cedars. He said he would deliver the deer to our motel, ah hah, in a half hour."

"Did Jones deliver the deer."

"He sure did, him and another, ah hah, man who we did not know."

"You then bought the deer?"

"Yes we each paid him $75 for the two, ah hah buck deer."

"Did Larry appear drunk when he delivered the deer?"

"No he seemed, ah hah, belligerent."

"I have nothing further, your witness Mr. Begger."

"Mr. Miller," began Begger "You and Mr. Chizek came to Crandon to induce someone like my client Larry Jones to commit a crime? Is that correct?"

"No sir we, ah ah, came to Crandon to investigate the illegal sale of deer in the area."

"You owned the fancy Thunderbird car bearing Illinois plates to entrap Mr. Jones. Is that correct?"

"It is correct that my wife, ah hah, owns the Thunderbird bearing Illinois plates–"

"Is that not using subterfuge?"

"I object your honor," cut in Gossens, "The defense has asked a question and won't allow him to answer it fully."

Judge Fowle agreed, "Let him answer the question."

"O.K., Go ahead Mr. Miller. Do you remember the question?"

"Yes, ah hah, The car was used to fool people as to our identity. It is, ah hah, not true that we entrapped Mr. Jones. We provided him the opportunity to, ah hah, sell us a deer. But we did not ask him to sell one to us. He, ah hah, was the one who suggested it."

"He suggested it after you bought him enough drinks to muddle his mind, Is that not correct?"

"No sir, ah ah, we bought him a few drinks prior to the 26 when the deer was purchased, but none on the, ah ah, 26. We were only in

Ducks about, ah ah, 15 minutes that evening."

"You were wearing deer hunting clothing as a part of your entrapment scheme, is that right?"

"No sir, We in fact, ah hah, were wearing deer hunting clothing to make them think we were hunting."

"You entrapped Mr. Jones?"

"We may have, ah ah, trapped him but not entrapped him."

"This is no place for smart answers."

"Your honor," intoned Gossens, "I have been very patient but Mr. Begger is badgering the witness. I think Mr. Miller has answered the defense attorney's questions sufficiently as to entrapment."

Judge Fowle interceded, This court is going to impose an objection based on an orderly proceeding. I'm asking both counsels to calm down and quit arguing."

"Very well your honor, I have no more questions of this witness."

As the day wore on, the building began to fill raising the temperature considerable. Slowly the elegance of the old building was sullied as the deer began to thaw and swarms of flies began to awaken and gather around the gaping openings where the deer had been gutted and where the tails had been cut off. Watching this display worried Chizek. *I wonder if the defense attorney is going to take notice that the tails have been cut off the deer? Could we be questioned on this? After all if the tails have been cut off could he not question whether the evidence also could have been tampered with.*

As the trial proceeded, each time Gossens presented testimony that was hurtful to the defense, Begger practically setting in the jury box, would whisper out loud something contradictory to the answer given by the prosecution.

Gossens noticing this asked for a conference in quarters where he asked that the defense attorney be reprimanded for verbalizing matters to the jury.

Denying the accusation did Begger little good as Judge Fowle told him he had indeed also heard the remarks.

Back in court Judge Fowle stated, "Members of the jury it has been brought to my attention that defense attorney Begger has been verbalizing things to you. I have personally heard these remarks and they are inappropriate. Any and all of his remarks will be disregarded by you and Mr. Begger there will be no more of that in my court. Proceed My Gossens."

By noon, the court house was a buzz with spectators. Harter said he knew most of them and most of them were violators who were there to cheer Jones on and use the case as a sort of inservice training for their own purposes. In pointing these people out, he named each one. As wardens not working the area on a regular basis, it was quite surprising that the investigators recognized most of the names. Chizek chuckled, "They have statewide recognition."

The fly population around the deer increased proportionately with the crowd and now was noticeable to everyone. Jim continued to worry that the flies would focus John Beggar on the deer and finally remind him to use the missing tails as a defense in attempting to throw the evidence out by questioning who had handled the deer and who had access to them. *Wonder who cut the tails off? I suppose there could have been a number of employees at the hatchery who could have. We still have tags on them, so maybe we could withstand Begger's questioning.*

After the state had presented their case, the defense moved for dismissal on the grounds of entrapment. This was denied by Judge Fowle who then called a recess. During the recess he called Gossens aside. "See those people sitting in the front row?"

"Why yes, they look like some of the backwoods people I recently saw in the movie Deliverance."

"Do you know why they are here? They are here to see what's going to happen to them next."

The defense called several witnesses. All of their testimony was basically the same. They all said they had been in Duck's bar and saw the two game wardens who they all called the cane man and the fat man approach Larry Jones and buy him many drinks and offer to buy deer from him. One was a very heavy set man who was obviously lying and showed it by his nervousness and heavy perspiration. The jury watched intently as he constantly dabbed at his face with a handkerchief. During a break while he was still on the stand, a court clerk approached Ed Hill and in her Kentucky accent said, "He's a-ly-en."

After Hill told Gossens this, he really hammered the man and accused him of lying and warned him that he could be charged with perjury. The man squirmed on the stand, practically admitting that some of his testimony was untrue. Finally, the man so choked up he could barely speak, was excused by Gossens from the stand.

After listening to the witnesses constantly call the two wardens the cane man and the fat man for a time, Miller complained to Gossens. "Why don't you object to the way they are demeaning us?"

"Object, why should I object? They're helping our case. Look at the jury, There are several overweight people over there and one who looks as though he don't get around to well. I just hope they keep it up. I'm surprised that Begger doesn't stop it himself."

Finally George Patak took the stand. Rubesch had told Gossens that Patak had been a good witness several years earlier when he was charged with selling a deer and had hung the jury. He testified that he also saw the cane man and the fat man buy many drinks for Jones to the point of such drunkenness he could not resist their inducement to sell them deer. "Mr. Patak can you describe an incident on November 26, 1971."

"I came in from hunting and went into Ducks Bar —"

"Is that here in Crandon?"

"Yes and these two gentleman," pointing, he continued, "the cane man and the fat man were sitting in a booth with Larry Jones."

"By the cane man and the fat man, you mean Mr. Miller and Mr. Chizek sitting over there?"

"Yes, everyone in Crandon called them the cane man and the fat man."

"Do you know about what time of day this was?"

"It was just before dark, about 4:30 a.m. in the deer season."

"And what if anything was going on?"

"They were trying to buy a deer from Larry."

"What made you draw this conclusion?"

"They were talking about the price of the deer and they were buying Larry drinks."

"And Larry agreed to get them the deer."

"Yeah he was drunk out of his mind."

On cross-examination, Gossens began by warning Patak of the penalties of perjury. While Patak told the same story as the prior witnesses and referred to the wardens as the cane man and the fat man he seemed to become more and more nervous. Hearing Gossen's continued dire warning of the penalties of perjury had a noticeable effect on his demeanor.

"Now Mr. Patak, you claim the investigators bought Mr. Jones many drinks. How long were they in the bar?"

"I don't know I didn't watch the clock. Long enough to buy a bunch of drinks."

"Did you hear the wardens testimony that they bought no drinks for Jones on November 26?"

"Yes."

"And you still say they did buy drinks?"

"Yes."

The investigators also testified that you assisted Jones in selling the deer. Do you know you could be charged as aiding and abetting in the commission of a crime?"

"No, I didn't help Larry. I just talked to them."

"Are you lying to the court? There are serious penalties for committing perjury."

As the questioning continued with frequent objections by the defense, Patak became increasingly distressed, his voice barely audible. Finally after much sweating and squirming he said, "I'm through. I'm not answering any more questions." Without an objection from Gossens he got up, left the witness stand and walked out of the court house.

As Larry Jones took the stand, the flies swarming around the deer had increased in size and an audible buzz permeated the huge hall. Still Begger did not pick up on the only possible defense that could clear his client. Chizek squirmed on the wooden court bench. *God I hope Begger doesn't question us on who could have tampered with the evidence. No evidence, no conviction.*

"Now Mr. Jones Begger intoned, "Did you in fact sell these deer to these two wardens?"

"Yes sir I did but— —?"

"And did these wardens get you drunk in Duck's bar?"

"Yes sir, several nights running."

"Did you know who they were?"

"I just knew them as the fat man and the cane man. They constantly asked me to get them a deer."

"By get them a deer what did you take that to mean?"

"Well I didn't really know. But they offered to buy deer from me."

"And what did you respond to this request?"

"I told them, I would not sell them a deer. It's illegal."

"And what finally made you decide to get them the deer?"

"I just sort of got sick of listening to them. I knew where I could get a couple deer so I finally relented, being half or all the way in the bag they talked me into doing a foolish thing."

"Did you shoot these deer?"

"No sir."

"Where did you get them?"

"I can't tell that."

"O.K., how much did they offer you for these deer?"

"$75 each."

"Are deer worth that much?"

"No sir. They offered way more than the deer are worth."

"In other words they tempted you with exorbitant remuneration."

"Yeah and if they had not got me drunk, I never would have done it."

"Just how many drinks did they buy you?"

"I'd say eight or 10 each night they were in Ducks."

"And that's enough to make you drunk and make a mistake. Is that correct?"

"Yes sir."

"I'm through with this witness."

The flies late in the afternoon had continued to increase to an alarming number, as the court house had filled up and raised the temperature. The flies drew everyone's attention to the deer. People whispered about the spectacle. After all, there should be no flies in March. There must have been an ideal place for the insects to spend the winter in the vast spaciousness of the grand old building. Begger didn't seem to heed the spectacle that may have given him a good defense. Jim continued to worry. *Glad this thing is about over. It seems I'm the only one who has thought that the evidence could be thrown out of court because of tampering.*

Gossens began with his cross-examination. Now Mr. Jones who killed the deer you sold?"

"I can't tell you that."

"You can't or won't?"

"I won't."

"If they weren't your deer to whom did you give the money you received?"

"No one."

"Did you spend the $150."

"I certainly did."

"You heard the testimony of both wardens. Do you agree as to what happened at Ducks Bar?"

"I do not. The fat man and the cane man both bought me a bunch of drinks the night I sold them the deer. They got me drunk."

"In 15 minutes they got you drunk?"

"They were there a lot longer then that. They were out to get me."

"What time did you go into Ducks Bar on November 26, 1971?"

"About 4.30 p.m."

"What time did the investigators enter Ducks that night?"

"Guess it was about 5 p.m. as they testified."

"What time did you deliver the deer to the motel at Hiles?"

"About 7 p.m.?"

"So in two hours the investigators got you drunk; you went to the Cedars and talked to them while they were eating; you went and picked up the deer and drove to Hiles and sold them the deer."

"Guess so, you've got it all figured out."

"Does it make sense to you?"

"It's good enough for me."

"Good enough for you, but does the jury believe you?"

"Yeah they'll believe me."

Begger interceded, "He's badgering the witness your honor. The witness answered his question."

"Objection sustained."

"You testified that you were offered and paid more than the deer were worth to induce you to sell. Do you consider $75 too much for a deer?"

"I would never pay $75 for a deer?"

"O.K., do you consider $75 too much for a car-killed deer?"

"I never sold them a car killed deer."

"Come now Mr. Jones. The wardens know a car-killed deer when they see one. You sold them a car-killed deer and bragged about it in Ducks Bar. Did you not?"

"Objection your honor cut in Begger, "There has been no testimony presented that Mr. Jones was even in Ducks Bar after the delivery of the deer. My client has already answered the question."

"Objection sustained. The witness has answered that he did not sell the wardens a car-killed deer. Continue Mr. Prosecutor."

Pointing to the buck with the mangled legs Gossens stated, "We'll let the jury decide if this is or is not a car-killed deer. I have nothing further."

Jim breathed a sigh of relief as the testimony concluded at 5 p.m., the flies buzzing a medley around the deer. *Glad that's over, too late now for a defense claiming evidence tampering.*

While the jury was sent out for supper, the court thrashed out the jury instructions. Begger asked that the judge instruct them on a defense of intoxication as a complete defense. He chose to instruct them on a limited defense of intoxication. He refused Begger's request to instruct the jury on the law of entrapment stating, "I haven't heard testimony that would make me believe there were any of the elements of entrapment brought forth in this case."

The court reconvened shortly after 6:30 p.m. to a milling crowd filling the room to capacity. With several raps of the gavel Judge Fowle settled the crowd down. All the seats were taken with the remaining people standing along the walls.

Because Judge Fowle refused to instruct the jury on entrapment, Paul Gossens summed up the state's case by comparing the credability of the prosecution's witnesses with the creditability of the defense witnesses. He stressed the fact that both undercover wardens had no interest in fabricating testimony. He continued, "Both wardens testimony has been consistent with each other. The defendant did in fact admit selling the deer that could only have been poached to be sold. The defense has consistently tried to make a case for the defense of entrapment. The judge has not instructed you the jury on the law of entrapment, so it is not for your consideration. Remember one of the defense witnesses left the stand rather than continue lying and face charges of perjury. You soon will retire to consider this case and come to a finding which I believe can only be guilty on all charges. Thank you."

Defense Attorney John Begger began, "If it pleases the court and ladies and gentlemen of the jury, I would have to disagree with the prosecutor on several of the issues he has so blatantly described in his summary. My client Mr. Jones testified he did not kill the deer in question. While he did sell the deer, he did so only after the undercover agents had bought him numerous drinks on several occasions in Ducks Bar. So many drinks were fed him that he became drunk and unable to control himself. You see those two gentleman over there, Mr. Chizek and Mr. Miller they came to the Crandon area with one thought in mind, to get Mr. Jones to commit a crime. They being the moving party as agents of the state induced Mr. Jones to sell them the deer. Although the judge has not instructed you on the laws of entrapment, it goes without saying that these two gentleman did in fact entrap him."

On rebuttal Gossens reminded the jury that they could not consider the defense of entrapment. He stressed that the integrity of the state's witnesses should be weighed against the integrity of the defendant and his witnesses.

Instruction of the jury by Judge Fowle was undertaken about 7:30 p.m. and the jury sent to the jury room to deliberate.

As the jury left the room, people began circulating small pieces of paper around the room. When asked by Paul Gossens what was going on a court clerk replied, that a pool had been set up and each person would designate on his piece of paper a time when the jury would return. He as the clerk was to note the time when the jury room door knob was turned. The person guessing closest to the time would win the pot. He also told Gossens that it was a foregone conclusion that the verdict would be not guilty, because no one was ever found guilty of selling deer in Forest County. He said the jury would definitely be back within 15 minutes. As a half hour passed, a new set of lottery papers was distributed. An hour after the jury had retired another set of bets was made.

Passing through the crowd to go outdoors for a breath of air, Gossens heard whispered exclamations. "State's man! State's man!"

Waiting for the verdict, Chizek exclaimed, "I thought that case would never end. I thought for sure Begger would see that swarm of flies around those deer and realize he had a defense of tampering because the deer's tails had been cut off."

"I never considered that mused Gossens. They were tagged."

"Yeah but it would have given him something to chew on. We already have problems with juries in this county."

Gossens asked, "What do you think of the jury being out so long?"

Ed Hill answered, "I think it's good. They must actually be considering the evidence or else they would just have come right back with a not guilty verdict."

"What will happen if they do find him guilty?"

"There will be retribution in some way. Possibly forest fires yet tonight."

"Really, that doesn't seem possible."

"Anything is possible up here Paul," responded Hill.

The hours began to drag with more little pieces of paper being distributed as the clock over the bench pointed to 10 then 11. With the jury out well over four hours, the clerk noted the time as the door knob of the jury room turned as 11:55 p.m.

The judge pounded his gavel to settle down those in the packed courtroom. He then asked the jury if they had reached a verdict. When they replied in the positive he directed the court clerk to read the verdict. "We the jury find the defendant Larry Jones guilty of two counts of selling deer and guilty of two counts of possession of untagged deer."

Judge Fowle rapped his gavel as a ripple of astonishment and horror rolled across the room. “Order in the court. I will now pronounce sentence. Mr. Jones you have been found guilty on two counts of selling deer and two counts of possessing untagged deer. I sentence you to a fine of $200 plus $9 court costs and further to 20 days in the Forest County jail.”

“Your honor,” interjected Gossens, “The law requires a revocation of hunting and fishing privileges upon conviction.“

“Oh yes, thank you for reminding me Mr. Gossens. Mr. Jones I also revoke your hunting and fishing privileges for two years.”

Again, a roar like the wind rushing through a dry forest arose from the mass of people.

People were heard to say, “A fine and jail are fine. But to take his hunting license is just not fair. It’ll kill Larry not to hunt. He’ll hunt anyway. He won’t let a little thing like a license stop him.”

Immediately all the wardens and Ranger Dick Abney gathered around Gossens. Abney said, “Paul you’ll need an armed escort out of Crandon. The jury has also asked for an escort to their homes.”

Hill volunteered, “I’ll escort Paul back to Antigo.”

Amid the scurrying crowd, jurors were hurried to their vehicles where Forest County deputies and wardens waited to escort them safely to their homes.

While riding to their motel, Hill, Abney and Gossens listened to a radio call reporting two forest fires had been started and were burning near Crandon. Hill then called for an escort because his car was low on gas. A Langlade County deputy met and escorted them to the Cutless Motel. Immediately, the telephone lines were hot as wardens reported their success in finally prosecuting a second deer selling case at Crandon. Deputy Chief Warden Harold Hettrick was awakened with the glad tidings. He assured them every warden in the state would hear about their success in the morning.

The Game Warden and the Justice of the Peace

Irene Fleming

INTRODUCTION

Justice court stood at the bottom of the American state court system. Developed as a court of first instance in medieval England, justice court has a rich and varied history. Transplanted into this country during colonial settlement, justice court played a very important role as trappers and then loggers opened the country to settlement. Since transportation was marginal, justice court provided a means to settle disputes close to home in a expeditious, economical and effective manner. From 1879 until the 1960s, Wisconsin wardens and other law enforcement officers often arraigned defendants before justice courts.

Justice court was viewed as adequate during pioneer days, but not for an urban society. These courts were gradually and systematically eliminated through a series of laws, amendments and repeals beginning in the early 1960s. They culminated in a constitutional amendment in 1966. A few justices served out their time until 1969, when statutory chapters covering justices were repealed by the Wisconsin legislature.

Justice court was organized to conform to the theory of local self-government and required the popular election of all offices. Justices of the peace were elected at regular county elections and each county had several justices in various communities. Justices were compensated through a fee system. The office was most often held by a person living in the neighborhood. They typically had no legal training and served in their spare time.

The justice of the peace was an official court officer, yet they often let their personalities and individual beliefs guide them during appearances and trials. Their capabilities varied depending upon education and background.

Small communities demanded that justices walk a very tight line. Trying to please the arresting officer to insure further fees often was tempered by the fact that they had to live in their respective communities. They often were criticized when the rule of the state and the actions of wardens were not always in agreement with the local point of view.

Wardens could take defendants before any justice in the county of the violation. More than one justice gave wardens the liberty off shopping around. They eventually took cases before the one who gave them the best outcome. Wardens usually took violators immediately to court upon apprehension regardless of whether it was on a weekend, a holiday, or early morning. Upon arresting a person at 3 a.m. most wardens contacted their favorite justice of the peace for an immediate arraignment.

Coming from many walks of life, these down-to-earth people dealt with sometimes serious, but more often humorous and embarrassing scenarios. Most had no formal law training, thus presenting problems in the way cases were handled. Wardens often drew up criminal complaints and warrants and generally advised them on how to proceed in criminal prosecutions. Justices asked wardens questions in open court on how to proceed and how much to fine a person. These questions demonstrated that the justice did not know how to administer law–questions an attorney wouldn't have to ask. Somehow the openness in the way they were asked and the way they ran their courts seemed to satisfy most people being prosecuted. Exchanges of this type were embarrassing, but generally justice was swiftly and properly meted out.

Humorous happenings were carried by word-of-mouth around the state and added to the mystique of game enforcement:

- Upon arraigning a man before a northern Wisconsin justice of the peace on the charge of possession of a deer during the closed season, the warden was faced with a dilemma. Seeing the justice paging through the statute book in a puzzled manner, the warden volunteered, "Your honor the penalties are in section 29.63."

  Without a blink the justice continued his paging.

  "Your honor the penalty section is in 29.63 of the statutes."

  The justice continue to page. The warden offered the information a third time.

  With a frown now replacing the puzzled look, the justice deliberately folded the book in front of him, stared deliberately at the warden and stated emphatically,

  "Young man, I'm not looking for the penalty section, I'm looking for the place in this book that allows me to let this man go."

  The warden was again in a shopping mood for another justice, one that would look at the penalty section, or even though embarrassing, would at least ask him how much the fine should be.

• In Waterford between 1952-1957, a justice who was also barber, held court in his barber shop. He utilized his barber chair as a witness chair. While most justices would charge only one court fee for each appearance regardless of the number of actual counts charged, he always charged the violator his $7.22 justice of the peace court fee on each count. This was legal, but considered unethical.

• Warden Don Beghin reported that during the 1949 five-day deer season, violations were so extensive it called for extra means. Legal game included only does, fawns, spike bucks and forked-antlered deer with a fork less than two inches and the 15 wardens working out of the Trout Lake Conservation Headquarters picked up approximately 60 large-antlered deer. They had so many violators to prosecute that the local justice of the peace, rather than cluttering up his home, held court at the conservation headquarters in the evenings.

• Because of the informal manner many justices proceeded and where court was held, violators sometimes reacted in unusual ways. Arraigned by Warden Joseph Rubesch in a southwest Wisconsin justice court the justice asked, "How do you plea to the charge of having in your possession three squirrels during the closed season?"

The man replied, "Yah honah, Aye pleads fer mercy."

• From 1935 to 1949, Warden Frank Adamske, stationed at Baraboo, used one justice of the peace. A self-made man, the justice had only a fourth-grade education, but was respected as the mayor of Baraboo for many years. He handled his court cases very professionally, applying common sense to his decisions. Before arraignment, he always held a very informal and personal conversation with the defendants that went something like this.

"What are you doing in the Baraboo area? Oh, visiting relatives. I hope you're not sponging off them. Are you buying a few groceries? I think you should help out financially while visiting..."

At times he showed a little temper. Upon fining a man for possession of a fraudulent fishing license, the man objected to the amount and insisting he had no money stated that he would go to jail. As the justice laboriously pecked out the commitment papers one finger at a time on his old typewriter, the violator continued to harangue him about the high fine, insisting he would have to go to jail because he did not have enough money to pay the fine. As the paper was handed to Adamske, the man pulled a money clip from his pocket holding a large roll of bills. "O.K. I will pay the fine," he said.

"You mean you let me type out that commitment and now you're going to pay the fine. You know I have other things to do. I'm a very busy man." His voiced growing more stern he continued.

"I know another thing you're going to pay for. You'll pay the fee for me making out the commitment papers."

• In Oconto County, Warden Carl Miersch used a woman justice of the peace who although fluent in her speech could not pronounce the word confiscate. The word always came out confacate. Often a defendant would question what she meant when she confacated his fish pole or firearm. Her standard reply was to very slowly, deliberately and clearly enunciate, "It's gone buster."

Conversations at warden gatherings often centered on my judge and the latest bazaar happening in my court. These intriguing events provided wardens entertainment and constructive direction in how to proceed in justice court. A few of the more colorful stories are included this book.

I hope you enjoy this look at a bygone era of justice.

BUT YOUR HONOR I WANT TO PLEAD NOT GUILTY!

Wardens Owen Anderson, Patrick "Pat" Burhans and James "Jim" Chizek worked as special wardens for Ortis "O.K." Johnson at Shawano in the spring of 1955.

Cecil is a small community east of Shawano where Cecil Creek drains into Shawano Lake. Each spring, multitudes of spawning northern pike run up Cecil Creek and are joined by hundreds of spawning walleyes. The creek is inundated with people trying to illegally take these fish. Intermixed with the potential violators are scores of people who walk the banks to watch the spectacle Mother Nature provides, as the fish follow their irresistible age-old urge to procreate.

A community celebration of sorts results as violators challenge wardens to catch them taking illegal fish. The stream provides only a short span where poachers can effectively catch fish. Several wardens can watch this span, but of course can't be there all the time. Therefore, the local and traveling outlaw must know where the wardens are at all times.

The local citizenry, constantly alert, are always aware of how many special wardens are assigned each spring at Shawano. They also quickly know their names, what they look like, and where they are living. They know the wardens' priority is to protect sturgeon on the Wolf River while the protection of fish at Cecil is of lesser priority. Therefore, wardens work hard to keep their whereabouts unknown. Doing so, they provide a deterrent and give some protection to fish populations.

Every night during the spawning season, a group of children would systematically search the small town of Cecil for wardens. Wardens rarely showed themselves and often parked their cars miles out of town in hidden locales and snuck into town on foot in an attempt to catch a violator or two off guard. Often, they found wardens hiding behind buildings, under porches, behind bushes shrubs or hedges, even on roofs of the few local people willing to assist.

People used every devious means to catch fish. Some are taken by hand while wading the creek. Some are thrown on shore and later retrieved when the coast is clear. Others are picked up and hid in the violators clothing. The larger female fish are sometimes teased into reach by using a long, thin tree branch to rub them under the belly. If her urge to spawn is great enough, she'll mistake the stick for a male fish bumping into her to make her release her eggs. As the stick is slowly withdrawn, the fish is coaxed, moving ever against the stick, toward the bank. When close enough, the enticer reaches down, rubs her under the belly, grasps her tightly and throws her on the bank, or just walks off with her. Others use spears and snaghooks of every description that they conceal under their clothing. Many spawning fish are injured and killed this way.

Justice courts played an important part in how a warden performed in the field, just as the courts affect their decisions today. Wardens knew justice courts in Shawano County, as directed by the district attorney, would not prosecute a person for taking an illegal fish unless the person was apprehended with a fish in their possession. The violators also knew this and adjusted their actions. Often, they would take fish and follow the shoreline closely. They called this "following the water." At the approach of a person even suspected of being a warden, they would throw the fish back into the creek. At times, if they thought a warden was in the area, they would blatantly hold up a fish for the warden to see, sometimes long enough to seriously injure the fish. After making what they felt were appropriate comments toward wardens, they returned the fish to the water. Occasionally the fish would float belly up and die, far beyond where a warden could retrieve it for evidence.

Faced with the uncertainty of the court, wardens reverted to devious methods to ensure a prosecution.

This night, Burhans had been found early in the evening hiding under a porch near the stream. When found, the searchers broadcast his presence loudly about town. Some of the searchers cursed Burhans using very coarse language. Later, it was reported that Burhans had returned some of their retorts in language as colorful as their own.

After being found, Burhans left town and made sure his departure was noted by the townspeople. He wanted them to think that there were no wardens in town. The creek in their mind would be open to the taking of as many fish as they pleased. The search for wardens continued for about another hour.

Emboldened by not finding any more wardens, they began to take fish.

Chizek watched a man tease a large walleye to shore with a stick, pick it up and shove it under his coat. The area between him and the violator was too great, especially since the area was illuminated by nearby house lights. As he ran from cover to apprehend the man, the violator bolted toward uptown. With Chizek just a few feet behind, the culprit veered swiftly toward the water. He quickly fumbled the fish from under his clothing and dumped it unceremoniously into the creek with a splash. At that juncture a lively discussion took place with Chizek inclined to arrest the man, regardless of whether he had a fish in possession or not. Discretion being the best part of valor, he decided that being a permanent warden was important to him.

He would follow O.K.'s orders.

Meanwhile Anderson was hiding behind a large cinder pile where he saw a man spear a large northern. As the man left the creek and the lights of the city, Anderson was able to get quite close to him. He was about 10 feet away when some cinders rolled under his feet. The man turned and spotted Anderson and began to sprint down the steep pile. Anderson pursued him, fast closing in on the young man. A final burst of speed brought him close enough for a mid-body tackle. The man came down hard with an audible whooosh, knocking the wind out of him. Anderson rode the man down the long, steep cinder bank. His legs bleeding profusely from sliding on the rough cinders, breathless and completely cowed, the young man surrendered meekly.

After retrieving the fish and spear, Anderson walked the man uptown to a place where he knew Chizek could see him. Together, they marched the man out of town with the spear and northern in plain view to broadcast their success.

They drove to Shawano and went directly to the justice's house. They sheparded the young man into his office about 1 a.m. The Justice Tom Jones was an elder, short, wizened man who walked with a severe limp that could be classified as a severe lurch. His office of Justice of the peace was his only means of support. Hobbling down the hall of a dark office building he asked, "Does anyone have a flashlight as he fumbled with the lock."

With the light beam on the lock, he opened the door.

"Looks like you guys have been burning the midnight oil."

Jim mused, "Yah, catch them in the night time and go to court at night."

"You boys can get me up anytime of the night. I'm always available," he breathed.

As they entered the court the justice said, "Why hello John, what have the wardens got you for?"

"They say I've been spearing fish."

"By the looks of your pant legs, it looks like you've been praying."

Pointing at Anderson he said, "He jumped on me. I'm bleeding bad and my legs hurt. Are they allowed to jump on me like that?"

"Were you running away from the warden?"

"I was running. Is there a law against running?"

"Look John, I'm not discussing this further. Take a seat, the wardens and I have a little office work to do."

After the complaint and warrant were typed up the justice said, "Move over here John in front of my desk. The wardens told me you were spearing fish tonight. I see they have your spear and a speared fish. That will be $50 and costs."

Twisting nervously on his rickety chair, John replied, "But Tom, I want to plead not guilty and have a trial."

"While in court you will refer to me as your honor."

"Yes, your honor, but I would like a trial."

In a stern voice, the justice said. "You've just had a trial, that will be $50 and costs."

John protested, "Your honor I believe I'm entitled to have a trial in front of a jury and to be represented by an attorney."

"I will make that decision as to whether you are entitled to a jury trial or not," reprimanded the justice sternly. The wardens wouldn't bring you here in the middle of the night with a spear and a speared fish if you were not guilty. You are fined $50 and costs. If you can't pay, I will have the wardens deliver you to jail until you can. Court adjourned."

Hanging is head and muttering something about the justice being a friend of his, John paid the fine and left.

TWO ROUNDS FOR THE HOUSE!

On a fall evening in the late 1920s, a warden arrested two men for the illegal killing of a deer and took them to the local justice's home to arraign them. Finding no one at home, the warden took them to the local saloon where the justice was known to frequent. Upon entering the tavern he noticed the justice at the bar commiserating with some congenial companions. Springing into action he left his bar stool. Assuming his office of justice of the peace, he ordered the two to sit down at a saloon table and promptly convened court. Without the formality of issuing a complaint or warrant he asked. "Well, are you guilty?" Heads hanging, both admitted they had indeed killed the deer in question.

The justice said, "I accept your pleas of guilty and hereby find each of you guilty and fine you each $50 and costs and confiscate the deer in the name of the State of Wisconsin."

He smiled and turned to his appreciative audience at the bar. The patrons clapped gleefully. The justice continued, "I also order you to buy two rounds of drinks for the house."

Feeling as if they had been treated fairly, they both gladly paid the fine. A rousing cheer arose from the gathered throng as they laid their money on the bar to comply with the justice's order.

SEARCH WARRANTS FOR BILL

On a bitter cold February night in 1951, Warden Bill Hiebing received a telephone call after midnight regarding the illegal killing of a deer. He left his warm, Alma home to investigate. Circling the fish camp and walking the shoreline where the alleged violator, Harley Litcher lived, Hiebing found deer hair and blood where a deer had been dragged, enough evidence outside the broken down camp to substantiate the complaint that an illegal deer may be on the premises. Back in Alma, still shivering from the bitter cold, he contacted Justice of the Peace Earl Hawthorn and requested a search warrant for the commercial fishing camp and its outbuildings.

Hawthorn was a gung-ho justice who was pleased to be called on to do his duty as an elected officer of the court. He quickly filled out an affidavit. Hiebing was sworn to its allegations and signed it. In a very short time, he was ready to make the search.

"Thanks Earl, I will make my return on this tomorrow," said Hiebing.

"Where does this Harland Litcher live?"

"Not far from here. He lives between Alma and Nelson, about a 15 minute drive."

"Could I come along? I would like to see how you do this."

"That's fine with me. Its now 2:30 in the morning. Do you have to work tomorrow?"

"Yeah, but it'll be worth losing sleep to see you serve the search warrant."

"O.K., lets go."

As they motored through the cold, starry night Hiebing asked, "Will your boss be mad if you're late for work."

"Yep, but I won't be late. One is never late when you work for Buffalo County."

"You work as a highway auditor?"

"Ever since I got out of school. I like it. But what about your job. Aren't you afraid? Going out at night alone like this?"

"Not really. See the shield I wear on my breast? It protects me. Ha! My Mama never raised any dummies. She always told me to never 'moon a werewolf or squat with my spurs on.' Seriously, I am very careful. I work alone a lot and adjust my actions accordingly."

Arriving at the group of shaky looking buildings making up the fish camp, he announced, "We're here. Come on."

At their knock a voice bellowed, "Who's there?"

"This is Bill Hiebing, I'm a conservation warden. I want to talk to you."

"Be right out. Hang on a minute."

After a short pause, a bewhiskered, shirtless man wearing bib overalls shiny with dried fish slime remaining from fall fishing, swung the plank door open just enough to peek out.

"Well Hi Bill. To what do I owe the honor of a visit in the middle of the night?"

"I have a search warrant for your house and outbuildings. I have information that you have an illegal deer on the premises."

Gulping several times, Litcher sighed in a barely audible whisper, "I was afraid, that was it. It's in the back shed Bill. Let me get my boots on and I'll take you to it."

Entering the ramshackle shed, Hiebing's flashlight gleamed off the newly skinned, frozen carcass of a buck hanging by his antlers from a ceiling joist.

"Nice deer Harley. Too bad you can't keep it. Where did you kill this deer?"

Visibly shaking from the cold and his frazzled nerves Litcher blurted, "In the Nelson bottoms. Man it's cold out here. I'm freezing."

"O.K. Harley, I'm cold too. We'll have to go to Alma where we'll hold court."

"Is Earl Hawthorn still the justice of the peace over there?"

"Yep, he's standing right there."

"You brought the justice with you?"

"Yeah, I'm prepared for court right now. Help me load this carcass and we'll be on our way to Earl's house."

A properly dignified court was held. The defendant was required to remove his hat and call Hawthorn "Your honor."

"How do you plead Harley?"

"I'm guilty your honor. I hope you will go easy on me. I was going to eat the meat. It wasn't for sale."

"I'm taking that into consideration, and upon your plea of guilty, I find you guilty and fine you the minimum of $50 and court costs or 30 days in the Buffalo County jail. The deer is confiscated in the name of the state. Bill you'll take possession of it and dispose of it as required by law."

"Yes your honor."

Litcher broke in, "Your honor, I've got the money and don't want to spend any time in jail."

Accepting payment Hawthorn said, "Just step outside a minute. I want to talk to Bill."

After Litchers left the room he spoke to Hiebing in a quiet conspiratorial voice.

"Bill, there's no need for you to contact me each time you need a search warrant." Reaching into his desk, he brought forth a handful of blank search warrants. Quickly signing them he handed them to Hiebing.

"Just fill them in when you need them, and bring the violator to me. I've got to change clothes now and get ready for work. Don't forget. Bring all your cases to me. I'll treat you right."

NO SPEAKA DE ENGLISH

In the early 1960s many displaced persons were entering the United States. Warden Kenneth “Ken” Kazmar, stationed at Dunbar, received a telephone call from Loyal “Dick” Abney, a fire control dispatcher at the Wausaukee Ranger Station regarding the killing of a pheasant during the closed season near Wausaukee.

“I talked to the informant and it appears a man named Polotski is the shooter. The informant tells me the guy can speak very little English as he’s a displaced person from Poland.”

“My dad’s visiting. He speaks fluent Polish and can interpret for us. I will ask him to ride along. Would you come along with me and help me pick this guy up?”

“Yeah, I’ll be waiting for you at the station.”

Arriving at the Wausaukee Ranger Station, Kazmar and his father were picked up Abney and proceeded to the informants house. Upon questioning the man, Kazmar asked if he would sign an affidavit for a search warrant, stipulating that he had witnessed the illegal act. He agreed and accompanied them to Justice of the Peace Robert Perrin’s home where the search warrant was issued. The warrant alleged that a Mr. James Polotski had on July 17, 1961, shot a rooster pheasant near Wausaukee in Marinette County during the closed season.

En route to serve the warrant Kazmar explained, “Now dad as we discussed on the way down, we will proceed very slowly with this man. When we get there, I will introduce myself and Dick. You tell him in Polish what I’ve said. We will go one sentence at a time so he will be sure to understand.”

A smiling middle-aged man opened the door and greeted them in Polish, gesturing with upturned palms, “No speaka de English.”

Kazmar explained why they were there and displayed the search warrant.

His father interpreted and explained in Polish, “My name is Walter Kaczmarski. This is my son Kenneth Kazmar and Dick Abney. They are game wardens and have a search warrant stating you have in your possession a pheasant. The season is closed on pheasants. You must allow them to search. They have a legal document, allowing them to enter your home."

Reading the warrant one line at a time Kazmar waited as his father patiently interpreted in Polish. Often asked if he understood, Polotski always responded in the positive. When the warrant was finally read Kaczmarski asked in Polish, "Are you sure you understand what the warrant means?"

The answer came in Polish, "Yes." Polotski stepped aside and with a flourish of both arms he gestured for them to enter.

Glancing at his son for more instruction Kaczmarski inquired, "Is there more I should ask?"

"Ask him where the pheasant is."

The response was turned up palms and a shrug of the shoulders.

"Well, we'll look around. Glancing around, he pointed toward a pail turned upside down on the kitchen floor. "Dick, take a look under that pail."

"Here it is Ken."

After much excited conversation,with Kaczmarski interpreting, Polotski was told he was under arrest and would be required to appear in justice court in Wausaukee.

"Do you understand?"

"Yes."

Justice Perrin who ran a very dignified court accepted the arrangement with Kaczmarski interpreting for Polotski and for the court.

After reading the criminal complaint to Polotski, Perrin handed it to Kaczmarski who reread it and translated Polotski's plea of guilty from Polish to English.

Perrin's decree of $25 and costs seemed to be understood by the defendant as he dug in his back pocket for his check book.

"No, no," stated Perrin holding up his hands in dissent. "The court will except no checks. Cash only." This began a long explanation, with Kaczmarski making long interpretations of the justice's words. Finally the justice's point was interpreted to the defendant's satisfaction and Mr. Polotski was allowed to go to a nearby grocery store to cash his check. Abney would accompany him.

Upon his return, Polotski paid the fine and costs.

On the lawn outside the justice's office, Polotski asked Kaczmarski a number of questions in Polish. "How is it you speak Polish? Are you from Poland?"

"No I was born in Cleveland, Ohio. My folks were immigrants. After moving to the south side of Milwaukee when I was young, my folks continued to speak Polish as there were many Polish speaking people living there. After becoming an electrical engineer and working there, I also continued to speak Polish."

"If Ken is your son, how come your names are different?"

"Ken changed his last name from Kaczmarski to Kazmar for professional reasons with my O.K. many years ago. People in this country have difficulty pronouncing Polish names."

Continuing in Polish he said, "I see. Thank you."

As Polotski walked toward the street, a thoughtful expression overcame his face. He turned and walked back toward Kaczmarski, hesitated for a moment, and with a smile grasped and shook his hand and said in perfect English, "Mister Kaczmarski, thank you, I have been in the United States several years now and you speak the most fluent Polish I've heard since I left Poland."

FIFTY-NINE WALLEYES

After his discharge from the United States Army in 1958, Warden Owen Anderson found himself in limbo, waiting for a warden station to open. During this wait he worked for Oliver "Ollie" Valley at Cassville. Working the Mississippi River was a rewarding challenge, quite different than his prior experience in other parts of the state.

Responding to a complaint of overbagging of walleyes on a fish for a fee barge found Anderson across the river, from Dubuque, Iowa. Basking in the beautiful spring sunshine, binoculars hanging around his neck, he posed as a fisherman a short distance up stream from the large anchored, steel fishing barge, with a large fo'c's'le type structure in its center. Dressed in coveralls as any other fisherman, he dangled a line for effect as he observed fisherman coming and going, and fishing from the barge. Dabbling with his fishing pole enough to convince the people on the barge that he was just another fisherman, he kept a ready eye on the fishermen on the barge. Occasionally lifting his binoculars when it appeared no one on the barge was watching, he spent the entire day observing the fishing activity.

As Valley had predicted, the fish were hitting and a number of fishermen came and left with bag limits of nice walleyes.

One fisherman in particular drew Anderson's attention–a middle aged man who stayed well beyond the others who constantly caught fish. Twice he saw him fillet fish and place them in a red cooler. Toward evening he left the barge via a gangplank between the barge and the dock.

As he unlocked his car Anderson sauntered up to him. "Hi, I'm a state game warden. I saw you fishing from the barge. How'd you do?"

"Oh I got a few."

"Good, could I see your fishing license please?"

"Oh sure, I was just going for some beer. My buddy who owns the boat, and I were going to tip a few."

"Your license is in order Mister Johnson, I see you are from Iowa. I would like to see your fish."

"Could you wait while I pick up the beer? My buddy has a great thirst."

Starting for the boat Anderson, his voice now a command answered, "No, I would like to see your fish now. I don't have time to wait. Lets go aboard and take a look."

"Well...o.k.. I have a bag limit."

On the barge, Johnson led him to a live-box hanging over the gunwale. In it were two stringers containing 10 walleyes. "Well it looks like you are in excess of the daily bag limit of five fish here George."

"This is my possession limit. I can possess 10 walleyes."

"Not here on the water and not caught in one day."

"Well then I've made a mistake. I thought I could possess two daily bag limits."

"As I've told you, you may catch only five per day. Now lets take a look at your cooler."

"What cooler?"

"I saw you fillet a number of walleyes and place them in a red cooler."

"Ah...don't have...Ah what's the use. I'll show you the cooler."

Directing Anderson to a storage compartment in the fo'c's'le, he opened a door and took out the red cooler. As he opened the lid, Anderson exclaimed, "Wow! How many fillets do you have in there?

"You will count them anyway. Might as well tell you. There are 98."

"Ninety-eight! I guess you would now agree that you're over the daily bag limit and the possession limit."

"Ah...guess so...what's the damage?

"You must accompany me to Lancaster where we will meet with the justice of the peace for court. What do you do in Iowa?"

"I sell fishing tackle for a large concern. Where did you say we were going?"

"We will meet Warden Ollie Valley at the Grant County jail where the justice will convene court."

"Guess I should tell you then that I don't really sell fishing tackle. I'm a police officer in Iowa. If you'd just give me a ticket, I would gladly pay the fine for this violation. I don't like the idea of going to court or jail."

"As a police officer, you surely know why we must take care of this right now. If you leave the state, we'd have a difficult time getting you back."

"I would come back. I know what you're talking about, but just between us couldn't I just pay the fine and leave?"

"Sorry, but I just can't do that. We must take care of this now."

"O.K. I know where you're coming from. Where were you watching me from?"

"Just upstream from the barge fishing from shore. I watched you all day. You must have seen me there."

"I don't remember seeing you, but I do remember your shoes. New Redwings aren't they?"

"Ha! You remember my shoes?"

"Yeah, I like Redwing shoes and I can spot them a mile away."

"Strange that you'd remember my shoes, but not me. Will you follow me into Lancaster with your car?"
"What will be will be. I'll follow you."
En route Anderson radioed Valley. He told him he was bringing in a prisoner and to meet him at the sheriff's office with the justice of the peace.
Walking into the jail, Valley greeted the prisoner. "Well hi George, what does Anderson have you for?"
With a fallen face he answered, "Oh hell Ollie, I made a mistake."
Making out the criminal complaint and warrant Anderson asked, "Do you know this guy Ollie?"
"Yeah, he's a police lieutenant from over in Iowa. A little embarrassing, but damn it he sure knows how to count."
When arraigned, Johnson pled guilty to the charge of possessing over the bag limit of walleyes.
Asked to describe the circumstances of the violation Anderson related what he saw while watching the barge. He continued, "Your honor, George here had in his possession 10 walleyes on stringers and 98 walleye fillets in his cooler."
"Wow! How many walleyes does that total?"
"Fifty-nine walleyes your honor."
"My God! Fifty nine walleyes! What were you thinking man?"
"Ah...your honor. I make a mistake, and...Er...would just like to pay for it and have this thing over."
"Well I would think so. I believe you are a real fish hog."
Paging through the statute book, scratching his head, he leaned forward toward Valley.
"Ollie, am I reading the penalty section correctly? Is the maximum penalty only $100 for this charge?"
"Yes your honor, $100 or 30 days in jail or both."
"I don't feel the penalties fit this case, taking into consideration the number of fish this man had in his possession. I suppose I could sentence him to jail."
"Your honor, interrupted Johnson, "I should tell you, I'm a police officer over in Iowa and a jail sentence would be disastrous to my career."
"You should have thought of that before you looted our river of fish. I do understand your problem though."
Returning his attention to Valley he asked, "Is there any other charge that could be placed against Mr. Johnson?"
"Well, Anderson said he threw fish guts in the water."
"Is that a violation?"
"Yes. He could be charged with that."
Paging more furiously through the large tome, the justice's finger suddenly stopped on a passage.
"Mr. Johnson you are also charged with illegally disposing of fish

offal in the waters of this state. The fine is the maximum of $100 on each charge plus court costs on each charge. The fish are confiscated and turned over to the state for disposition. Take possession Mr. Valley. Court dismissed."

RISING STAR–FALLING STAR

Donald "Donny" Riles, a middle aged entrepreneur, was elected as a second justice of the peace in the city of Portage in the late 1950s. His jurisdiction covered Columbia County. In an effort to divide his cases with the other justice in the city, Conservation Warden Jim Chizek came to his court with a simple case of several fishermen fishing with too many lines.

Delighted to receive the business, Riles asked the accused men to wait in the hall outside his dingy upstairs office. "How do I proceed Mr. Chizek?"

"Do you have the necessary forms, criminal complaints and warrants?"

"I ordered a number of forms I thought I would need. Will you help me look them over?"

Noticing the stacks of forms on his desk, Chizek pulled two familiar appearing piles toward him. "These are complaints and warrants. Do you have a typewriter? I will help you fill them out."

Pointing to a dusty Underwood in the corner he replied, "Right there, I haven't used it for a long time, but I think it works."

Blowing the dust off the ancient machine, Chizek seated himself, rolled in a complaint and began to type. "Seems to work fine. Could use a new ribbon but we'll make out O.K.." Finishing the two forms he instructed Riles, "Now read the complaint to these men and ask for a plea. If they plead guilty, which I expect, you tell them that upon your plea of guilty, I find you guilty. You then fine them as prescribed by the statutes and assess them your court costs which are also prescribed by the statutes."

"Are court costs the money I get to keep?"

"Yep, court costs are yours to keep. Warden fees I send into my department"

"What do I do with the rest of the money?"

"The fine is sent through Columbia County into the state, I'm sure you have forms here for their remittance"

"What happens if these guys can't pay the fine"

"First you type up a commitment form.." Leaning forward he pulled another form from the pile. "This done, you remand them to the county jail where I will take them. It's really not too complicated once you get used to handling the cases"

"For how long a period do I sentence them too?"

"In this case 30 days. The statutes will tell you how long in each case. After these cases are disposed of, I suggest you thoroughly read the statutes as to your authority. If they plead not guilty, you must set a trial date. If and when that happens we will cross that bridge."

"O.k., Jim bring them in. Wait, how much should I fine them?"

"That's your decision. The penalty section in this case calls for a fine of up to $100."

"What's a fair fine?"

"I'd say $25 and costs"

"O.K.. Let me get myself seated so I appear confident. Let them in."

Riles followed Chizek's instructions and the case was disposed of promptly with guilty pleas.

The scholarly type, Riles read the statutes and studied statutory state instructions on handling funds. Soon, he became efficient in handling court cases and his court ran with a dignity not ordinarily seen in justice court. He instructed each defendant that they must remove their caps, stand while speaking, and refer to him as your honor as befitted his office.

Chizek was highly pleased with how Riles handled his cases. Even though he still divided his cases between the two justices in the city, he favored Riles. When he wanted a little higher fine because of extenuating circumstances, he brought the violator before Riles who would always take his recommendation.

After several years, Riles' business picked up and Chizek began to notice him becoming less careful in his recording and filing of cases. His behavior was also noticeable different. It was obvious he was drinking. Often Chizek called him from the country club to hold court. It became harder for him to retain the dignity of the court, especially since at times he was partially inebriated. He always managed to be dressed in a suit while presiding over a case because he left a suit jacket in his office. At times he would ask Chizek to keep the violators down the hall while he slipped in the back way to slip on a shirt, tie and suit jacket over shorts. He would hurriedly turn his desk so no one could see his bare legs.

"Now Jim, when the case is over, you usher the people out so they never know I am wearing shorts."

After each case was disposed of, Riles always asked for a critique on how he had handled the case. "Was my handling of the case dignified? Did I fine them enough?"

Like a sports coach, Chizek always told him the areas where he could perform better.

"Donny, please don't ask me what the fine should be in open court.

If you must ask, please do it when the defendants can't hear us."

"When you make out the complaint, always note on the upper corner the amount of the fine. If you don't, is it alright for me to ask for a recommendation?"

"You may do that."

"While I will not mention an amount, I will comment on the facts of the case, the defendants behavior and attitude. Then you can make a decision based on the statutes."

While some things about Riles still bothered Chizek, he still he held good court and he was pleased with the penalties meted out. Even though he occasionally still asked in open court how much the fine should be, he felt at least the violators were being properly penalized.

Then there came the unexpected knock on the door, "Are you James Chizek the conservation warden?"

"Yes I am, why?"

"We are state auditors. Do you keep copies of all your arrest records?"

"Why yes I do. Why?"

"We are investigating a justice of the peace that you have been taking cases before. We feel he isn't remitting fine moneys to the state."

"Is it Donald Riles?"

"Yes, how long have you been taking cases before him?"

"Oh, at least several years. I have all the records, come on in"

Examining Chizek's card file, the auditors found Riles had embezzled approximately $2,600 in conservation fines. His office was found to be a disaster of piles with cash mixed into the piles. A significant amount of the missing money was never found. The auditors felt it was more a problem of negligence than theft. Never-the-less, they took their report to the district attorney for a possible prosecution.

Strange things began to happen as Riles, scared for his life, began to contact all and anybody who might get him out of his jam. Riles was a cousin of Emmy Dallman, who was the wife of Royce "Smoky" Dallman, the warden at Milton Junction. Emmy Dallman and Riles were first cousins to the famed Wisconsin movie actor Dennis Morgan. These cousins were contacted to see if they could influence the county not to prosecute. Dennis Morgan offered to repay all the fine moneys embezzled. The offer was accepted along with Rile's resignation in lieu of a prosecution.

PERILOUS PAULINE

The lady justice of the peace in Solon Springs was a retired school marm named Pauline Draper who proudly proclaimed this to anyone who questioned her qualifications. Pauline was a proud, astute woman in her late 70s who was well respected in her community. Her osteoporosis-riddled, humped shoulder, hooked nose and sharp cheek bones stood out in a stark manner making her appear somewhat different. With no formal law training, she never-the-less understood criminal law and quite ably administered it in a fair, if unorthodox manner. Her firm actions left no doubt that she was in charge in her courtroom.

Elected as justice of the peace by the people of Solon Springs, Pauline served as an official of Douglas County. She usually ran a very dignified court, but her somber appearance sometimes led to inconsistency in control.. She often befuddled defense attorneys with her unorthodox style.

Warden Tony Jelich, stationed at Solon Springs, brought all of his cases before Justice Pauline.

When the defendants story and Warden Jelich's differed, she would ask, "Are you calling the game warden a liar?" Most times they would back off and try to make a deal to settle the case.

On an October afternoon in 1954, Jelich brought five cases dealing with illegal grouse hunters before her.

One of them involved the son of a local businessman. The local businessman was held in high regard by the community and held himself in even higher regard. He brought with him personal friends, the village president who also was a conservation department forester, and his friend Conservation Commissioner Spiegel, who proudly proclaimed himself to be a river rat attorney from St. Croix Falls. Commissioner Spiegel was a controversial critic of conservation wardens who had attempted to limit warden's authority through legislation. The scene was set for dynamics. His goal was to have charges dropped against son. He was charged with carrying a loaded gun in an auto while hunting grouse.

As usual, Jelich furnished Pauline transportation to the village hall where she routinely held court. Pulling up in front of the office, he dutifully rounded the car and opened the rear door for her. She got out and hobbled into the building. On her back was her husband's timber-cruiser packsack containing her outdated statute books and court forms.

Justice Pauline always appointed Jelich as bailiff to maintain order in her court. Thus he played the double role of arresting officer and officer of the court. Before Justice Pauline entered the court room, he draped a dark black cloak around her shoulders. As she stepped into the court room, he announced, "Let me have your attention. Court is now in session. The Honorable Justice Pauline Draper presiding." He continued, "Please stand."

In an attempt to disguise her jerky pace, Pauline entered with a flourish, regally whipping her black cape.

"Everyone raise their right hands," she announced as she solemnly swore in everyone in the room. She then reviewed the law on perjury and advised that anyone caught lying would pay a severe penalty.

The first case called was the young man charged with carrying a loaded firearm in a car. Immediately, the young man's father arose and asked that his son be cleared of the charge.

Pauline said, "Please be seated while I read the complaint. It appears that this young man did what he is accused of and he must answer for it. I will not listen to any further discussion of this case except evidence of guilt or innocence." She then read the charge to which the man pled guilty.

Again the man's father arose, "I don't think there should be a penalty for this."

"Sit down. I told you there would be no more discussion of this case. If you have evidence to offer I will listen. This man has pled guilty and I find him guilty."

"Now just a minute. Are you aware of my family's status in this community?"

"I'm well aware of your status, but I expect you to honor the sanctity of this court. Sit down and shut up or I'll hold you in contempt of court."

"Contempt of court. I hold this court in contempt."

Very gently and clearly enunciating each word she responded, "Shut up and sit down."

"Do you realize who is in attendance here? This man is conservation commissioner Spiegel. This is a kangaroo court if I ever saw one. Let's see if you can stand the contempt of this community. I could buy this community."

"That does it. I respect Mr. Spiegel for his office, but he has no standing in this court. I'm sure you could buy this community, but you can't buy this court. You are held in contempt of court and I fine you $50."

"Fifty dollars! I suppose you will pocket that."

"Do you want to try for a hundred. Shut up and pay the bailiff"

Chagrined, the man reluctantly paid the $50 to Jelich, who in an embarrassed manner held up two fingers to signal a $20 fine for man as charged.

"Young man upon your plea of guilty, I will fine you $20 and costs or 30 days in the Douglas County jail."

Leaving the room the father yelled, "I'm taking this thing further. I will complain in Madison about this court. I will take it to the Supreme Court."

"I wish you well and if you would like to discuss this further come back in. I must remind you though that you are still under oath."

Afraid to try Pauline further, the man waved his group out the door.

The silence of the court room was broken by a whisper from the assemblage, "Man I don't like the looks of this."

"Yeah, she looks like 20 miles of corduroy road."

"Silence in the courtroom," intoned bailiff Jelich.

After witnessing Pauline's wrath, The remaining people waived the reading of their complaints and pled guilty. As they left, one of them turned at the door and yelled, "Judge would you like to hire out for Halloween?"

Justice Pauline shouted, "Come back in here and we'll discuss it."

Visibly paling, he whipped out the door.

Leaving the courtroom Commissioner Spiegel summoned Jelich aside and shaking his finger in his face he proclaimed, "This whole procedure is illegal and should be abolished."

"Would you like to talk to Judge Draper about this?"

His shaking finger now almost in Jelich's eye he shouted in fury, "You can bet I'll see this court is abolished."

Meanwhile, supervising Warden D. W. Waggoner and Warden Cliff Freeman had been sent to the city hall by Jelich's wife to finalize a bear damage settlement. They didn't expect to meet warden nemesis Spiegel. As they entered city hall, they spotted him storming out of the court room. Not wanting to be caught in any discussion with Spiegel, the wardens flushed a clerk out of the woman's bathroom to escape his wrath. Nearly every warden in the state soon heard of their bravery.

Shortly after this court encounter, Jelich received a memorandum from the deputy chief warden saying he would no longer serve as bailiff.

I'LL BUY THE DRINKS!

In the early 1960s, the Necedah National Wildlife Refuge area was receiving notoriety because of its large deer population. Hunters came from all parts of the state and nearby states, especially during the late bow season in early December. Over, 5,000 hunters swarmed the area creating a circuslike atmosphere.

Ronald "Ronnie" Kubisiak was stationed at Necedah and faced with enforcing the laws on the area laying just outside the village limits. These laws were enforced on a cooperative basis with the U.S. Fish and Wildlife Service, since both state and federal law applied.

It was a cold blustery day on the first Saturday of December on the opening day of the late bow season in the early 1960s when Kubisiak came upon two bow hunters in an area closed to hunting.

Amid much grousing as to how both state and federal regulations could apply to the area, Kubisiak wrote citations. Since they were non-residents, he escorted them to Necedah for court.

During arraignment, before Justice of the Peace Bernice Burns the complaining continued. She read the criminal complaint and charged them with unlawfully hunting deer in a closed portion of the Necedah National Wildlife Refuge. When she asked for a plea, she was greeted with more complaining about the complexity of the laws. Listening patiently, Burns allowed them to voice their complaints. Finally they pled guilty.

"To your plea of guilty I am finding you guilty of hunting in a closed area and fine each of you $50 and costs or 30 days in the Juneau County Jail."

"Your honor we have the money to pay the fine, but think we should be given a break considering we didn't understand the law."

Becoming flustered over the grousing she explained, "I...Well...The area was posted...and .... I...see no reason for you to have been in that area. I did fine you the minimum under the law."

"We saw no signs."

"Ah...I guess it's your responsibility to know where you're hunting. I've been out to the refuge and I've seen the signs. I know the area is well posted."

"We're strangers to this area. We saw no signs."

They continued to complain as they paid their fine and court costs.

Becoming more flustered and not knowing how to handle the situation, she floundered around for the proper response. “I...just don’t know. It appears we’re getting nowhere. Actually this case is over. You have pled guilty. You are guilty and you’ve paid your fines. Which, I...must point out are the minimum allowed by the law. Pointing out her front window she arose. “Tell you what. There’s a bar across the street. Lets go over there and I’ll buy the first drink.”

Some years later Burns failed a state audit of her books and resigned her office.

WHO EATS WOODPECKERS!?

Patrolling north of Portage on a balmy October day in 1964, Warden Jim Chizek answered a radio call. A farmer had seen some hunters kill a hen pheasant near Date's Mill Pond in Columbia County. Chizek quickly arrived at the farmers home, which abutted the 1,600-acre French Creek Public Hunting Ground. The farmer told him that four black people had killed a hen pheasant on his land. He said he had granted them permission to hunt his land, but when he saw three of them shoot at and kill the hen, he rushed into his field to evict them. An argument ensued and one of the four unceremoniously threw the dead bird in the back seat of the car. They sped off in a huff.

The farmer described the car as a 1963 black Pontiac.

"They went south on Wilcox Road"

"I came up Wilcox, and met that car. Too bad I didn't have a description on it. I could have stopped it easily. Oh well, I'll swing down that way. I may still bump into them."

After calling in the license number, Chizek discovered that the owner was from the Milwaukee area. He contemplated where the suspect car could have gone. *Let's see its only about noon, they won't go back to Milwaukee this early. They're strangers in the area, so they may hunt the public hunting ground.*

Circling the perimeter of the French Creek Public Hunting Ground took a considerable amount of time, poking as he did into all the old field roads entering it. On one of the dirt trails, he was surprised to meet the auto he was looking for. The car was past him in a cloud of dust before he could block it. Braking to a halt, he looked back to see the Pontiac spin its wheels and speed toward the main road.

Dog-gone-it they recognized me, and they're running. Got to get turned around in a hurry. In desperation, he slammed the car back into an open slot between several trees. A sickening thump greeted him, bringing him to a sudden stop. He through the vehicle into forward and slammed the gas pedal down. To his dismay, he stood still. One of his rear wheels was spinning. *I'm hung up on an a stump. Damn it, why do I have to be so clumsy? Got to get out of here.*

He rammed the car back and forth in a frenzy and finally shook it free. Dirt flying from his rear wheels, he sped after the fleeing car. Sluing onto the main road, he turned right and followed the skid marks left by the fleeing auto.

Realizing the car now had a giant lead, he opened up the 309 Ford to well over 100 m.p.h. He strained to look ahead and was unable to see the fleeing car. After several miles of high speed driving, he was saw a wheel skid mark entering one of the public hunting grounds roads. *Oh, oh...they're playing possum. They're back in that road. I've got them now.*

Braking the speeding and overshooting the road, he swiftly backed up and headed in. Driving very slowly, alert and ready to block the car should they attempt to leave, he saw their car parked at the end of the dirt road facing his direction.

Driving close to their auto, he effectively blocked it from leaving. Sweat beaded his forehead as he left his vehicle, somewhat from the warm temperature, but mostly from the stress of the fast chase. Identifying himself to the gathered troupe he asked. "Well now guys, what seems to be the big hurry?"

The leader, a tall raw-boned man who towered head and shoulders over the others responded. "Whad all you mean? We been huntin' here for a cupla 'ourers."

"You don't expect me to believe that do you?" Pointing at the raw boned man he continued. "I recognize you. You were driving the car when you passed me back on the public hunting ground road. Is your name Ozebia Adams? This is your car isn't it? I know why you were running. You guys shot a hen pheasant back by Date's Pond. I would like to look your car over."

Grinning the tall man said, "Go aheeed. We 'ons don't have any 'ol pheasant. We only shoots the pretty ones ennaway."

"O.k. you fellows, stand up in front of your car while I search it." Digging through the assorted hunting gear in the vehicle, Chizek found a loaded gun inside a case. "Looks like you fellows left the farmers' place in quite a hurry. You didn't take time enough to unload this shotgun. That's a good way to get someone shot." Unloading it and laying it aside, he continued the search.

"You guys just stay up front there until I'm through. Keeping a wary eye on the suspects, he continued the search. He found several pheasant feathers, but no bird. Digging further, he found several hunting vests and jackets, with suspicious bulges in them. "What do we have here?" he asked. "Looks like some woodpeckers." He threw them into a neat pile near the hunters. "Lets see now, I have a grand total of five flickers, and two red-headed woodpeckers. You know these birds are protected and illegal to kill or possess. Now where did you fellows throw the hen pheasant?"

Again, the leader spoke for the group. "We 'ons don't have no pheasant."

After extensive questioning, it was obvious to Chizek that they were not about to admit to shooting the pheasant.

"O.K., you four can follow me back to the farm. We're going to look for that pheasant.

Chizek ran his labrador retriever around the area where the pheasant had been shot and where the car left the field to no avail.

"Guess you threw it out down the road someplace. I'll tell you fellows something. You may not pay for killing a pheasant, but you will pay for killing these woodpeckers. Why would you kill a woodpecker?"

"Man we eats 'em. We babbacues 'em."

Disgusted with anyone who would kill woodpeckers, Chizek bit his tongue and wrote a summons for all of them. He took their guns and left.

Appearing before Justice of the Peace Norman Stowers in Portage the next week, one of them pled guilty to carrying a loaded gun in a vehicle and all of them pled guilty to possession of protected song birds. In making his decision on sentencing, Stowers questioned their intent in killing the birds.

"Why in the world would you men shoot a bunch of woodpeckers?"

"Man, we told the warden, we eats 'em."

"Come on, you don't eat woodpeckers. No one eats them."

"I begs yawh paadon mister justice, but we babbacues woodpeckas and they's delicious."

"You mean you hunt them all the time?"

"Yes suh, we 'ons didn't know they's potected."

"Ha, ha...I just can't believe you guys shoot and eat woodpeckers. This is the goofiest case I've ever handled."

Regaining his composure he continued, "You do know hen pheasants are protected?"

"Well yeah, but we didn't have no 'ol hen pheasant."

"The warden tells me you shot a hen and could he could have proved it if the farmer would have testified."

"Mista justice, weons don have no hen pheasant."

"Well, you're not charged with it anyway, but I will take it into consideration when sentencing you. I just can't get over the fact that you not only kill woodpeckers, but eat them."

"You 'ons come on down to Milwaukee and we'll babbacue these birds for you. Y'all will luv 'em, especially the yella hammas."

"There's a difference in the flavor of these birds?"

"Yes suh. Them with the all red head taste woody."

"Ha, ha...excuse my humor, but you mean to tell me yellow hammers are better eating then red-headed woodpeckers?"

"They sho is."

Chizek interrupted, "Have you tried other woodpeckers?"

"We sho have and yella hammas are the best eaten."

Straightening himself in his chair, clearing his throat and struggling to wipe the smile off his face, Stowers returned the court to its somber tenor.

"We won't come to Milwaukee and the woodpeckers are confiscated by the state. You won't have them either."

"Mista justice, y'all means we can't have these birds even afta we 'on pays for 'em?"

"They're confiscated."

"Will y'all eat them birds? They's goo..ood."

"No one will eat them."

Turning to Chizek, the tall man said, "Will you eat 'em?"

"God no, I would never consider eating a woodpecker. They'll be buried."

"You's a worse violator then us 'ons. We don't waste ann...ything."

TWO DOLLARS FOR SERVICE RENDERED

In the early 1950s, wardens Arthur "Art" Gillette stationed at Hayward and John "Johnny" Helsing from Winter responded to a complaint near Couderay. Arriving at a shack where the alleged violator lived, they followed a fresh man track through deep snow into a woods job. They found a man busily wielding a swedesaw and sawing poplar into pulpwood sized lengths. Looking up from his labors, the man spotted the badges and grunted "Oh oh, am I in trouble?"

"Is your name Hans Baker?" asked Gillette.

"Yep, what can I do for you guys?"

"We have a complaint that you have some illegal venison in your house."

"Well, can't deny it. I have some venison in my shack."

"Do you own this land?"

"Naw, it belongs to Louie Spray. I work for him. This is his wood I'm cutting. He lets me live here."

"Are you referring to the Louie Spray? The man holding the record for catching the world's largest musky?"

"Yeah, that's the guy. I'm working off rent for his cabin."

"Oh, I see. Well Hans, let's go down to your place and get the venison."

Removing several quarters of frozen venison from a meat box attached to his shack, the two wardens escorted Baker to their auto. You'll have to go to Winter with us and appear before Justice of the Peace Mike Johnson," said Helsing.

With Gillette driving and Helsing riding behind Baker in the rear seat they journeyed toward Winter. Noticing Baker holding his jaw Gillette asked, "What's wrong with your jaw?"

"I've got a terrible toothache."

"What a coincidence, the justice is also a dentist. Maybe he can help you."

Setting in the old fashioned dentist chair where Johnson practiced his trade, Baker pled guilty to the violation of possessing venison during the closed season.

"The fine will be $50 and costs or 30 days in the county jail. Can you pay the fine?"

Pacing around the room, he grimaced noticeably at the amount. Baker instinctively clutched his jaw even tighter at the double injury he was suffering.

"Maybe Louie will pay the fine for me," he mumbled. "Could I call him?"

"Why yes, use my phone."

Assured that Spray would pay the fine and costs, Johnson turned his attention back to Baker, who continued to hold his jaw. "What's with your jaw?"

Gillette interjected, "Hans has a toothache. Perhaps you can help him."

"Sure, get back in the dentist chair and I'll see what I can do."

Baker eyed the forceps, still dirtied with the dried blood of Johnson's last patient, laying on the dining room table beside the Wisconsin statute book. Baker hesitated, "I don't know..."

"Just get in the chair. I won't hurt you. I'll help you get rid of your toothache."

Reluctantly, the pain-ridden logger sat uneasily in the dentist's chair.

"Let's see now. Open up wide. Ah ha...This is the one ain't it?" Johnson asked as he jabbed a probe deep into his mouth.

Baker jerked away as the probe hit the tender tooth, sending throbbing pain throughout his body.

He gagged out a "yeach" and nodded in the affirmative.

"Ah haw, thought so."

Reaching for the filthy forceps, Johnson clamped it on the offending molar and gave it a sudden twist and wrench. Baker bounced to his feet in agony and Johnson backed away proudly holding the bloody tooth in the forceps.

"There ain't that better?"

Gasping in pain and holding his jaw, Baker paced around the room spitting blood. "My God man, you just about killed me. Couldn't you have given me some novocaine or something?"

"Novocaine is expensive. You said you had no money. Can you pay me for pulling your tooth?"

"I don't have much."

"How much do you have with you?"

Pulling his wallet from his pocket Baker counted, "One...two dollars. Two dollars, that's all I have."

"That's just right. I'll except two dollars for services rendered. Be sure you send Spray over to pay your fine."

CALL ME YOUR HONOR

In the fall of 1954, wardens Arthur "Art" Gillette of Hayward and John "Johnny" Helsing of Winter, approached Justice of the Peace Mike Johnson of Winter. They asked for a warrant to search the home and outbuildings of Jacob Pilek, who lived near Draper. Johnson recorded all the information and drew up an affidavit. He alleged that Pilek had in his possession parts of an untagged deer. Johnson decreed that the information was sufficient to issue a search warrant for Pilek's premises.

While not receptive to the wardens, Pilek reluctantly allowed the two lawmen to enter and search. Finding nothing in the house, they extended the search to the outbuildings. In an old shed, partially hidden in a brushy area behind the house, hung a young buck deer.

"Well now Jake," said Helsing, "It looks like you'll have to accompany us to Winter."

"I suppose you'll take me before Johnson? I don't like the idea of appearing before him. I know him personally. This is really embarrassing for me."

"You should have thought of that before you shot the deer. Johnson is the justice of the peace and you must appear before him."

Loading the deer, the wardens transported Pilek to the home and real estate office of Mike Johnson. Assuming the role to which he had been elected, Johnson very formally presided over the case pending before him. After reading the criminal complaint typed up by Gillette, he explained, "Mr. Pilek you're being charged with possessing an untagged deer. How do you plead?"

"Mike, I plead..."

"Wait," Johnson interrupted. "You don't call me by my first name in court. You may call me your honor or judge, but please do not use my given name. I represent Sawyer County and the State of Wisconsin. The office of justice of the peace should be shown the same respect as a circuit court or the supreme court."

Chagrined, Pilek stuttered, Yes, yes your honor, I plead not guilty."

"Not guilty! How can you plead not guilty? The wardens have your deer."

"I'm entitled to a trial and would like to plead not guilty. I want a trial."

"You want a trial! You just had a trial. I wouldn't have issued a search warrant if I thought you were innocent."

"I don't care. I'm entitled to a trial and I want one. I'm entitled to have my case heard before a jury. I believe I can contest the issuance of your search warrant."

"I'll make that determination. A jury would just find you guilty when they realize I have issued a search warrant. An attorney and trial would cost you a bundle. I'm just saving you money. As I said, you just had a trial and I fine you $50 and costs. Can you pay the fine? If not, you can sit 30 days in the county jail."

Reaching for his wallet, Pilek resigned to his fate and replied, "I still think I'm entitled to a trial, but I'll pay the fine. To think, I had to call you your honor."

BRINGING UP JUSTICE JONES

In the late 1950s, George Jones, after retiring from many years of working on the railroad was elected to the office of Justice of the Peace in Sauk City, having jurisdiction over Sauk County. He began his new career as most other justices, with no law training. Recognizing his inexperience, he proceeded with his cases by going slowly.

The tall distinguished man in his sixties, ran his court as his appearance would dictate. He proceeded with a great deal of patience, in a demure, quiet manner, belaying his lack of law training and experience in running a court. Very exacting in everything he did, he prided himself on the very accurate summation of every case he wrote into his docket.

When a defendant could not pay a fine, he would methodically fill out a commitment order hand it to warden Owen Anderson who was stationed at Sauk City, and firmly order the man to jail, usually for 30 days or until the fine was paid. Because of his inexperience he always discreetly asked Anderson what the penalty for each specific charge should be, out of hearing of the defendant.

After arraigning an Illinois man, who Anderson apprehended running an illegal set line on Lake Wisconsin. justice Jones accepted Robert Binham's plea of not guilty, and required he leave an appearance bond and set a trial date.

After the man had left he asked, "Well, how did I do?"

Anderson replied, "Fine. Have you ever held a trial before?"

"No. But I guess I can handle it."

The man hired a local attorney who promptly called Jones, and asked if the charge against his client could be dismissed, and transferred to his wife, who would gladly appear and plead guilty to it and pay any fines levied.

Not knowing what to do, Jones called Anderson, and asked if this was possible.

"The man was alone when running the line," responded Anderson, "His wife was not even in the area. I could not prove his wife ran the line. What reason does he give for this action?"

"It seems he has a very responsible job, and does not want a criminal conviction on his record."

"Tell the attorney, we can't go along with his suggestion."

With the court date fast approaching, Anderson began to worry, knowing the justice had not handled a trial before, he began to dread what an experienced trial attorney could do to him. Making a trip to the Law Library in Baraboo, he picked up several statute books with the chapters describing how trials are to be conducted, and delivered them to Jone's home where he held court. "George I'm worried. I'm afraid that Binham's attorney may twist you up on court procedure. Seeing you've never handled a trial before, I think you should bone up on court procedure, so you can hold your own and control the trial."

"I suppose there are things in those books I should know. Leave them here and I'll study them."

He then reviewed what would happen at the trial. "Briefly George, the district attorney will present my side of the case, and the defendants attorney will present his side of the case. It is your job to control the testimony, listen to the testimony and make decisions, as to what is evidence and what is not. After both sides rest, you will because there is to be no jury, be required to make a decision as to the man's guilt."

Gazing at Anderson, in a firm voice he stated, "Oh well he's guilty, or you never would have brought him in here."

"Well, yeah George," chuckled Anderson, "But you must make the finding. The district attorney is prepared for this case. I believe it is important that you do not let the defense attorney shake you so you lose control of the trial. Remember even if you are wrong, or are not sure of something it is your court and you control it."

Anderson monitored his protege until satisfied, that Jones had the court procedure well in mind. His mind was finally at ease, sure that the justice could handle the case. Then he received a call from Jones, stating the defendants attorney had changed his plea to guilty, and Binham had paid the fine ending the need of all the in-service training.

BETCHA $5

On a bright October day in the early 1940s Warden Arthur "Art" Gillette stationed at Spooner received a telephone call from Webster. Louis "Louie" Simons was on the line,

"Art, this is Louie. How about coming over tomorrow morning. You know that trapper I pinched three weeks ago for trapping rats during the closed season? Well he's at it again."

"You mean he's trapping again?"

"Yup, trapping on Loon creek. At least that's what my informer tells me."

"God that's the same creek you caught him on. Wasn't his name Sam Johnstown?"

"Yeah, same guy, same creek. Can you give me a hand?"

"Did he have any muskrats when you pinched him?"

"He had two in his traps. I searched his house and out buildings, but I couldn't I find any more."

"What time?"

"Meet me at Webster about 5 a.m. Sam usually runs his traps at sunrise."

Scratching the early morning frost hastily off his windshield, Gillette swiftly drove west on highway 70 meeting Simons, who was munching on some burned early morning toast. Hurrying out the door, coffee cup in hand, he muttered, "We'll use your car Art. Head her north toward Danbury while I finish my coffee."

Turning east off state highway 35 the two proceeded several miles to an old logging road, where Simons directed Gillette to turn right. Bumping along the old trail he exclaimed, "I can see why you left your car at home."

"Now Art, I know every one of these miles will be on your expense account."

"Yeah, but I may have to buy a new car before this day is done."

"Hell Art, you'd kick if you were hung with a silk rope." Gesturing at a log landing he intoned, "Park her here Art. We only have about a half-mile to walk. I'll lead the way."

Brushing the hazel nut brush aside, he led the two through the dark frosty woods as if he knew exactly where he was at all times. This fallacy was soon dispelled as he stopped, glanced at his glow in the dark compass and whispered, "Should hit the creek soon if we continue straight south."

Art began to worry. *Wonder if my hero is about to lose us out here?*

"Here we are Art," came the low whisper as they approached a small stream. "The traps should be right around here." He continued to whisper, "Sun is beginning to rise. Should have enough light in a few minutes to find them."

Hurrying to assure themselves that they would find the traps before Sam arrived, the two pushed through the heavy alder brush, rime frost cascading down and thawing on their clothing. Soon their clothing was soaked through.

Shivering and teeth chattering Gillette muttered, "Only a couple of game wardens would be dumb enough to come out here at this time of day."

"Yeah, breathed Simons, but just look at that beautiful sunrise streaming through the trees. Ain't it a serene scene?"

"You shoulda been a poet Louie. Oh, oh here's a trap. It's got a rat in it. Lets see, no tag. Be pretty stupid to tag a trap set during the closed season. There's good cover here Louie. Think I'll stay right here. I'll hide behind that clump of alders. He won't be able to see me regardless of which way he comes."

"O.K. Art. I'll continue upstream until I find more traps and find a place to lay. Good luck."

Gillette let his thoughts wander. *Sure is cold and wet out here, but Louie is right. That sunrise is a wondrous sight.* Snapping limbs brought him out of his reverie. Glancing apprehensively downstream toward the breaking brush, he watched as a slim, tall young man with a dark complexion materialized from the maze. Simons had described the man perfectly. Swinging along at a swift pace, as most trappers do, the man's eyes continually searched each nook and cranny on the ground for sign.

Suddenly warmed by anticipation, he thought, *glad there's no snow. Hard to fool a trapper when it comes to reading sign.* About 50 feet from Gillette, the trapper stopped, squatted, reached down and quickly reset a small trap in his hands. He carefully positioned it in the water. Standing up he gazed straight at the clump of brush where Gillette knelt. His heart suddenly began hammering against his ribs. Does he see me? As if answering him, the thin man glanced around and strode forward, eyes down again searching for sign. Directly in front of Gillette he stopped at the trap, knelt and deftly depressed the trap spring to remove the muskrat. He placed it in a canvas sack hanging under his arm.

He whirled around at the unmistakable sound of a man swishing through the frosty grass. He stared in disbelief at the man with the badge quickly closing the distance between them.

"Good morning Sam, I' m a conservation warden and you my friend are under arrest for trapping during the closed season."

Confused, trap still in hand Johnstown muttered, “Where's Louie?”

“He's here with me. You show me the rest of your traps. We'll walk downstream and pick them up.”

After picking up all the traps, Gillette led the way back upstream.

Stepping out of the thick alders, Simons loomed large and within arms reach of the trapper. “Good morning Sam, We meet again.”

Startled, he stepped back awkwardly into a nearby thicket and blurted,

“Yeah, thought you'd leave me alone after you arrested me a couple of weeks ago.”

“Don't look like we can leave you alone Sam. Did you get all the traps up to here Art?”

“We went back and Sam showed me all his traps. I have quite a bunch here.”

Glancing at the stream bank Simons mused, “Do you have more along here Sam?”

“A few, I won't fool you. I have just a few. I'll show you all of them. No use monkeying around now. You're pretty good Louie, caught me twice in three weeks.”

“You wouldn't do it again would you Sam?”

“Never can tell. I may be smarter than you think.”

“Well lets get out of here. The justice of the peace must be up by now.”

Riding toward Webster, Simons again inquired, “You really wouldn't try trapping again before the season would you Sam?”

“Why not, I think I'm a pretty smart trapper. I have to admit you're good Louie to catch me twice in three weeks, but you could never catch me again in three weeks.”

“I'll bet you $5 I won't catch you again in the next three weeks?”

Chuckling, Johnstown, announced, “Don't count on me not trapping, but that would be a dumb bet anyway. Why would I bet that you'll catch me again in three weeks.”

A smile creasing his face Simons continued, “Put up or shut up Sam. I said I'll betcha five bucks we won't catch you again in three weeks.”

Suddenly cowed, Johnstown went silent as he was led into the justice's house for court. At the arraignment he pled guilty to trapping muskrats during the closed season. Simons had an arrangement with the justice that everyone knew about including Johnstown. He always wrote the penalty he wanted on the top of the criminal complaint.

After his plea of guilty, the justice said, “I accept your plea of guilty and therefore find you guilty of trapping muskrats during the closed season. The 18 traps and three muskrats are confiscated in the name of the state of Wisconsin.” Glancing down at the complaint, he continued. “I sentence you to 30 days in the Burnett County Jail.”

“Jail!? But your honor, I'll gladly pay the fine as I did the last time.”

"There's no fine this time. You're sentenced to 30 days. Court adjourned."

"I don't think this is fair your honor. I saw Louie write on the top of that paper. He wrote to sentence me to jail. Louie wanted to bet me $5 that he wouldn't catch me trapping illegally in the next three weeks."

"It's a good thing you didn't take the bet. You're going to set for 30 days. Take him to jail Louie."

Turning to Simons Johnstown blurted, "No wonder you wanted to bet you S.O.B."

"There will be none of that in my court," retorted the justice. "Take him to jail Louie."

A twinkle in his eye, Simons turned to Gillette and winked, "I knew we wouldn't catch him again in three weeks."

Wardens sometimes see the most unusual things. Warden Bill Waggoner and outdoor writer and conservationist Gordon MacQuarrie told photographer Stabor Reese that three Albino deer were feeding at a conservation department feeding station near Boulder Junction. For six days in March of 1950, Reese shivered in his blind to get this shot. The photograph was published worldwide in *Pic* and *Life Magazine*. *Life Magazine* awarded it "Photo of the Year," stating that Reese had beaten the odds, said to be 79 billion to one of photographing three pink-eyed albino deer.

Order Form

PROTECTORS OF THE OUTDOORS

Sold to (please print clearly):
Last name ____________________________ First ________________
Middle _________
Street ________________________________ City ________________
State______ Evening phone (_____) ______________________________

Author will personalize your book as indicated below. All books will be signed.
To: ____
Personal message:____
____

Please send me _____ book(s) $16.95 each = _____ . __
Shipping:
1 book @ $2.25 = ... ______. __
2 books @ $3.25* = ... ______. __

Total enclosed in U.S. funds. . . . . ______. __
(Check or money order)

*Resellers please call publisher for quote.

Send orders to:
Flambeau River Publishing
W10298 Wells Road
Lodi, WI 53555
(608) **592-3752**